THE BRITISH POLITICAL TRADITION

Edited by

Alan Bullock *and* F. W. Deakin

Fellow of New College, Oxford *Fellow of Wadham College, Oxford*

BOOK TWO

THE DEBATE ON THE FRENCH REVOLUTION 1789–1800

The Debate on the French Revolution 1789 – 1800

EDITED BY

Alfred Cobban

Reader in Modern French History
in the University of London

NICHOLAS KAYE
LONDON

First published by Nicholas Kaye, Ltd.
Trebeck Street, London, W.1. 1950

Gift of a member of the faculty

Printed for Nicholas Kaye Ltd., at the St Ann's Press, Timperley
Altrincham, and entirely produced in Great Britain

GENERAL PREFACE

ONE of the unique contributions the English people have made to civilisation has been the discussion of political issues which has been going on in Britain continuously since the sixteenth century. It is a discussion which has ranged over the whole field of political thought and experience. It began with the relation of the State to the individual in religious matters; for the last half century it has been increasingly preoccupied with the relation of the State to the individual in economic matters. The strength of tradition, the right of rebellion; the demand for equality, the rights of property; the place of justice and morality in foreign policy, the relations between Britain and her overseas territories; the claims of minorities, the value of civil and religious freedom; the rule of law, the Rule of the Saints; the rights of the individual, the claims of the State—all these have been the subject of passionate and incessant argument among Englishmen since the time of the Reformation.

This debate has never been of an academic character. There are, it is true, masterpieces of political philosophy in the English language: Hobbes' *Leviathan* is an obvious example. But the true character of this debate has been empirical: the discussion of particular and practical issues, in the course of which a clash of principle and attitude is brought out, but in which the element of abstract thought is always kept in relation to an immediate and actual situation. The riches of British political thought are to be found less in the philosophers' discussions of terms like 'The State', 'freedom' and 'obligation'—important though these are—than in the writings and speeches on contemporary political issues of men like Lilburne, Locke, Bolingbroke, Burke, Tom Paine, Fox, the Mills, Cobden, Disraeli, Gladstone, and the Fabians. No other literature in the world is so rich in political pamphlets as English, and the pages of *Hansard* are a mine not only for the historian of political events but also for the historian of political ideas. It is in the discussions provoked by the major crises in British history—the Civil War, the Revolt of the American Colonies, the Reform Bills of the nineteenth century—that our political ideas have been hammered out.

One unfortunate result of this is that much of the material which anyone interested in English political ideas needs to read is inaccessible. Pamphlets and speeches are often only to be found in contemporary publications hidden away on the more obscure shelves of the big libraries. Even when the reader has secured a volume of seventeenth-century pamphlets or of Gladstone's speeches, he may well be deterred by the large amount of now irrelevant detail or polemic through which he has to make his way before striking the characteristic ideas and assumptions of the writer or speaker. It is to meet the need of the reader who is interested in English political ideas but has neither the time, the patience, nor perhaps the opportunity, to read through a library of books to find the material he is looking for that this present series of books is designed. Its aim is to present from sources of the most varied kind, books, pamphlets, speeches, letters, newspapers, a selection of original material illustrating the different facets of Englishmen's discussion of politics. Each volume will include an introductory essay by the editor together with sufficient explanation of the circumstances to make each extract intelligible. In some cases it has seemed best to make a particular crisis the focus of the discussion: this has been done with Mr. Beloff's volume, 'The Debate on the American Revolution', and with Dr. Cobban's 'The Debate on the French Revolution'. In other cases the development of a particular view has been traced over a long period of years: this is the case for instance with the volumes on the Conservative, the Liberal, and the Radical Traditions. In a third case, that of the volume on 'Britain and Europe', our idea has been to single out a recurrent problem in English politics and trace its discussion from Pitt's day to our own.

To begin with, we have concentrated our attention on the period between the Revolt of the American Colonies and the Great War of 1914. When that has been covered we hope to treat the earlier period in the same way, notably the political discussions of the seventeenth century.

We do not believe that any one of these facets can be singled out and labelled as in some particular way more characteristic than others of the British Political Tradition: the rebels have as great a part in our political tradition as those who have argued the case for the claims of prescription and established authority. The wealth of that tradition is that it includes Lilburne, Tom Paine, Richard Cobden and the Early English Socialists as well as Locke, Burke and Disraeli.

We have tried to hold the balance even. In no sense do we wish to act as propagandists or advocates. While each editor has been given complete freedom to present his material as he wishes, we have been concerned as general editors to see that equal representation is given to different views in the series as whole. Only in this way, we believe, is it possible to display the British Political Tradition in its unequalled richness, as built up out of a variety of political opinions and out of the clash between them, as the great and continuous debate of the nation to which, in its very nature, there can be no end.

ALAN BULLOCK

F. W. DEAKIN

Oxford

TABLE OF CONTENTS

PART III. *NATURAL RIGHTS AND SOVEREIGNTY:* THE RIGHTS OF MAN

SOVEREIGNTY OF THE PEOPLE

THE TREASON TRIALS

TABLE OF CONTENTS

CHURCH AND STATE

PART VII. *THE REVOLUTIONARY WAR*

INTRODUCTION

I

THE eighteenth century for Great Britain was an age of progress and prosperity at home, and victory and expansion abroad. The loss of the American colonies, regarded by many as inevitable, especially after it had occurred, left no serious scar on the prevailing national complacency. Agricultural productivity was mounting and with it population; the beginnings of a new industrial revolution were making themselves felt; trade was expanding, and—at least until the last quarter of the century—all classes shared in the general economic improvement. The desirability of maintaining a political and economic system which had such consequences seemed the mere dictate of common sense. Eighteenth-century England, therefore, without abandoning the revolutionary principles which it had inherited from the previous century, transformed them into a profoundly conservative social and political creed.

It would not be correct, however, to suggest that the eighteenth century was merely concerned to preserve the past. On the contrary, the very climate of political and economic stability provided growing weather for social experiment. Politically conservative, the prevailing utilitarianism was socially progressive, and in this soil were sown many seeds which were to bear fruit later. Even in the eighteenth century the list of effective reforms, which culminates between 1784 and 1789 in the administrative changes of the younger Pitt, was not inconsiderable, and more were rapidly maturing. Reform was in the air, but revolution was conspicuously absent. It is true, a political agitation, which might have developed on dangerous lines, appeared in the 'eighties.[1] This was, Burke alleged much later, in his *Letter to a Noble Lord*, " one of the most critical periods in our annals". " There was, indeed," he said, " much intestine heat; there was a dreadful fermentation. Wild and savage insurrection quitted the woods, and prowled about our streets in the name of reform. Such was the distemper of the public mind, that there was no madman, in his maddest ideas, and maddest projects, who might not count upon numbers to support his principles and execute his designs. Many of the changes, by a great misnomer called parliamentary reforms, went, not in the intention of all the professors and supporters of them, undoubtedly, but went in their certain, and, in my opinion, not very remote effect, home to the utter destruction of the constitution of this kingdom. Had they taken place, not France, but England, would have had the honour of leading up the death-dance of democratic revolution." There was some exaggeration in this picture. The crisis, in any case, passed over, and the country settled down to a generation of peace and economic progress.

Although the general agitation subsided, and Pitt, after one abortive effort, abandoned the cause of parliamentary reform, the demand was continued in a narrower circle, especially by members of the old dissenting sects, amongst whom the Unitarians played a prominent part. Their religious ideas easily took on

[1] Cf. H. Butterfield, *George III, Lord North and the People, 1779-80*, 1949.

a political form, their prime object being to obtain equal citizenship with members of the Established Church.

To justify their political aspirations they turned back to seventeenth-century ideas of natural rights and the sovereignty of the people. Thus, though their chief aim as Dissenters was the removal of the disabilities imposed by the Test and Corporation Acts, they joined in the campaign for parliamentary reform, of which Christopher Wyvill was the chief political organizer and Major John Cartwright the most persevering propagandist. The Dissenters had been behind Pitt in 1784, but his failure to support the repeal of the Test and Corporation Acts in 1787 and 1789 changed their attitude and caused them to look with greater favour on the Foxite opposition. The approach of the centenary of the Revolution of 1688 stimulated the formation of societies for its commemoration. In this movement the Dissenters took the lead, and their influence, as an educated community containing a large number of literary men and scientists, and controlling the leading literary journals, was greater than their numbers would have suggested. In the conservative society of eighteenth-century England, thus, they formed an important body of opinion, which was prepared to look with favour on a revolution in France, especially one justified on the principles of natural rights and the sovereignty of the people, and proclaiming the ideal of political and religious equality.

In this sense it might be said that the Dissenters were ready to welcome the Revolution. Of course, neither they nor anyone else anticipated it. The revolutionary storm came out of a blue sky. The initial reaction varied between enthusiasm and indifference. Even those who from the beginning were hostile to the new political ideas, at least experienced a mild satisfaction at the thought that the Revolution would eliminate French economic and political rivalry with Great Britain for an indefinite time to come. "*Snug* was the word," wrote Windham later, "People were for leaving other nations to shift for themselves."[1] Practically all, critics and admirers alike, were as mistaken as they well could be, and a glance at some of the early comments on the revolution is sufficient to show why. Information about political and social conditions in France was in most cases quite inadequate for the formation of any reasoned judgment at all. What was happening in France was read in the light of English conditions, and even these rather the conditions of an idealized past than of a rapidly changing present. The enthusiasm of a small minority was all the greater because it was unhampered by any real understanding of the situation in France. Apart from the pamphlets, sermons, articles, letters, published in the opening stages of the Revolution by this minority, largely composed of Dissenters, the Press reported the happenings in France with considerable interest and surprise but little comment of value.

The debate over the Revolution did not really begin until the mind of a great man was directed, not so much to the actual circumstances—it could hardly have been to these, for he was supremely ignorant of them—but to the basic theoretical issues raised by the Revolution. Burke's *Reflections on the French Revolution* was at the same time the greatest and most influential political pamphlet ever written, and a

[1] Windham, *Speeches*, 1812, III, p. 420. (13 May 1802.)

classic contribution to the political theory of western civilization. It set the terms of the whole subsequent discussion.

The *Reflections* has often been interpreted as a repudiation of all the causes for which Burke had fought earlier. The superficiality of this view need not be demonstrated again here. The *Reflections* is the crowning work of his career. It is ill-informed, in striking contrast to his writings and speeches on America, India and Ireland; it is prejudiced, violently unfair, grossly unhistorical. Its vices have won more disciples than its virtues. Every petty politician defending the principle that whatever is, if it be to his own interest, is right, has sheltered himself behind the great name of Burke. His more meretricious passages have provided splashes of colour in the drab patchwork put together by would-be followers. *Saying ditto to Mr. Burke* has been a substitute for thought for generations of English political writers. There are, indeed, too many passages in which Burke seems to justify not thinking, or at least not on the kind of subjects on which he permitted himself to think. But when all that can be said in criticism has been said, the *Reflections* remains one of the world's great treatises on politics. No British writer except Locke has exercised such a mighty influence over political thinking, or left such a deep imprint on the political mind of the country.

Burke took as the starting-point for his attack on the English admirers of the Revolution the sermon delivered at Old Jewry in commemoration of the Revolution of 1688, by the unfortunate Dr. Price. The choice was not merely fortuitous. As a minority, the Dissenters were an obvious target. They had vociferously welcomed the Revolution and justified it on native English principles. Before Burke could effectively denounce the doctrines of the French Revolution, therefore, he had first to dispose of the Dissenters and their claim that it merely continued the traditions of the English Revolution. He did this thoroughly—moderation was the virtue which he most preached and least practised—by throwing overboard the classic Whig theory of the Revolution and adopting what had been in effect the Tory interpretation. An uneasy awareness that he had endangered his own claim to represent Whig traditions was shown subsequently by his rather disingenuous *Appeal from the New to the Old Whigs.* The re-interpretation of the Revolution of 1688 was, however, essential to his argument, for this involved setting up an historical utilitarianism in opposition to the doctrine of inherent natural rights, which Burke attributed to Rousseau and the *philosophes* of the eighteenth century, but which he might, more correctly, have laid at the feet of Locke and the intellectual forbears of his own Whig theory of government.

Burke's discussion of rights falls into three distinct parts. First, he condemns the whole conception of natural or abstract rights as a meaningless and dangerous delusion. Secondly, since he finds it difficult to deny altogether the existence of rights—had he not defended them eloquently in the past?—he insists that they are not abstract and universal rights, but specific social rights to the particular advantages which society can procure the individual. For this reason they are related to his social position, and though equal rights are not rights to equal things. And thirdly, refusing to derive these rights from a fundamental natural right, he insists that they are an inheritance from the past and embodied in constitutional precedent. He refrains from saying what should be done in a country where there are no such precedents. Indeed, the assumption is that no such country exists. It follows that France should have started with the rights recognized in her old Constitution and built on these. The view that the *ancien régime* had no constitution, since all powers were summed up in the *bon plaisir* of the King, and that the function of the National Assembly was to make one, he repudiates with indignation.

The theory of rights which Burke substitutes for the principle of natural rights includes two alternative and to some extent rival conceptions—the interpretation of rights in terms of past traditions, and their interpretation in terms of present interests. In the first of these he was anticipating the historical school of the nineteenth century; in the second he was truer to the utilitarian spirit of the eighteenth century than were his political opponents, who were still clinging to the natural right theories of an older school of thought. Both variants of Burke's theory of rights were capable of justification on utilitarian grounds. Survival over a long period of time, he could argue, is the best evidence of the utility of an institution. But this doctrine easily turned into the principle of prescription, which assumed for Burke its outward and visible form in the shape of property. Property was both an inheritance and a present advantage—Burke did not ask whose advantage. Some of his opponents were able to point out that the French Revolution had also proclaimed in unqualified terms the rights of property; but Burke was not mistaken in thinking that there was an important difference. The kind of property which was sacred above all for him, the estates of the landed aristocracy and the Church, was precisely that which the revolutionaries had challenged in the name of a newer kind of property right, that of the enterprising acquisitiveness of bourgeois society. To a property right based on prescription, they opposed one based on social utility. The conflict of property rights, in fact, concealed a conflict of classes in France. The same conflict never emerged clearly in England, but the alarm of the corresponding classes to those expropriated in France was natural, even without a Burke to play upon their fears.

This is not the whole explanation, however. There are schools of historical interpretation, and these not merely Marxist, which seem to imagine that once the magic words " class " or " interest " have been uttered, all historical problems are solved. The motives of the rawest country squire in the revolutionary age are not to be understood in terms of such a superficial simplification.[1] Even the proprietor of Beaconsfield is not to be treated as a mere defender of vested interests. Burke's impassioned indignation against the Revolution was the child of a conviction that two intrinsically hostile views of life were in mortal combat. Underneath his historical utilitarianism, at a deeper layer of his mind, was the belief that what is useful for man has been laid down from all time by divine providence. His politics begins with the sentence, " Man is a religious animal". He had a deep awareness of the movement, beneath the conscious, calculating intellect, of more fundamental, non-intellectual, unconscious forces in the life of society. In this respect, it may be observed, the difference

[1] Cf., *inf.*, p. 17.

between Burke and the revolutionaries was perhaps less than it seemed at the time. The great currents of thought in any age rise from the same springs, though they run in different channels and turn different wheels. The revolutionaries, too, appealed to forces beyond simple reason and utility; but they set up as the ultimate authority the sovereignty and rights of the people as a nation or state. The State in this way became for them an end in itself; whereas for Burke it could never be more than a means to the realization of the eternal values implanted in human nature.

Both Burke and the revolutionaries were moving away from the rationalism and utilitarianism of the eighteenth century to the romantic values of the nineteenth: both were in danger of sacrificing the real, concrete, present interests of the people, to which an unromantic, eighteenth-century Bentham continued to hold fast. But whatever happened to Burke's ideas at the hands of nineteenth-century worshippers of the State, he himself never completely lost touch with the rational utilitarianism of his own century. The same can hardly be said of the revolutionaries. If Burke's criticisms were unfair to the idealists who began the Revolution, events, leading through the Reign of Terror and the corrupt oligarchy of the Directory to the tyranny of a Bonaparte, justified him in the end. If accurate prophecy is the test of a political thinker, Burke stands supreme. Basing himself on a theoretical analysis, with a totally inadequate knowledge of the facts, he prophesied that France would first fall under the control of an oligarchy of *nouveaux riches*, made wealthy by the acquisition of confiscated estates, and then by way of terror and disorder would pass into the hands of a military despotism, more powerful, more destructive of the peace of the world, and more disastrous in its historical sequel than any that Western civilization had known.

II

When Burke published his *Reflections*, his views on France were as yet mere speculation, and to his critics wild and wanton speculation. There was little inclination in responsible political quarters to heed his call. Pitt and the majority in Parliament remained indifferent. The French monarchy was a traditional enemy: a development that seemed to rob it of its power for aggression was not unwelcome. Burke's own party for the most part failed to follow his lead. Fox, in particular, seems to have interpreted the Revolution in the light of the Whig struggle against royal influence. A good illustration of his attitude is provided in a letter to Lord Holland, " If you admit that the Jacobins, having the confidence of the Assembly and country, ought to be Ministers, what can be said for the Feuillans, who encouraged and supported the King, in maintaining an Administration of an adverse faction, in using his veto and other prerogatives in opposition to the will of the Assembly and the nation ? He who defends even this, cannot be a Whig. . . . That they (the Feuillans) gave into the idea of availing themselves of the letter of the Constitution, and of the King's using his prerogatives, independently of, and hostilely to the Assembly, is what they themselves would not deny, and what I must disapprove, unless I abandon every political principle of my life."[1] On the whole, however, the difference

[1] *Memorials and Correspondence of Charles James Fox*, II, pp. 373–4. (12 October 1792.)

between Pitt and Fox at first was only that between unsympathetic and sympathetic neutrality. Active hostility to the Revolution developed slowly. It would doubtless have appeared in any case, but its formation was precipitated by Burke, who gave the controversy an emotional content which it might not have acquired so soon without him. The tendency to appeal from reason to emotion was shared by sympathizers and opponents of the Revolution alike. Uncritical admiration was countered by impassioned denunciation, while the breach in the former intimate relations between Burke and the Foxite Whigs added the acerbity of broken friendship to political disagreement, though Fox himself never lost his innate generosity of spirit.

The debate was now well begun. It turned first, naturally, on the reasons for the Revolution. Was it, as the *émigrés* were claiming, the result of a deep-laid plot against Church and Crown ? Or was it the spontaneous uprising of an oppressed people against a cruel despotism, a corrupt Church and a worthless *noblesse* ? Initial prejudices were on the side of the Revolution: the contrast of English liberty and French slavery was an eighteenth-century commonplace. We hardly meet with an unqualified defence of the *ancien régime* until Burke in the *Reflections* put forward the claim that France possessed before the Revolution " the elements of a constitution almost as good as could be desired". To support his view he idealized Louis XVI, romanticized Marie Antoinette, white-washed the upper clergy, and re-dressed the *noblesse* in the garb of English country gentlemen. The most widely-read attempt to present the other side of the medal was Mackintosh's *Vindiciæ Gallicæ*; but Mackintosh, like most of Burke's critics, was as ill-informed of the facts as Burke, and at the same time lacked his intellectual and emotional powers. Polemists on either side were at one only in their common ignorance of the real conditions in France, while the effect of the development of controversy upon reasoned judgment may be seen by a comparison of the sane, balanced views of Arthur Young in his *Travels in France* with his later wild denunciation of the Revolution and all its works.

A particular source of misunderstanding among the supporters of the Revolution was the tendency to interpret it in terms of the Glorious Revolution of 1688. Political developments in England and France were, of course, not unrelated; and the democratic movement, which appeared towards the end of the eighteenth century in Western Europe and America, was not unconnected with political ideas which had first been clearly stated in the course of the English Civil War, and had been lying latent until economic and political changes produced a situation in which they could have practical meaning.[1] Though the Revolution of 1688 introduced an age of political conservatism, the ideas of its chief theorist, Locke, and even more those of the extremer writers of the Commonwealth, could not easily be reconciled with the government of a small land-owning oligarchy. Towards 1789, Whig principles, after lying fallow for a century, had shown signs of coming to life and producing a crop of reforms, in which, however, abstract ideas were strictly subordinated to considerations of expediency. It was on such grounds that the Younger Pitt put forward his unsuccessful proposal for parliamentary reform in 1785. British opinion, to begin

[1] See the volume in this series by Max Beloff, *The Debate on the American Revolution.*

with, tended to regard the French Revolution as a similar attempt to provide practical remedies for practical grievances, and one of its first results in England was to stimulate a revival of the demand for parliamentary reform. Fox himself always remained a little disingenuous in his public references to reform, and the conversion of many of the Foxite Whigs to the cause was not unrelated to the fact that while the existing system lasted Pitt, with royal patronage at his command, and an unlimited supply of peerages with which to reward his supporters, was invincibly entrenched in power. There were, however, many sincere and persevering advocates of reform, headed by Christopher Wyvill and the eccentric Major Cartwright.

The case for a moderate parliamentary reform might easily have been argued, and in due course won, on the grounds of practical expediency, if it had not been for the impact of the French Revolution, and the positive dangers it seemed to present. It was Burke who made the theoretical issue the dominant one. His mind inevitably moved in the sphere of political principles. "His greatness," declared Matthew Arnold, "is that he lived in a world which neither English Liberalism nor English Toryism is apt to enter;—the world of ideas, not the world of catchwords and party habits."[1] If this was his greatness for posterity, it was his weakness for his contemporaries. Indeed they would hardly have listened to his insistent exposition of the theoretical issue, had not the English democrats from the beginning of the Revolution concentrated their attention on questions of abstract principle, and

[1] Matthew Arnold, "The Function of Criticism at the Present Time", in *Essays in Criticism*, 1865, pp. 14–15.

driven the lesson home by attempting to apply French ideas to the British Constitution. For, as well as the moderate Whigs who wanted a reform of some of the more obvious imperfections of the representative system, there was an extremer school of thought which advocated universal suffrage, and based itself on an assertion of absolute principles more characteristic of the seventeenth than of the eighteenth century. In the early stages of the agitation, Dissenters, such as Price and Priestley, played the leading part in the revival and propagation of abstract political ideas. Richard Price was perhaps the closest to his spiritual ancestors of the Civil War. He best deserves to be remembered as a moral philosopher, but he has come down to history as the exponent of a millenarian theory of politics. Burke, in his *Reflections*, chose a good victim, but one who was far from typical of the English democrats. In 1790 Price was an anachronism. Far more characteristic was Joseph Priestley's combination of a doctrine of natural rights with utilitarianism, but even Priestley was only the writer for a political coterie. For the real popularizer of democratic ideas it was necessary to wait until 1791. Just as Burke's *Reflections* crystallized opinion on one side, so Paine's *Rights of Man* brought out in a clear light the basic principles on the other side.

Against constitutional rights Paine asserted natural rights, against the claims of monarchy and aristocracy, the sovereignty of the people. Although his political theory had its roots in the Lockian doctrine of natural rights, between the Liberalism of Locke and the Jacobinism of Paine there was an immense gulf. Locke stood for the toleration of all tolerant churches, and behind the rule of law envisaged the eternally valid decrees of a deistic universe. Paine had moved on to a complete denial of the place of religion in society. Locke and Paine both began with an assertion of natural rights, and then in the application of their political principles turned to the criterion of utility. But for Locke this meant the adoption of constitutional forms which restricted the exercise of political power; for Paine the principle of utility was embodied in the unlimited sovereignty of the people.

It should not be thought that in this assertion of sovereignty Paine was in any way different from the other English democrats of his time. "In every state," wrote Priestley, "as in every single person, there ought to be but one will, and no important business should be prevented from proceeding by any opposite will."[1] We must not exaggerate their conception of sovereignty, however. Paine and Priestley still belong to the eighteenth century and envisage the sovereignty of the people in terms of a strictly individualist society, in which the natural identification of interests is allowed to operate with as little interference from government as possible. If Paine's thought has connections with the authoritarian Jacobinism of the Committee of Public Safety on the one hand, it joins with the anarchic individualism of Godwin on the other. But there can be no doubt which affiliation was of the greater practical importance. Godwin, whose *Political Justice* deserves its later neglect almost as little as its contemporary exaggerated reputation, was as pure a theorist as ever wrote. Pitt's common sense rightly refused to see any political danger in his writings. Paine was the true prophet of

[1] J. Priestley, *A Political Dialogue on the General Principles of Government*, 1791, p. 96.

the new radicalism. With his *Rights of Man* the moderate conclusions of a Priestley were replaced by a direct attack on Church and Crown. He crystallized extreme opinion on one side of the controversy, as Burke did on the other. In the thought of both there was a large measure of eighteenth-century utilitarianism, but in both it was subjected to more absolute conceptions of political right that linked the seventeenth century with the twentieth. Meanwhile, in obscurity, Jeremy Bentham was working out the practical implications of a stricter utilitarian outlook, and laying the foundations of the nineteenth century.

III

The ideas of Paine appealed to only a small faction among the people. In Great Britain, once the issues had been stated in these terms, the cause of the democratic party was doomed. Its handful of agitators, in spite of increasing social distress, found fewer and fewer to listen to them. The Dissenting interest, which had provided the main body of supporters of the movement for political reform, was alarmed by attacks on religion and the social order. Paine's writings alienated the middle classes, whose leadership was necessary to a successful popular movement. The social resentment of the English "Jacobins" against the wealth of court and aristocracy contributed to radical tradition in the following century; but in the 'nineties, so far as democratic writers transferred the idea of equality from politics to economics they merely completed the antagonism of the middle classes. On the whole, however, the discussion concentrated on political rights. To interpret it as a conflict of economic interests would be to read back into the eighteenth century ideas which only became an effective force subsequently. There was, indeed, little difference of opinion on questions of economic principle. In England, as in France, though they condemned the extravagance of courts and nobles, the democrats for the most part stoutly upheld the rights of property and were quite as strong individualists as their opponents. On the other side, the "panic of property" is more evident in the writings of historians than in contemporary literature. It is not unreasonable to suggest that Englishmen of the last decade of the eighteenth century saw the menace before them, not in the light of social-revolutionary movements of the future, but in the terms with which their own generation was familiar—a generation which remembered the Gordon Riots, and read horrific accounts of the September massacres in Paris. They were afraid of the peril they knew: anarchy, not socialism, was the gulf they saw opening at their feet.

It must also be remembered that religion still exercised a great influence over the minds of men. A study of lists of eighteenth-century publications soon reveals the predominance of theological and devotional works. Political and religious opinions were closely linked. Priestley claimed, not without justification, that the Birmingham riots were stirred up by the High Church party, and that he and his friends suffered as Dissenters rather than as supporters of the Revolution. When the revolutionary movement came to be associated with a general attack on religion, especially after Paine's *Age of Reason* was published in 1794, outraged religious feelings added fuel to the anti-revolutionary fire. The banner of Church and State was raised, the Dissenters were frightened out of political activity, and the Evangelicals driven back into the arms of the Church. Anti-Catholic feeling was slow in dying down, as was shown by the suspicion with which the activities of the *émigré* clergy were regarded, but as the Revolution went on and Protestants found themselves in the same camp with Catholics, even this diminished.[1]

The most effective argument against the Revolution, however, was none of these, but the simple appeal to facts. Seen from this side of the Channel the benefits of the Revolution were hypothetical, and indeed its real achievements were largely ignored, by supporters whose eyes were dazzled with abstract principles as well as by opponents. The price paid was only too apparent. The popular disorders that accompanied its early stages could be explained away as an inevitable part of the struggle for liberty; but when the Terror, instead of declining with the destruction of the *ancien régime*, became fiercer, many of those who had at first welcomed the Revolution abandoned their

[1] The fear, among the English Catholics, of an outbreak of anti-Catholic feeling appears clearly in a letter sent by Lord Petre to Grenville in December 1792—" My Lord, Being well acquainted with your Lordships favourable dispositions towards the Catholics of this country I have ventured to break in upon your much engaged time to state a circumstance which gives me considerable uneasiness.

" The convent of Nuns from Montargis have engaged a house within three miles of this place, where they propose to live in community, the report of this importation of Nuns has already spread, and the hard fate of these respectable ladies are exceedingly to be lamented, and will call on every feeling mind for protection, yet I apprehend the people of the country will see in them, the establishment, of what, they will call, a Popish nunnery; and as your Lordship knows, tho' rendered a great deal firmer by the liberality of government, we still stand on slippery ground with respect to the prejudices of the people. Should this neighbourhood conceive that I was instrumental in bringing them into the country . . . I fear the lower ranks of people will attribute the introduction of what they conceive Popish superstition, to me. . . . I am convinced that the whole Body of Catholics would soon again become the objects of Popular cry and odium, if anything like Religious Establishments were to be perceived fixing themselves in this country." Buckenham House, near Brandon, Norfolk, 26 December 1792. (Record Office, H.O. 32/2.)

illusions, and old prejudices against the French as a treacherous and cruel nation, incapable of freedom, revived. Revolutionary principles became indissolubly connected in the public mind with mob violence, and the combination only required a name to constitute a fully-formed political stereotype. The name was provided by Jacobinism, in which was summed up everything that was feared and hated in the Revolution. Political opinion is not discriminating, and the temptation to supporters of the government to label all opposition Jacobinism, and to discredit reform by identifying it with revolution, was too great to be resisted. The English reformers for long closed their eyes to the facts and denied the reports of terrorism; but evidence of the excesses of the Revolution, which it was difficult to deny, was provided out of the mouths of revolutionaries themselves, in the indictment of the Robespierrist Jacobins by their Thermidorean successors. Finally, the favourite excuse, that the Terror was a consequence of the threat of foreign invasion, lost its validity when French armies passed from the defence to the offensive and France became an invader in her turn.

IV

While moderate opinion was turning against the Revolution, those who persisted in their sympathies followed Paine in the path of extreme ideas, and to the alarm of the Government began to organize themselves in societies. The initial welcome to the Revolution had come from the Dissenters gathered to celebrate the memory of 1688 in the London Revolution Society and similar bodies in the provinces. In 1792 more advanced societies appeared. The Society for Promoting

Constitutional Information, founded in 1780 but dormant by 1791, was revived. The London Corresponding Society, with the shoemaker Hardy as its Secretary, was formed to spread the gospel of parliamentary reform among working-men; and at the other end of the social scale Charles Grey and the aristocratic Whig reformers founded the Friends of the People. The same name was adopted by various local societies, such as the Friends of the People in the Borough, meeting at the Three Tuns in Southwark. Most important provincial towns had their own societies—the Manchester Constitutional Society, the Norwich Revolution Society, the Derby Society for Political Information, and the like. The scope of the movement in Scotland is shown by the fact that a Convention—sinister name—could be held in Edinburgh in December 1792, with delegates from eighty different societies. The appeal that some of these bodies made to individuals from the lower strata of the populace was from the point of view of the authorities their most dangerous feature, and for the future the most significant new development. The London Corresponding Society, with its subscription of one penny a week, was composed largely of craftsmen and petty shopkeepers. Similar societies were to be found in towns such as Sheffield and Birmingham. To supply the demand they stimulated, a cheap, popular, political literature appeared. This was the real beginning of working-class politics in Great Britain, and it was evidence of a political maturity in advance of anything that Revolutionary France could show. The features which were to be characteristic of its development throughout the nineteenth century were already present—the effective part played by working-men in the organization of their own political movement, the emphasis on political reform as the path to social improvement, reliance on moral force and general opposition to the use of physical violence; and already a tendency was apparent to shift away from the abstract theorizing of the school of Paine, and concentrate on specific political issues.

In all this, it may be said, there was nothing to alarm a reasonable government, less indeed than in 1780 or 1830. One of the remarkable features of the British situation during the Revolutionary decade was the absence of serious social disorder in the presence of generally deteriorating economic conditions. But in the light of the French Revolution any popular political movement assumed a dangerous appearance. Reactions are seldom moderate, and there was enough evidence of revolutionary sympathies in the country to alarm more temperate politicians than Windham and more liberal ones than Dundas. Since Jacobinism in Great Britain never reached the stage of open resistance to the Government, opinion had to be the main object of repression. Acts against treason and sedition, and prosecutions under them in the courts, were the Government's chosen weapon. To facilitate arrests and prosecutions, Habeas Corpus was suspended. Though they had little sympathy with the aims of the English Jacobins, the members of the small Foxite opposition in Parliament, where Grey was still persisting in his periodic motions for a parliamentary reform, were indignant at the persecution of opinion.

The cause of freedom of speech brought out all their latent fire. In speech after speech, which rank among the greater glories of the anthology of English freedom, Erskine in the courts, and Fox in the Commons, defended the constitutional liberties of the subject, and left a memory as golden as that of Pitt's Home Secretary, Dundas, is dark.[1] It was lucky, indeed, that there were Whig aristocrats to speak for freedom, for the judges in the Scottish courts, and the Anglo-Irish in Dublin, seemed to have forgotten, if they ever knew, its meaning. The English courts of law, with an Erskine to keep them up to the mark, never lost their judicial character. Few things are more striking, among the records of the time, than the contrast between the Scottish sedition trials under Braxfield and similar trials in the English courts. Dundas, with his spies, was doing his best to secure convictions and exemplary sentences, and the foolishness or simplicity of the English Jacobins often seconded him well; but the English Judges, though their sympathies were hardly in doubt, were honest and sensible men. One cannot read trials such as those of Hardy, or Horne Tooke, without being moved by the humane and gentlemanly way in which they were conducted by the judges, and the moderation even of the prosecuting lawyers. At the same time the Revolutionary Tribunal in Paris was exhibiting a very different conception of the judicial function. Horne Tooke's trial ended in mutual felicitations between Lord Chief Justice Eyre and the accused; even the prosecuting lawyers could scarce forbear to cheer, and the crowd outside carried the defendant in triumph to his lodgings. It was clear that no London jury would find a man guilty on the kind of evidence that the agents of Dundas could gather. The trial of Mr. Walker, in which the prosecution's chief witness ignominiously collapsed and

[1] It is only fair to state that Dundas himself seems to have regretted the brutal behaviour of Braxfield in the sedition trials. Holden Furber, *Henry Dundas, first Viscount Melville, 1742–1811*, 1931, p. 88.

revealed himself as a drunken liar, taught the same lesson in Manchester.

V

In the course of the revolutionary decade, however, domestic controversies tended to sink into the background. The London Corresponding Society declined and was finally suppressed. Newer and more revolutionary groups, the United Englishmen and United Scotsmen, unlike their prototype in Ireland, developed no vitality. The war became all-important, and under war conditions the crowd rapidly came round to Burke's view. When he started his crusade against Jacobinism he was almost a solitary figure. During the first months of the Revolution, he scarcely dared to mutter his Cassandra warnings in the midst of general rejoicing. After the initial enthusiasm subsided in all except the professed democrats, there ensued a period of indifference, while the reactionary wave was gathering strength before it broke. The aspect of the Revolution which aroused most interest among practical politicians, as distinguished from men of theory, was the problem of its influence on the future course of international relations, and there seemed little doubt about this. To a country which had just emerged, after many victories though with a final set-back in the War of American Independence, from its second Hundred Years' War with France, and which was still profoundly suspicious of French ambitions, the apparent collapse of the traditional enemy could not be unwelcome. Windham, soon to be one of the most fervent opponents of the Revolution, maintained, as late as 1792, that, " France, our ancient rival, was in a situation which, more than at any other period, freed us from apprehension, on her account."[1] Pitt, in his Budget speech of the same year, uttered the famous declaration that, " Unquestionably there never was a time in the history of this country, when, from the situation in Europe, we might more reasonably expect fifteen years of peace than at the present moment."[2]

In the course of the year the basis of such calculations was drastically changed by the French declaration of war against Austria, the annexation of Nice and Savoy, and the successes of Custine on the Rhine and Dumouriez in Belgium. With Brissot and the Girondin ministry in power, the belief that France had been cured of the lust of conquest began to seem over-optimistic. Adherents of the Revolution were naturally unwilling to admit this, but their arguments had to be re-adjusted when French armies assumed the offensive and French leaders were uttering bellicose threats. The English Jacobins still refused to admit that a nation which was in charge of its own destinies could be warlike: kings and aristocrats might make war, a people was peaceful in the nature of things. If the behaviour of the French seemed to contradict this thesis, it was because the attacks of their enemies had driven them to war in self-defence. Against this the opponents of the Revolution argued that, as Windham put it later, " the French Revolution did not need to be provoked to become mischievous . . . the aggressions were not the consequence of the resistance, but the resistance of the aggressions."[3]

War and the Terror combined to turn public opinion finally against the Revolution. The September

[1] Windham, *Speeches*, 1812, I, p. 201. (29 February 1792.)
[2] Pitt, *Speeches*, 3rd ed., 1817, I, p. 350. (17 February 1792.)
[3] *Windham Papers*, 1913, II, p. 270. (7 October 1805.)

massacres, and the trial and execution of the King, were the decisive events in this evolution. Pitt's policy, on the other hand, was mainly determined by considerations of national interest. The preservation of the independence of the Netherlands was one of the two prime objects of his policy. The other was to stop the organization of sedition from abroad, which had been openly proclaimed by the decree of 19 November 1792, inviting all the peoples of Europe to revolt with the promise of French assistance. This threat continually appears and re-appears in Pitt's justification of the war with France. How could we live at peace with a government acting like the French, he asked, perpetually encouraging other nations to revolt, teaching the peoples of the world that they were slaves and their rulers tyrants, enticing the poor with the loot of society, threatening by force and sedition every nation in Europe. Not only was Jacobinism a subversive opinion, it was an *armed* opinion, and by this consideration he defended himself against Fox's charge of having made war on opinion.[1]

However unwilling the Whigs were to admit it, Pitt had the facts on his side in claiming that the war between Britain and France had been begun by French aggression. Their knowledge that in essentials their policy had been one of peace and non-intervention, and that the war had been forced upon them, was not the least element in the strength of mind which kept Pitt and Grenville firm through dark days. Pitt justified the continuance of the war on the ground that the Revolution had proved itself essentially annexationist in principle as well as in practice. The revolutionaries,

[1] Pitt, *Speeches*, I, pp. 409–10 (1 February 1793); II, p. 76 (26 January 1795); III, pp. 99 and 118 (3 February 1800).

he said, had rejected the Law of Nations and claimed the right to supersede it.[1] That was a claim no British government could accept, and until it was abandoned peace with France was impossible. But what was this Law of Nations that Pitt imagined himself to be defending? A man of affairs, neither a jurist nor a philospher, he cannot have been upholding a merely abstract scheme. Yet Sorel has shown that nearly every feature of Revolutionary and Napoleonic diplomacy had its precedents in the history of the preceding century. The one difference—but a very important one—was that the Revolution did from principle what the *ancien régime* had done from lack of principle. The revolutionaries rationalized their passions and imagined that they had thereby moralized self-interest. The theorists of the Assembly would not be satisfied until they had evolved a doctrine to cover their ambitions: they were consequently compelled to generalize the principle of annexation. Other governments might well ask, in the words of Sorel, "*S'ensuivait-il que toute population qui prétendait former un corps de nation séparé ou, en s'affranchissant, déclarerait en constituer un, pourrait, par cela seul, disposer de soi, se détacher de l'État auquel elle était liée et s'unir à un autre État, sans que le souverain de fait fût admis à s'y opposer ou même à protester?*"[2] As if this were not enough, it was supplemented by the doctrine of the inalienability of all territory, new or old, incorporated in the French Republic.[3] Against this Pitt protested, elevating the custom of normal international relations into a contrary principle: "When in the course of war any nation acquires new possessions, such nation has only

[1] E.g. Pitt, *Speeches*, III, p. 97. (3 February 1800.)
[2] Sorel, *L'Europe et la Révolution française*, II, pp. 97–8.
[3] *Id.*, II, p. 104; cf. III, p. 236.

temporary right to them, and they do not become property till the end of the war. This principle is incontrovertible, and founded upon the nature of things."[1]

At last we reach the great idea, for whose sake year after year Britain was pouring out her life-blood. The observer may well find it difficult to say which was the more absurd, Pitt, who might so much more easily, as indeed he did when pushed, have based his argument on the necessities of self-defence, or Fox, who clothed French aggressions in the chaste robes of popular sovereignty and self-determination. But Pitt had the practical logic of events on his side, and there was in fact one international convention on which he might well have based his case. That international relations are between governments and governments alone, was the first assumption of international law. Revolutionary diplomacy aimed at establishing direct relations with other peoples without the intervention of their governments. The French Government was necessarily the enemy of all other governments so long as it pursued this policy. At bottom, Pitt's justification was a plain one, and on occasion he could state it plainly enough. It consisted simply in the need for security as a preliminary to peace with France. Whenever hard pressed for an argument he always reverted to this. Where is our security for the performance of a treaty, he asked, where we have neither the good faith of a nation, nor the responsibility of a monarch?[2]

This argument had far-reaching implications. It led logically to the conclusion that since security could

[1] Pitt, *Speeches*, II, p. 260. (30 December 1796.) ; cf. III, p. 113. (3 February 1800.)

[2] Pitt, *Speeches*, II, p. 6. (17 June 1793.); II, pp. 74–5. (26 January 1795.)

not be expected from a revolutionary government, the main object of the war must be to secure the overthrow of the Republic and the restoration of monarchy in France. Pitt admitted, in a speech of 1801 on the Preliminaries of Peace, that at times he had hoped to be able "to put together the scattered fragments of that great and venerable edifice",[1] the *ancien régime*. In 1793 he had suggested to Grenville the desirability of an open declaration that monarchy was "the only system in the re-establishment of which we are disposed to concur".[2] Windham and the extreme anti-Jacobins went much farther than this. They were hot for intervention inside France, and their writings and speeches show what Burke's theories could lead to in the minds of lesser men.

There was, however, one practical difficulty in the policy of intervention. If assistance to the royalists was not to do them more harm than good, it was necessary that their foreign allies should renounce the idea of making acquisitions from France. But the Continental powers were wedded to schemes of aggrandisement, and, as Windham wrote to Grenville in 1795, England could hardly protest in view of her own proceedings in French overseas possessions.[3] Pitt had adulterated his main object of security with, as he modestly put it, "a little mixture of indemnification".[4] The influence of Dundas in this field, as in domestic policy, was, according to Wilberforce, Pitt's great misfortune,[5] but Pitt's own bias led him in the same direction. Moreover, though no statesman was

[1] Pitt, *Speeches,* III, p. 278. (3 November 1801.)
[2] Historical Manuscripts Commission, Fortescue MSS. at Dropmore, II, p. 438. (5 October, 1793.)
[3] *Windham Papers,* I, p. 285. (13 February 1795.)
[4] Pitt, *Speeches,* III, p. 85. (7 June 1799.)
[5] R. J. and S. Wilberforce, *Life of Wilberforce,* 1839, II, p. 92.

ever less prone than Pitt, by the natural bent of his mind, to ideological strife, the war was bound to include this. The conditions of a contest cannot be determined by one side without reference to the policy of the other. So long as the French made use of the appeal to revolutionary principles, so long their opponents had to do their best in a war of ideas as well as of arms.

VI

As the war continued considerations of power, however, came increasingly to dominate all others. As early as 1793 a number of the more important Foxite Whigs found the call of national unity stronger than their allegiance to Fox, and joined Pitt's government.[1] The rise of Napoleon to personal power completed the change in the nature of the war. By this time all the essential issues had been brought out clearly and argued to exhaustion. The phase of vigorous original discussion had passed. There was nothing new left to be said, and the debate, so far as it

[1] Lord Malmesbury wrote to the Duke of Portland, on 16 January 1793, " You will, I am sure, forgive my repeating what you have often heard me say, that it is my opinion that the Government of this country ought to be cordially and strenuously supported under all the circumstances, and in all the measures arising from the present crisis; and as this crisis is one which cannot pass away suddenly, but must be depending as long as any attempts are made to maintain elsewhere, or introduce here, the French doctrines, I conceive this support cannot be confined to any fixed term, but must be unlimited as to its duration, and given without a drawback. . . .

" I am heartily sorry that it is not also the sentiment of Fox. I have such a deference for his judgment, respect for his abilities, and so strong a personal regard for him, that it gives me great pain to differ from him on a point of such magnitude, and in its nature so conclusive, that I do not see a possibility of our living long enough for us ever to meet again in our public opinions; for Fox must either be sincere or insincere in what he has done, and is doing. If he is sincere he is dangerous, *acting upon principle*; if insincere he is dangerous, *acting without principle*. . . . It grieves me to separate from him; it grieves me still more to see how completely he has set the whole country against him, and how far he has driven himself from a probability of holding a high office in it." (*Diaries and Correspondence of the Earl of Malmesbury*, 1844, II, pp. 499–500.)

continued, degenerated into vain repetition. The spirit of reaction triumphed, and proposals for reform, which before the Revolution had met with a moderate and open-minded reception, withered in the hard climate of the new Toryism. They were not to revive until the Napoleonic Wars were over and Europe had recovered from their immediate effects, when in a more peaceful and settled world, the harvest of methodical, practical reform, submerged when the revolutionary flood had burst its banks, could be taken up again.

It was taken up with a difference. The years of revolution and war had not been entirely wasted. The discussion of fundamental principles stimulated by the Revolution had deepened and broadened political ideas. Burke could not take part in any controversy, right or wrong, without enriching the political thinking of the world. The experience of the Revolution, seen it is true from the outside and in the light of Burke's prejudiced but profound intuitions, had killed the idea of Jacobin democracy so far as British opinion was concerned. If the principle of popular sovereignty ever had a chance of replacing the English liberal ideal in politics, that chance was lost in the course of the debate over the French Revolution. On the other hand, the traditional liberties of England had been preserved by the small aristocratic clique that found its inspiration in Charles James Fox; and Grey's obstinate and futile struggle acquired significance nearly forty years later, when he became the head of a government pledged to reform of Parliament. If the Foxite Whigs had not staked out the claims of liberty so firmly in the 'nineties, much might have been lost that could only have been regained by a long and bitter conflict.

The French Revolution put back reform in Great Britain by a generation, but in the course of the debate to which it gave rise, the theoretical foundations of British political progress in the nineteenth century were more soundly laid. This was perhaps the last real discussion of the fundamentals of politics in this country. Great issues were worthily debated. The general level of discussion was a high one, and would seem higher still did not the stature of Burke dwarf all other contributors on either side. Issues as great have been raised in our day, but it cannot be pretended that they have evoked a political discussion on the intellectual level of that inspired by the French Revolution. There is a danger, indeed, that we may transfer the contemporary lack of interest in political principles into the past, and because theory seems of little significance to us, forget that it was very important to our ancestors—not only to Burke but to the whole political world of his day. Political theory, to-day an academic by-path, was in the seventeenth and eighteenth centuries still the study of politicians, theologians, historians and lawyers. The close connection of theory with practical affairs was part of its strength: it was also a part of the strength of the English political system. A consciousness of the fundamental principles at stake upheld Pitt in the defence of one aspect of the national ideal in the face of apparently overwhelming forces abroad, and the Foxite Whigs in maintaining another aspect of the same inheritance through a generation of apparently hopeless opposition at home. If Charles James Fox had not defended the traditional liberties of England with all the force of his generous mind in the first and decisive crisis of the war of ideas, what Pitt saved might have been much less worth saving. And if, against the oratorical triumphs of Fox and Erskine and Sheridan, Pitt had not been secure in his own mind, and in the support of a people that saw, if only as through a glass darkly, something of the shape of the warring ideas, there might have been no liberties left to save.

Note

This book is intended to illustrate political opinion in the course of the Revolutionary decade, not the general history of the period. It is confined to the leading questions raised by the impact of the French Revolution on Great Britain. Subjects such as the Irish Rebellion and the agitation against the slave trade, which although inevitably influenced by the Revolution raise fundamentally separate issues, have been excluded. The extracts are chosen (with one or two exceptions) from the period between the outbreak of the Revolution and the Treaty of Amiens. Though some specimens of the more extravagant type of comment have been included, on the whole they have been taken from the more serious and rational contributions to the discussion. An attempt has been made to represent both what has permanent theoretical value and what was of significance at the time. A thinker such as Bentham, whose writings only became an effective force at a later date, is not included. The temptation to add comments on the extracts has been resisted, and apart from the Introduction and brief biographical notes, they have been left to speak for themselves. The aim has been to present selected, but not pre-digested, material. Finally, it should be noted that considerations of space have necessarily restricted the choice of extracts and limited their length.

CHRONOLOGY OF EVENTS

1789

May	The States-General meet at Versailles
June	The Third Estate declares itself a National Assembly
July	Fall of the Bastille
October	Louis XVI and the Assembly move to Paris

1790

March	Motion of Flood for Reform of Parliament
July	Civil Constitution of the Clergy in France
November	Burke's *Reflections on the Revolution in France*

1791

April	Grenville becomes Foreign Secretary
June	Louis XVI's unsuccessful flight to Varennes
July	The Birmingham Riots
September	French Constitution voted and National Assembly dissolves

1792

January	London Corresponding Society founded
April	France declares war on Austria
	The Friends of the People founded
May	Fox's Libel Act
August	The Paris mob attacks the Tuileries
	Louis XVI imprisoned
September	September Massacres in Paris
	Battle of Valmy
	The National Convention meets
	The French Republic proclaimed
November	Dumouriez occupies Austrian Netherlands
	France proclaims the opening of the Scheldt and offers armed aid to any country wishing to free itself
December	The Edinburgh Convention
	Prosecution of Paine's *Rights of Man*

1793

January	Louis XVI condemned and executed
February	France declares war on England and Holland
March	France declares war on Spain
	Outbreak of revolt in the Vendée
May	Decree of the Maximum
July	The Great Committee of Public Safety
August–September	Trials of Muir and Palmer in Scotland
October	Trial and execution of the Girondins
	Execution of Marie Antoinette

1794

May	Suspension of the Habeas Corpus Act
	Arrest of Hardy, Horne Tooke and other members of the Constitutional Society and the London Corresponding Society
	Portland Whigs enter Pitt's Government
June	French Victory at Fleurus
July	Thermidor
	Robespierre and his followers guillotined
October–November	Trial and acquittal of Hardy and Horne Tooke
November	The Jacobin Club closed
November–December	The British Convention at Edinburgh

1795

January	French troops occupy Amsterdam
	Trial of Skirving and Margarot in Scotland
April	Treaty of Basle between France and Prussia
May	Holland capitulates
July	Peace between France and Spain
October	Belgium incorporated in France
	The Convention dissolved
November	The Directory established

November–December Pitt's "Two Acts" (Seditious Meetings Act; Treasonable Practices Act)

1796

April Bonaparte opens his Italian campaign
May Conspiracy of Babœuf suppressed
December French expedition under Hoche sets sail from Brest for Ireland

1797

April—May Mutiny of the Fleet at Spithead and the Nore
July—September Unsuccessful negotiations of Lord Malmesbury at Lille
Austria signs the Peace of Campo Formio
Bonaparte appointed to organize the invasion of England

1798

January French invasion of Switzerland
April Suspension of the Habeas Corpus Act
May Bonaparte sails for Egypt
August Battle of the Nile
December Formation of the Second Coalition

1799

October Bonaparte returns to France
November *Coup d'état* of Brumaire
December The Consulate established

PART I

THE DEBATE BEGINS

First Impressions

1: SAMUEL ROMILLY. Letter to M. Dumont

28 July 1789

Sir Samuel Romilly (1757–1818), sucessful lawyer and Member of Parliament, was descended from a Huguenot family. He was a follower of Rousseau, a friend of Dumont and Bentham, and waged a long and fruitful struggle to mitigate the severities of the criminal law. He welcomed the Revolution and published a translation of letters describing the events of 1789 written by Dumont, to whom this letter is addressed. Later he turned against the Revolution, without however becoming an opponent of all change.

Etienne Dumont (1759–1829), was a Genevan preacher, proscribed in 1783 because of his political opinions. In 1785 he came to London as tutor to Lord Shelburne's sons and there met Fox, Sheridan, and Romilly. In 1788 Dumont visited Paris with Romilly and returned there the next year. He contributed to Mirabeau's journal, *Courrier de Provence* and helped him in writing his speeches. On his return from Paris he carried through the laborious work of preparing a series of Bentham's works for publication, and translating them into French. (*Memoirs of Sir S. Romilly*, 1840, I, p. 356.)

I AM sure I need not tell you how much I have rejoiced at the Revolution which has taken place. I think of nothing else, and please myself with endeavouring to guess at some of the important consequences which must follow throughout all Europe. I think myself happy that it has happened when I am of an age at which I may reasonably hope to live to see some of those consequences produced. It will perhaps surprise you, but it is certainly true, that the Revolution had produced a very sincere and very general joy here. It is the subject of all conversations; and even all the newspapers, without one exception, though they are not conducted by the most liberal or most philosophical of men, join in sounding forth the praises of the Parisians, and in rejoicing at an event so important for mankind.

2: JOHN CARTWRIGHT. Letter to the President of the Committee of Constitution of the States General

18 August 1789

John Cartwright (1740–1824) was a naval officer and country gentleman, for which he was excused much. He discovered parliamentary reform in 1775, and devoted the remainder of his life to a campaign for universal suffrage, secret ballot and annual parliaments. The eighteenth century produced many such eccentrics, who gave up their lives to causes which proved in the end not quite so eccentric as was supposed at the time. (*Life and Correspondence of Major Cartwright*, edited by F. D. Cartwright, 1826, p. 182.)

DEGENERATE must be that heart which expands not with sentiments of delight at what is now transacting in the National Assembly of France. The French, Sir, are not only asserting their own rights, but they are also asserting and advancing the general liberties of mankind.

3: WILLIAM WORDSWORTH. *The Prelude*, Book XI

Wordsworth's great autobiographical poem, *The Prelude*, was begun in 1799 and finished in 1805. Book VI deals with his first visit to France, with Robert Jones, in the summer of 1790, while he was still an undergraduate at Cambridge. Books IX, X and XI deal with the year he spent in France from November 1791 to December 1792. Wordsworth passionately defended the Revolution in his early years. His disillusionment appears to have been complete after the French invasion of Switzerland in 1798. Of his interest in politics, Coleridge's daughter, Sara, wrote: " How gravely and earnestly used Samuel Taylor Coleridge and William Wordsworth and my uncle Southey also to discuss the affairs of the nation, as if it all came home to their business and bosoms, as if it were their private concern! Men do not canvass these matters now-a-days, I think, quite in the same tone." (*The Prelude*, Book XI, lines 105–44.)

O pleasant exercise of hope and joy!
For mighty were the auxiliars which then stood
Upon our side, us who were strong in love!
Bliss was it in that dawn to be alive,
But to be young was very Heaven! O times,
In which the meagre, stale, forbidding ways
Of custom, law, and statute, took at once
The attraction of a country in romance!
When Reason seemed the most to assert her rights
When most intent on making of herself
A prime enchantress—to assist the work,
Which then was going forward in her name!
Not favoured spots alone, but the whole Earth,
The beauty wore of promise—that which sets
(As at some moments might not be unfelt
Among the bowers of Paradise itself)

The budding rose above the rose full blown.
What temper at the prospect did not wake
To happiness unthought of? The inert
Were roused, and lively natures rapt away!
They who had fed their childhood upon dreams,
The play-fellows of fancy, who had made
All powers of swiftness, subtilty, and strength
Their ministers,—who in lordly wise had stirred
Among the grandest objects of the sense,
And dealt with whatsoever they found there
As if they had within some lurking right
To wield it;—they, too, who of gentle mood
Had watched all gentle motions, and to these
Had fitted their own thoughts, schemes more mild
And in the region of their peaceful selves;—
Now was it that *both* found, the meek and lofty
Did both find, helpers to their hearts' desire,
And stuff at hand, plastic as they could wish,—
Were called upon to exercise their skill,
Not in Utopia,—subterranean fields,—
Or some secreted island, Heaven knows where!
But in the very world, which is the world
Of all of us,—the place where, in the end,
We find our happiness, or not at all!

4: HANNAH MORE. *Remarks on the Speech of M. Dupont*

1793

Hannah More (1745–1833) earned her living as a governess until she was emancipated by an annuity bestowed on her by the guardian of two pupils in lieu of his hand in marriage. The youthful friend of Garrick, Johnson, and Reynolds, a blue-stocking and much esteemed writer, she devoted the latter part of her life to the propagation of reading and morality in the villages, and the composition of cheap tracts and moral tales for the poor. (*Works of Hannah More*, 1818, VI, pp. 284–5.)

MUCH, very much is to be said in vindication of your favouring in the *first instance* their political projects. The cause they took in hand seemed to be the great cause of human kind. Its very name insured its popularity. What English heart did not exult at the demolition of the Bastille? What lover of his species did not triumph in the warm hope, that one of the finest countries in the world would soon be one of the most free? Popery and despotism, though chained by the gentle influence of Louis the Sixteenth, had actually slain their thousands. Little was it then imagined, that anarchy and atheism, the monsters who were about to succeed them, would soon slay their ten thousands. If we cannot regret the defeat of the two former tyrants, what must they be who can triumph in the mischiefs of the two latter? Who, I say, that had a head to reason, or a heart to feel, did not glow with the hope, that from the ruins of tyranny, and the rubbish of popery, a beautiful and finely framed edifice would in time have been constructed, and that ours would not have been the only country in which the patriot's fair idea of well-understood liberty, the politician's view of a perfect Constitution, together with the establishment of a pure and reasonable, a sublime and rectified Christianity, might be realized?

5: WILLIAM BLAKE. *The French Revolution*

1791

William Blake (1757–1827) was employed by the bookseller Johnson to design plates for a book of stories for children by Mary Wollstonecraft. Through Johnson he met Price, Priestley, Paine, Godwin and other revolutionary sympathizers. Only the first book of his *French Revolution* was printed, and it was for long forgotten. He subsequently wrote much more violently against kings, but on the whole his interest in contemporary politics was overborne by his prophetic spirit. (*Political Works*, ed. John Sampson, Oxford, 1913, pp. 266, 275–7.)

But the dens shook and trembled: the prisoners look up and assay to shout; they listen,
Then laugh in the dismal den, then are silent; and a light walks round the dark towers.
For the Commons convene in the Hall of the Nation; like spirits of fire in the beautiful
Porches of the Sun, to plant beauty in the desert craving abyss, they gleam
On the anxious city: all children new-born first behold them, tears are fled,
And they nestle in earth-breathing bosoms. So the city of Paris, their wives and children,
Look up to the morning Senate, and visions of sorrow leave pensive streets.

But heavy-brow'd jealousies lour o'er the Louvre; and terrors of ancient Kings
Descend from the gloom and wander thro' the palace, and weep round the King and his Nobles;
While loud thunders roll, troubling the dead. Kings are sick throughout all the earth!

The voice ceas'd: the Nation sat; and the triple forg'd fetters of times were unloos'd.
The voice ceas'd: the Nation sat; but ancient darkness and trembling wander thro' the palace.

Then the valleys of France shall cry to the soldier: " Throw down thy sword and musket,
And run and embrace the meek peasant." Her Nobles shall hear and shall weep, and put off
The red robe of terror, the crown of oppression, the shoes of contempt, and unbuckle
The girdle of war from the desolate earth. Then the Priest in his thund'rous cloud
Shall weep, bending to earth, embracing the valleys, and putting his hand to the plough,
Shall say: " No more I curse thee; but now I will bless thee: no more in deadly black
Devour thy labour; nor lift up a cloud in thy heavens, O laborious plough;
That the wild raging millions, that wander in forests, and howl in law-blasted wastes,
Strength madden'd with slavery, honesty bound in the dens of superstition,
May sing in the village, and shout in the harvest, and woo in pleasant gardens
Their once savage loves, now beaming with knowledge, with gentle awe adornèd;
And the saw, and the hammer, the chisel, the pencil, the pen, and the instruments
Of heavenly song sound in the wilds once forbidden, to teach the laborious ploughman
And shepherd, deliver'd from clouds of war, from pestilence, from night-fear, from murder,
From falling, from stifling, from hunger, from cold, from slander, discontent and sloth,
That walk in beasts and birds of night, driven back by the sandy desert,
Like pestilent fogs round cities of men; and the happy earth sing in its course,

The mild peaceable nations be openèd to heav'n, and men walk
with their fathers in bliss."
Then hear the first voice of the morning: " Depart, O clouds of
night, and no more
Return; be withdrawn cloudy war, troops of warriors depart, nor
around our peaceable city
Breathe fires; but ten miles from Paris let all be peace, nor a
soldier be seen! "

6: MRS. BARBAULD. *An Address to the Opposers of the Repeal of the Corporation and Test Acts*

1790

Anna Letitia Barbauld (1743–1825) was a learned and poetical lady, whose marriage to a dissenting clergyman doubtless explains the fervour with which she defended the cause of the Dissenters in the pamphlet cited. Her writings and associations were for the most part literary rather than political. (Pp. 30–6.)

WE appeal to the certain, sure operation of increasing light and knowledge, which it is no more in your power to stop, than to repel the tide with your naked hand, or to wither with your breath the genial influence of vegetation. The spread of that light is in general gradual and imperceptible; but there are periods when its progress is accelerated, when it seems with a sudden flash to open the firmament, and pour in day at once. Can ye not discern the signs of the times? The minds of men are in movement from the Borysthenes to the Atlantic. . . .

The genius of Philosophy is walking abroad, and with the touch of Ithuriel's spear is trying the establishments of the earth. The various forms of Prejudice, Superstition and Servility start up in their true shapes, which had long imposed upon the world under the revered semblances of Honour, Faith, and Loyalty. Whatever is loose must be shaken, whatever is corrupted must be lopt away; whatever is not built on the broad basis of public utility must be thrown to the ground. . . .

Man, *as* man, becomes an object of respect. Tenets are transferred from theory to practice. The glowing sentiment and the lofty speculation no longer serve " but to adorn the pages of a book"; they are brought home to men's business and bosoms; and, what some centuries ago it was daring but to think, and dangerous to express, is now realized, and carried into effect. Systems are analysed into their first principles, and principles are fairly pursued to their legitimate consequences. The enemies of reformation, who palliate what they cannot defend, and defer what they dare not refuse; who, with Festus, put off to a more convenient season what, only because it is the present season is inconvenient, stand aghast; and find they have no power to put back the important hour, when nature is labouring with the birth of great events. Can ye not discern?—But you do discern these signs; you discern them well, and your alarm is apparent. You see a mighty empire breaking from bondage, and exerting the energies of recovered freedom. . . .

Nobles, the creatures of Kings, exist there no longer; but Man, the creature of God, exists there. Millions of men exist there who, only now, truly begin to exist, and hail with shouts of grateful acclamation the better birth-day of their country. Go on, generous nation, set the world an example of virtues as you have of talents. Be our model, as we have been yours.

7: ARTHUR YOUNG. *Travels in France, During the Years* 1787, 1788, 1789

1792

Arthur Young (1741–1820), a Suffolk squire, failed as a farmer, but succeeded as an agricultural writer. He was a leading advocate of enclosures and scientific farming. His *Travels in France* are described by his French editor, Henri Sée, as " one of the most precious documents we possess on France at the end of the *ancien régime* and the beginning of the Revolution ". (pp. 105–6.)

THE 11th (June, 1789). I have been in much company all day, and cannot but remark, that there seem to be no settled ideas of the best means of forming a new constitution. Yesterday the Abbé Syeyes made a motion in the House of Commons, to declare boldly to the privileged orders, that if they will not join the commons, the latter will proceed in the national business without them; and the House decreed it, with a small amendment. This causes much conversation on what will be the consequence of such a proceeding; and on the contrary, on what may flow from the nobility and clergy continuing steadily to refuse to join the commons, and should they so proceed, to protest against all they decree, and appeal to the King to dissolve the states, and recall them in such a form as may be practicable for business. In these most interesting discussions, I find a general ignorance of the principles of government; a strange and unaccountable appeal, on one side, to ideal and visionary rights of nature; and, on the other, no settled plan that shall give security to the people for being in future in a much better situation than hitherto; a security absolutely necessary. But the nobility, with the principles of great lords that I converse with, are most disgustingly tenacious of all old rights, however hard they may bear on the people; they will not hear of giving way in the least to the spirit of liberty, beyond the point of paying equal land-taxes, which they hold to be all that can with reason be demanded. The popular party, on the other hand, seem to consider all liberty as depending on the privileged classes being lost, and outvoted in the order of the commons, at least for making the new constitution; and when I urge the great probability, that should they once unite, there will remain no power of ever separating them; and that in such case, they will have a very questionable constitution, perhaps a very bad one; I am always told, that the first object must be for the people to get the power of doing good; and that it is no argument against such a conduct to urge that an ill use may be made of it. But among such men, the common idea is, that anything tending towards a separate order, like our House of Lords, is absolutely inconsistent with liberty; all which seems perfectly wild and unfounded.

8: EDMUND BURKE. Letter to M. Dupont

October 1789

The best comment is Hazlitt's: "The only specimen of Burke is, *all that he wrote*." (*Correspondence*, edited by Earl Fitzwilliam, etc., 1844. III, pp. 104–8.)

YOU may easily believe, that I have had my eyes turned, with great curiosity, to the astonishing scene now displayed in France. It has certainly given rise in my mind to many reflections, and to some emotions. These are natural and unavoidable; but it would ill become me to be too ready in forming a positive opinion upon matters transacted in a country, with the correct political map of which I must be very imperfectly acquainted. Things, indeed, have already happened so much beyond the scope of all speculation, that persons of infinitely more sagacity than I am, ought to be ashamed of anything like confidence in their reasoning upon the operation of any principle, or the effect of any measure.

I have nothing to check my wishes towards the establishment of a solid and rational scheme of liberty in France. On the subject of the relative power of nations, I may have my prejudices; but I envy internal freedom, security, and good order, to none. When, therefore, I shall learn that, in France, the citizen, by whatever description he is qualified, is in a perfect state of legal security, with regard to his life,—to his property,—to the uncontrolled disposal of his person, —to the free use of his industry and his faculties:— When I hear that he is protected in the beneficial enjoyment of the estates to which, by the course of settled law, he was born, or is provided with a fair compensation for them;—that he is maintained in the full fruition of the advantages belonging to the state and condition of life in which he had lawfully engaged himself, or is supplied with a substantial, equitable, equivalent:—When I am assured that a simple citizen may decently express his sentiments upon public affairs, without hazard to his life or safety, even though against a predominant and fashionable opinion:— When I know all this of France, I shall be as well pleased as every one must be, who has not forgot the general communion of mankind, nor lost his natural sympathy, in local and accidental connexions.

9A: THE ANALYTICAL REVIEW

1789

This review, founded by Thomas Christie (see note to No. 27), was published by Joseph Johnson (1738–1809), a bookseller in St. Paul's Churchyard, who published for Priestley, Mrs. Barbauld, Horne Tooke and Mary Wollstonecraft amongst others. The first number came out in May 1788, the last in 1799.

WHAT are the machinations of despots, or the intrigues of worthless statesmen, when compared to the object now before us? A nation of 24 millions of people raising their unanimous voice in favour of liberty, and the rights of human nature! . . . As men, and as Britons, we most sincerely wish them success; and pray that no dissentions amongst themselves may obscure the glorious prospect before them. We are confident, indeed, that it cannot long be obscured. . . . There are some who are of opinion that if the French become a free and commercial people, it will be much against the interest of this country; but for our part we declare this a narrow and ill-grounded idea. . . . The emancipation of France may be followed by a restoration of their ancient rights to the Austrian Netherlands; and in time, by the emancipation of Spain and other countries of Europe. We seem to be advancing to a great aera in the history of human affairs. The papal power, that scourge of nations, is declining. . . . More liberal ideas, both in politics and religion, are everywhere gaining ground. . . . The Genius of Commerce is gone forth amongst the nations of the earth; everywhere carrying Peace and Plenty, and Freedom in her train.

9B: THE SCOTS MAGAZINE

October 1789

(*The Scots Magazine*, LI, pp. 474–6.)

Editor's Note. It may not be improper, by way of contrast to the above, to read the sentiments of a writer who draws very different conclusions from the view he takes of the present state of the world.

Sir,

. . . I would call the attention of your readers to the conformity of events, at this time, to the predictions of our Saviour, respecting the destruction of Jerusalem. . . . The comparison holds too strikingly in the leading features of the times: in infidelity, heterodoxy, luxury, dissipation, debauchery, excess and extravagance of every kind, total want of principle, impunity of crimes, and mistaken pretences and pleas of humanity;—in short, in the pride of human wit and wickedness: and universal passion to do what every one likes. . . . Man is left to universal liberty and unlimited speculation. Experiments have been tried, and are daily trying, with the dearest interests of Mankind, Religion, and Government, and at the dearest rate; Faction and Party, abusing the names of Liberty and Patriotism, and subverting established governments, without ability, authority, or temper to substitute better, or to maintain that subordination to the Law which can ensure men's lives and properties. . . .

IEROPHANTES.

10: THE MORNING POST AND DAILY ADVERTISER

22 October 1789

THERE are some people who seem to think that the mobs in the different parts of France, but particularly in Paris, are intitled to the appellation of Whigs.

But we who wish not to see so honourable a name disgraced, by its being bestowed on such SAVAGES, are anxious to prove, that the Antipodes are not further asunder than the principles by which those mobs have been actuated, if principles they can be called, are remote from those which GENUINE WHIGGISM inculcates. . . . And yet those who *would* be *Whigs*, if they knew how, who profess whiggism, but know not in what it consists, call those WHIGS who thus debase the MAJESTY of the PEOPLE, and think *we* are not WHIGS because we represent those MISCREANTS as in rebellion against the KING and the PEOPLE.

11: RICHARD PRICE. *A Discourse on the Love of our Country, delivered on 4 November 1789 at the Meeting House in the Old Jewry, to the Society for Commemorating the Revolution in Great Britain*

1789

Richard Price (1723–91) was a dissenting minister, a Unitarian, and the author of books on population and political economy. Among his works were a plan for the extinction of the National Debt, which influenced Pitt, political pamphlets in support of the Americans (he was a friend of Franklin), and *A Review of the Principal Questions in Morals*, which is still esteemed by moral philosophers. Burke chose the discourse quoted below for attack in his *Reflections*. (Pp. 31–4, 35–41, 49–51.)

WE are met to thank God for that event in this country to which the name of THE REVOLUTION has been given; and which, for more than a century, it has been usual for the friends of freedom, and more especially Protestant Dissenters, to celebrate with expressions of joy and exultation ... By a bloodless victory, the fetters which despotism had been long preparing for us were broken; the rights of the people were asserted, a tyrant expelled, and a Sovereign of our own choice appointed in his room. Security was given to our property, and our consciences were emancipated. The bounds of free enquiry were enlarged; the volume in which are the words of eternal life, was laid more open to our examination; and that *aera* of light and liberty was introduced among us, by which we have been made an example to other kingdoms, and became the instructors of the world. Had it not been for this deliverance, the probability is, that, instead of being thus distinguished, we should now have been a base people, groaning under the infamy and misery of Popery and slavery. Let us, therefore, offer thanksgivings to God, the author of all our blessings.

> *Had he not been on our side, we should have been swallowed up quick, and the proud waters would have gone over our souls. But our souls are escaped, and the snare has been broken. Blessed then be the name of the Lord, who made heaven and earth.*
>
> cxxivth Psalm.

It is well known that King James was not far from gaining his purpose; and that probably he would have succeeded, had he been less in a hurry. But he wanted courage as well as prudence; and, therefore, fled, and left us to settle quietly for ourselves that constitution of government which is now our boast. We have particular reason, as Protestant Dissenters, to rejoice on this occasion. It was at this time we were rescued from persecution, and obtained the liberty of worshipping God in the manner we think most acceptable to him. It was then our meeting-houses were opened, our worship was taken under the protection of the law and the principles of toleration gained a triumph. We have, therefore, on this occasion, peculiar reasons for thanksgiving.—But let us remember that we ought not to satisfy ourselves with thanksgivings. Our gratitude, if genuine, will be accompanied with endeavours to give stability to the deliverance our country has obtained, and to extend and improve the happiness with which the Revolution has blest us.—

Let us, in particular, take care not to forget the principles of the Revolution. This Society has, very properly, in its reports, held out these principles, as an instruction to the public. I will only take notice of the three following:

First; The right to liberty of conscience in religious matters.

Secondly; The right to resist power when abused. And,

Thirdly; The right to choose our own governors; to cashier them for misconduct; and to frame a government for ourselves.

I would farther direct you to remember, that though the Revolution was a great work, it was by no means a perfect work; and that all was not then gained which was necessary to put the kingdom in the secure and complete possession of the blessings of liberty.—In particular, you should recollect that the toleration then obtained was imperfect. It included only those who could declare their faith in the doctrinal articles of the Church of England. It has, indeed, been since extended, but not sufficiently; for there still exist penal laws on account of religious opinions, which (were they carried into execution) would shut up many of our places of worship, and silence and imprison some of our ablest and best men.—The TEST LAWS are also still in force; and deprive of eligibility to civil and military offices, all who cannot conform to the established worship. It is with great pleasure I find that the body of Protestant Dissenters, though defeated in their attempts to deliver their country from this disgrace to it, have determined to persevere. Should they at last succeed, they will have the satisfaction, not only of removing from themselves a proscription they do not deserve, but of contributing to lessen the number of our public iniquities. For I cannot call by a gentler name, laws which convert an ordinance appointed by our Saviour to commemorate his death, into an instrument of oppressive policy, and a qualification of rakes and atheists for civil posts.—I have said, *should* they succeed—but perhaps I ought not suggest a doubt about their success.[1] And, indeed, when I consider that in SCOTLAND the established church is defended by no such test—that in IRELAND it has been abolished—that in a great neighbouring country it has been declared to be an indefeasible right of all citizens to be equally eligible to public offices—that in the same kingdom a professed Dissenter from the established church holds the first office in the state—that in the Emperor's dominions *Jews* have been lately admitted to the enjoyment of equal privileges with other citizens—and that in this very country, a Dissenter, though excluded from the power of *executing* the laws, yet is allowed to be employed in *making* them.—When, I say, I consider such facts as these, I am disposed to think it impossible that the enemies of the repeal of the Test Laws should not soon become ashamed, and give up their opposition.

But the most important instance of the imperfect

[1] It has been unfortunate for the Dissenters that, in their late applications for a repeal of the Test Laws, they have been opposed by MR. PITT. He has contended that, on account of their not believing and worshipping as the Church of England does, they ought to be excluded from that eligibility to public offices which is the right of other citizens, and consequently denied a *complete* toleration; acknowledging, however, their integrity and respectableness, but reckoning it only the more necessary on that account to defend the national church against them. Such sentiments in these times can do no honour to any man, much less to a son of the late Lord CHATHAM. . . .

state in which the Revolution left our constitution, is the INEQUALITY OF OUR REPRESENTATION. I think, indeed, this defect in our constitution so gross and so palpable, as to make it excellent chiefly in form and theory. You should remember that a representation in the legislature of a kingdom is the *basis* of constitutional liberty in it, and of all legitimate government; and that without it a government is nothing but an usurpation.[1] When the representation is fair and equal, and at the same time vested with such powers as our House of Commons possesses, a kingdom may be said to govern itself, and consequently to possess to true liberty. When the representation is partial, a kingdom possesses liberty only partially; and if extremely partial, it only gives a *semblance* of liberty; but if not only extremely partial, but corruptly chosen, and under corrupt influence after being chosen, it becomes a *nuisance*, and produces the worst of all forms of government—a government by corruption—a government carried on and supported by spreading venality and profligacy through a kingdom. May heaven preserve this kingdom from a calamity so dreadful! It is the point of depravity to which abuses under such a government as ours naturally tend, and the last stage of national unhappiness. We are, at present, I hope, at a great distance from it. But it cannot be pretended that there are no advances towards it, or that there is no reason for apprehension and alarm.

What an eventful period is this! I am thankful that I have lived to it; and I could almost say, *Lord now lettest thou thy servant depart in peace, for mine eyes have seen thy salvation.* I have lived to see a diffusion of

[1] Except in states so small as to admit of a Legislative Assembly, consisting of all the members of the state.

knowledge, which has undermined superstition and error—I have lived to see the rights of men better understood than ever; and nations panting for liberty, which seemed to have lost the idea of it.—I have lived to see THIRTY MILLIONS of people, indignant and resolute, spurning at slavery, and demanding liberty with an irresistible voice; their king led in triumph, and an arbitrary monarch surrendering himself to his subjects.—After sharing in the benefits of one Revolution, I have been spared to be a witness to two other Revolutions, both glorious.—And now methinks, I see the ardour for liberty catching and spreading; a general amendment beginning in human affairs; the dominion of kings changed for the dominion of laws, and the dominion of priests giving way to the dominion of reason and conscience.

Be encouraged all ye friends of freedom, and writers in its defence! The times are auspicious. Your labours have not been in vain. Behold kingdoms, admonished by you, starting from sleep, breaking their fetters, and claiming justice from their oppressors! Behold, the light you have struck out, after setting AMERICA free, reflected to FRANCE, and there kindled into a blaze that lays despotism in ashes, and warms and illuminates EUROPE!

Tremble all ye oppressors of the world! Take warning all ye supporters of slavish governments, and slavish hierarchies! Call no more (absurdly and wickedly) REFORMATION, innovation. You cannot now hold the world in darkness. Struggle no longer against increasing light and liberality. Restore to mankind their rights; and consent to the correction of abuses, before they and you are destroyed together.

The Intervention of Burke

12: DEBATE IN THE HOUSE OF COMMONS ON THE ARMY ESTIMATES

5 February 1790

(*Parliamentary History*, XXVIII, pp. 353–67.)

BURKE

That France had hitherto been our first object, in all considerations concerning the balance of power. The presence or absence of France totally varied every sort of speculation relative to that balance.

That France is, at this time, in a political light to be considered as expunged out of the system of Europe. Whether she could ever appear in it again, as a leading power, was not easy to determine: but at present he considered France as not politically existing; and most assuredly it would take up much time to restore her to her former active existence.

In the last age, we were in danger of being entangled by the example of France in the net of a relentless despotism. It is not necessary to say anything upon that example; it exists no longer. Our present danger from the example of a people, whose character knows no medium, is, with regard to government, a danger from anarchy; a danger of being led through an admiration of successful fraud and violence, to an imitation of the excesses of an irrational, unprincipled, proscribing, confiscating, plundering, ferocious, bloody, and tyrannical democracy. On the side of religion, the danger of their example is no longer from intolerance, but from atheism; a foul, unnatural vice, foe to all the dignity and consolation of mankind; which seems in France, for a long time, to have been embodied into a faction, accredited, and almost avowed.

Fox

The scenes of bloodshed and cruelty which had been acted in France no man could have heard of without lamenting; but still, when the severe tyranny under which the people had so long groaned was considered, the excesses which they committed, in their endeavour to shake off the yoke of despotism, might, he thought, be spoken of with some degree of compassion; and he was persuaded that, unsettled as their present state appeared, it was preferable to their former condition, and that ultimately, it would be for the advantage of this country that France had regained her freedom.

Sheridan

Mr. Sheridan added some warm compliments to Mr. Burke's general principles; but said that he could not conceive how it was possible for a person possessing such principles, or for any man who valued our own constitution, and revered the revolution that obtained it for us, to unite with such feelings an indignant and unqualified abhorrence of all the proceedings of the patriotic party in France.—He conceived theirs to be as just a revolution as ours, proceeding upon as sound a principle and a greater provocation. He vehemently defended the general views and conduct of the national assembly. He could not even understand what was meant by the charge against them of having overturned the laws, the justice, and the revenues of their country. What were their laws? The arbitrary mandates of capricious despotism. What their justice? The partial adjudications of venal magistrates. What their revenues? National bankruptcy. This he thought the fundamental error of his right hon. friend's argument, that he accused the national assembly of creating the evils, which they had found existing in full deformity at the first hour of their meeting.

13: EDMUND BURKE. Substance of the Speech on the Army Estimates, House of Commons

9 February 1790

(*Works of Edmund Burke* [Bohn's British Classics, 1872–3], III, pp. 278–81.)

HE felt some concern that this strange thing, called a Revolution in France, should be compared with the glorious event commonly called the Revolution in England; and the conduct of the soldiery, on that occasion, compared with the behaviour of some of the troops of France in the present instance. At that period the Prince of Orange, a prince of the blood-royal in England, was called in by the flower of the English aristocracy to defend its ancient constitution, and not to level all distinctions. To this prince, so invited, the aristocratic leaders who commanded the troops went over with their several corps, in bodies, to the deliverer of their country. Aristocratic leaders brought up the corps of citizens who newly enlisted in this cause. Military obedience changed its object; but military discipline was not for a moment interrupted in its principle. The troops were ready for war, but indisposed to mutiny.

But as the conduct of the English armies was different, so was that of the whole English nation at that time. In truth, the circumstances of our revolution (as it is called) and that of France are just the reverse of each other in almost every particular, and in the whole spirit of the transaction. With us it was the case of a legal monarch attempting arbitrary power—in France it is the case of an arbitrary monarch, beginning, from whatever cause, to legalize his authority. The one was to be resisted, the other was to be managed and directed; but in neither case was the order of the state to be changed, lest government might be ruined, which ought only to be corrected and legalized. With us we got rid of the man, and preserved the constituent parts of the state. There they get rid of the constituent parts of the state, and keep the man. What we did was in truth and substance, and in a constitutional light, a revolution, not made, but prevented. We took solid securities; we settled doubtful questions; we corrected anomalies in our law. In the stable, fundamental parts of our constitution we made no revolution; no, nor any alteration at all. We did not impair the monarchy. Perhaps it might be shown that we strengthened it very considerably. The nation kept the same ranks, the same orders, the same privileges, the same franchises, the same rules for property, the same subordinations, the same order in the law, in the revenue, and in the magistracy; the same Lords, the same Commons, the same corporations, the same electors.

The church was not impaired. Her estates, her majesty, her splendour, her orders and gradations, continued the same. She was preserved in her full efficiency, and cleared only of a certain intolerance, which was her weakness and disgrace. The church and the state were the same after the Revolution that they were before, but better secured in every part.

Was little done because a revolution was not made in the constitution? No! Everything was done; because we commenced with reparation, not with ruin.

Accordingly the state flourished. Instead of lying as dead, in a sort of trance, or exposed, as some others, in an epileptic fit, to the pity or derision of the world, for her wild, ridiculous, convulsive movements, impotent to every purpose but that of dashing out her brains against the pavement, Great Britain rose above the standard even of her former self. An *aera* of a more improved domestic prosperity then commenced, and still continues not only unimpaired, but growing, under the wasting hand of time. All the energies of the country were awakened. England never presented a firmer countenance, nor a more vigorous arm, to all her enemies and to all her rivals. Europe under her respired and revived. Everywhere she appeared as the protector, assertor, or avenger, of liberty. A war was made and supported against fortune itself. The treaty of Ryswick, which first limited the power of France, was soon after made: the grand alliance very shortly followed, which shook to the foundations the dreadful power which menaced the independence of mankind. The states of Europe lay happy under the shade of a great and free monarchy, which knew how to be great without endangering its own peace at home, or the internal or external peace of any of its neighbours.

Mr. Burke said he should have felt very unpleasantly if he had not delivered these sentiments. He was near the end of his natural, probably still nearer the end of his political, career; that he was weak and weary; and wished for rest. That he was little disposed to controversies, or what is called a detailed opposition. That at his time of life, if he could not do something by some sort of weight of opinion, natural or acquired, it was useless and indecorous to attempt anything by mere struggle. *Turpe senex miles*. That he had for that reason little attended the army business, or that of the revenue, or almost any other matter of detail, for some years past. That he had, however, his task. He was far from condemning such opposition; on the contrary, he mostly highly applauded it, where a just occasion existed for it, and gentlemen had vigour and capacity to pursue it. Where a great occasion occurred, he was, and, while he continued in parliament, would be, amongst the most active and the most earnest; as he hoped he had shown on a late event. With respect to the constitution itself, he wished few alterations in it. Happy if he left it not the worse for any share he had taken in its service.

Mr. Fox then rose, and declared, in substance, that so far as regarded the French army, he went no further than the general principle, by which that army showed itself indisposed to be an instrument in the servitude of their fellow-citizens, but did not enter into the particulars of their conduct. He declared, that he did not affect a democracy. That he always thought any of the simple, unbalanced governments bad; simple monarchy, simple aristocracy, simple democracy; he held them all imperfect or vicious; all were bad by themselves; the composition alone was good. That these had been always his principles, in which he had agreed with his friend Mr. Burke, of whom he said many kind and flattering things, which Mr. Burke, I take it for granted, will know himself too well to think he merits from anything but Mr. Fox's acknowledged good nature. Mr. Fox thought, however, that, in many cases, Mr. Burke was rather carried too far by his hatred to innovation.

Mr. Burke said, he well knew that these had been Mr. Fox's invariable opinions; that they were a sure ground for the confidence of his country. But he had been fearful, that cabals of very different intentions would be ready to make use of his great name, against his character and sentiments, in order to derive a credit to their destructive machinations.

Mr. Sheridan then rose, and made a lively and eloquent speech against Mr. Burke; in which, among other things, he said that Mr. Burke had libelled the National Assembly of France, and had cast out reflections on such characters as those of the Marquis de la Fayette and Mr. Bailly.

Mr. Burke said, that he did not libel the National Assembly of France, whom he considered very little in the discussion of these matters. That he thought all the substantial power resided in the republic of Paris, whose authority guided, or whose example was followed by, all the republics of France. The republic of Paris had an army under their orders, and not under those of the National Assembly.

N.B. As to the particular gentlemen, I do not remember that Mr. Burke mentioned either of them—certainly not Mr. Bailly. He alluded, undoubtedly, to the case of the Marquis de la Fayette; but whether what he asserted of him be a libel on him, must be left to those who are acquainted with the business.

Mr. Pitt concluded the debate with becoming gravity and dignity, and a reserve on both sides of the question, as related to France, fit for a person in a ministerial situation. He said, that what he had spoken only regarded France when she should unite, which he rather thought she soon might, with the liberty she had acquired, the blessings of law and order. He, too, said several civil things concerning the sentiments of Mr. Burke, as applied to this country.

14: DEBATE IN THE HOUSE OF COMMONS ON THE QUEBEC GOVERNMENT BILL

21 April, 1791

(*Parliamentary History*, XXIX, pp. 366–88.)

Burke

The ancient Canadians were next to be considered, and being the most numerous, they were entitled to the greatest attention. Were we to give them the French constitution—a constitution founded on principles diametrically opposite to ours, that could not assimilate with it in a single point; as different from it as wisdom from folly, as vice from virtue, as the most opposite extremes in nature—a constitution founded on what was called the rights of man?

Fox

Mr. Fox said, he was sincerely sorry to feel that he must support the motion, and the more so, as his right hon. friend had made it necessary, by bringing on, in so irregular a manner, a discussion of a matter by no means connected with the Quebec bill.

On the French revolution he did, indeed, differ from his right hon. friend. Their opinions, he had no scruple to say, were wide as the poles asunder. But, what had a difference of opinion on that, which to the House was only a matter of theoretical contemplation, to do with the discussion of a practical point, on which no such difference existed? On that revolution, he adhered to his opinion, and never would retract one syllable of what he had said. He repeated, that he thought it, on the whole, one of the most glorious events in the history of mankind.

BURKE

The practice now was, upon all occasions, to praise, in the highest strain, the French constitution: some indeed qualified their argument so far, by praising only the French revolution: but in that he could see no difference, as the French constitution, if they had any, was the consequence and effect of that revolution. So fond were gentlemen of this favourite topic, that whoever disapproved of the anarchy and confusion that had taken place in France, or could not foresee the benefits that were to arise out of it, were stigmatised as enemies to liberty, and to the British constitution,—charges that were false, unfounded, misapplied, and every way unfair. Doctrines of this kind, he thought, were extremely dangerous at all times, and much more so, if they were to be sanctioned by so great a name as that of the right hon. gentleman, who always put whatever he said in the strongest and most forcible view in which it could possibly appear. Thus, it had become common to set the French constitution up against the English constitution, upon all occasions, when the comparison could be introduced; and then, he insisted, if the former was praised, the latter must be proportionably depreciated.

It certainly was indiscretion, at any period, but especially at his time of life, to provoke enemies, or give his friends occasion to desert him; yet if his firm and steady adherence to the British constitution placed him in such a dilemma, he would risk all; and, as public duty and public prudence taught him, with his last words exclaim, "Fly from the French constitution". (Mr. Fox here whispered, that "there was no loss of friends".) Mr. Burke said Yes, there was a loss of friends—he knew the price of his conduct—he had done his duty at the price of his friend—their friendship was at an end.

Mr. Fox rose to reply; but his mind was so much agitated, and his heart so much affected by what had fallen from Mr. Burke, that it was some minutes before he could proceed. Tears trickled down his cheeks, and he strove in vain to give utterance to feelings that dignified and exalted his nature. The sensibility of every member in the House appeared uncommonly excited upon the occasion.

15: EDMUND BURKE. *Reflections on the Revolution in France*

1790

(*Works*, II, pp. 289–92.)

WHATEVER may be the success of evasion in explaining away the gross error of *fact*, which supposes that his Majesty (though he holds it in concurrence with the wishes) owes his crown to the choice of his people, yet nothing can evade their full explicit declaration, concerning the principle of a right in the people to choose; which right is directly maintained, and tenaciously adhered to. All the oblique insinuations concerning election bottom in this proposition, and are referable to it. Lest the foundation of the king's exclusive legal title should pass for a mere rant of adulatory freedom, the political divine[1] proceeds dogmatically to assert, that, by the principles of the Revolution, the people of England have acquired three fundamental rights, all which, with him, compose one system, and lie together in one short sentence; namely, that we have acquired a right,

1. "To choose our own governors."
2. "To cashier them for misconduct."
3. "To frame a government for ourselves."

This new, and hitherto unheard-of, bill of rights, though made in the name of the whole people, belongs

[1] Dr. Price. See No. 11.

to those gentlemen and their faction only. The body of the people of England have no share in it. They utterly disclaim it. They will resist the practical assertion of it with their lives and fortunes. They are bound to do so by the laws of their country, made at the time of that very Revolution which is appealed to in favour of the fictitious rights claimed by the Society which abuses its name.

These gentlemen of the Old Jewry, in all their reasonings on the Revolution of 1688, have a Revolution which happened in England about forty years before, and the late French Revolution, so much before their eyes, and in their hearts, that they are constantly confounding all the three together. It is necessary that we should separate what they confound. We must recall their erring fancies to the *acts* of the Revolution which we revere, for the discovery of its true *principles*. If the *principles* of the Revolution of 1688 are anywhere to be found, it is in the statute called the *Declaration of Right*. In that most wise, sober, and considerate declaration, drawn up by great lawyers and great statesmen, and not by warm and inexperienced enthusiasts, not one word is said, nor one suggestion made, of a general right "to choose our own *governors*; to cashier them for misconduct; and to *form* a government for *ourselves*".

Unquestionably there was at the Revolution, in the person of King William, a small and a temporary deviation from the strict order of a regular hereditary succession; but it is against all genuine principles of jurisprudence to draw a principle from a law made in a special case, and regarding an individual person. *Privilegium non transit in exemplum.* If ever there was a time favourable for establishing the principle, that a king of popular choice was the only legal king, without all doubt it was at the Revolution. Its not being done at that time is a proof that the nation was of opinion it ought not to be done at any time. There is no person so completely ignorant of our history as not to know, that the majority in parliament of both parties were so little disposed to anything resembling that principle, that at first they were determined to place the vacant crown, not on the head of the Prince of Orange, but on that of his wife Mary, daughter of King James, the eldest born of the issue of that king, which they acknowledged as undoubtedly his. It would be to repeat a very trite story, to recall to your memory all those circumstances which demonstrated that their accepting King William was not properly a *choice*; but to all those who did not wish, in effect, to recall King James, or to deluge their country in blood, and again to bring their religion, laws, and liberties into the peril they had just escaped, it was an act of *necessity*, in the strictest moral sense in which necessity can be taken.

16: WILLIAM WINDHAM. Entry in his Diary for 7 November 1790

William Windham (1750–1810), a Foxite Whig, took Burke as his political guide and followed him in violent opposition to the French Revolution. He became Secretary at War in 1794 and was a strong advocate of intervention in France in support of the Royalists. He held a strange mixture of opinions and was immoderate in the expression of them. (*The Windham Papers*, with an introduction by Lord Roseberry, 1913, I, pp. 96–7.)

ON Thursday I conceive it was, that a material incident happened—the arrival of Mr. Burke's pamphlet.[1] Never was there, I suppose, a work so valuable in its kind, or that displayed powers of so extraordinary a sort. It is a work that may seem capable of overturning the National Assembly, and turning the stream of opinion throughout Europe. One would think, that the author of such a work, would be called to the government of his country, by the combined voices of every man in it. What shall be said of the state of things when it is remembered that the writer is a man decried, persecuted, and proscribed; not being much valued, even by his own party, and by half the nation considered as little better than an ingenious madman?

[1] The reference is to Burke's *Reflections*.

17: DR. PARR. *A Sequel to the printed paper lately circulated in Warwickshire by the Revd. Chas. Carter*

1792

Dr. Samuel Parr (1747–1825) was a schoolmaster and clergyman of the Church of England. His attachment to the Foxite Whigs robbed him of his hope of preferment. He defended Priestley, sympathized with the early ideals of the French Revolution, and criticized the repressive legislation of Pitt. (*Memoirs of the Life, Writings and Opinions of the Revd. Samuel Parr, LL.D.*, by the Rev. W. Field, 1828, I, pp. 310–11.)

UPON the first perusal of Mr. Burke's book, I felt, like many other men, its magic force; and, like many other men, I was at last delivered from the illusions which had " cheated my reason", and borne me on from admiration to assent. But though the dazzling spell be now dissolved, I still remember with pleasure the gay and celestial visions, when " my mind in sweet madness was robbed of itself". I still look back, with a mixture of piety and holy awe, to the wizard himself, who, having lately broken his wand, in a start of frenzy, has shortened the term of his sorceries; and of drugs so potent, as " to bathe the spirits in delight", I must still acknowledge that many were culled from the choicest and " most virtuous plants of paradise itself".

18: MARY WOLLSTONECRAFT. *A Vindication of the Rights of Men*

1790

Mary Wollstonecraft (1759–97) became a governess to escape from the house of her father who was ruining himself with drink. By her talent and character she established a reputation in London literary society. From 1793 to 1795 she lived with the American Gilbert Imlay in France and after his desertion tried to commit suicide. She enjoyed a brief but happy connection with Godwin, whom she married in 1797, and died after the birth of Mary Godwin, who was later to become the wife of Shelley. Her *Vindication of the Rights of Men* was a reply to Burke's *Reflections*. (2nd edition, 1790, p. 27.)

MISERY, to reach your heart, I perceive, must have its cap and bells; your tears are reserved, very *naturally* considering your character, for the declamation of the theatre, or for the downfall of queens, whose rank alters the nature of folly, and throws a graceful veil over vices that degrade humanity; whilst the distress of many industrious mothers, whose *helpmates* have been torn from them, and the hungry cry of helpless babes, were vulgar sorrows that could not move your commiseration, though they might extort an alms.

19: MARY WOLLSTONECRAFT. *A Vindication of the Rights of Men*

1790

(Pp. 151–3.)

SURVEYING civilized life, and seeing, with undazzled eye, the polished vices of the rich, their insincerity, want of natural affections, with all the specious train that luxury introduces, I have turned impatiently to the poor, to look for man undebauched by riches or power—but, alas! what did I see? a being scarcely above the brutes, over which he tyrannized; a broken spirit, worn-out body, and all those gross vices which the example of the rich, rudely copied, could produce. Envy built a wall of separation, that made the poor hate, whilst they bent to their superiors; who, on their part, stepped aside to avoid the loathsome sight of human misery.

What were the outrages of a day[1] to these continual miseries? Let those sorrows hide their diminished head before the tremendous mountain of woe that thus defaces our globe! Man preys on man; and you mourn for the idle tapestry that decorated a gothic pile, and the dronish bell that summoned the fat priest to prayer. You mourn for the empty pageant of a name, when slavery flaps her wing, and the sick heart

[1] The 6th of October [1789, on which Louis XVI was brought back to Paris by the mob].

retires to die in lonely wilds, far from the abodes of men. Did the pangs you felt for insulted nobility, the anguish that rent your heart when the gorgeous robes were torn off the idol human weakness had set up, deserve to be compared with the long-drawn sigh of melancholy reflection, when misery and vice are thus seen to haunt our steps, and swim on the top of every cheering prospect? Why is our fancy to be appalled by terrific perspectives of a hell beyond the grave?—Hell stalks abroad;—the lash resounds on the slave's naked sides; and the sick wretch, who can no longer earn the sour bread of unremitting labour, steals to a ditch to bid the world a long good-night—or, neglected in some ostentatious hospital, breathes his last amidst the laugh of mercenary attendants.

Such misery demands more than tears—I pause to recollect myself; and smother the contempt I feel rising for your rhetorical flourishes and infantine sensibility.

20: SIR BROOKE BOOTHBY. *A Letter to the Rt. Hon. Edmund Burke*

1791

Sir Brooke Boothby (1743–1824), the seventh baronet, had literary and botanical interests. He was a member of the Lichfield circle, to which Erasmus Darwin, the Edgeworths and Thomas Day belonged. An admirer of Rousseau, he defended the Revolution against Burke, but opposed the extreme principles of Paine.

IN your view of France you seem to have been so awe-struck with the magnificence of the court, and so enamoured of the rising beauties of the dauphiness, that you had no attention left to bestow upon the people. If at your return from Versailles you had looked into the Morgue, where the bodies of those unfortunate wretches whose miseries had drawn them to seek the last refuge from despair were daily exposed in frightful numbers; if you had followed the peasant or the artizan to his scanty meal on a morsel of black unsavoury bread, such spectacles would not have been lost upon a heart like yours. They would surely have abated something of your partial regard for the destructive splendour of a court, or the redundant and invidious wealth of a lazy and luxurious priesthood.

21: THOMAS PAINE. *The Rights of Man*

1791

Thomas Paine (1737–1809), came from an East Anglian Quaker family. After a varied but unsuccessful career he emigrated to America in 1774, and became a leading anti-English propagandist. His pamphlet, " Common Sense " (1776) helped to crystalize ideas of republicanism in America.[1] He bitterly attacked those Americans who did not join in the struggle for independence, especially the Quakers. Paine returned to Europe in 1787 and was inspired by the French Revolution to produce the *Rights of Man* in 1791–2. He fled England to escape trial, was imprisoned as a Girondin in Paris, and only released after the fall of Robespierre. He demolished Christianity in the *Age of Reason*, defended property in *Agrarian Justice*, and offered Napoleon advice on the invasion of England. His political ideas are a curious combination of assertions of individual rights with tendencies towards totalitarian democracy. (Part I, p. 24.)

NOT one glance of compassion, not one commiserating reflection, that I can find throughout his book, has he bestowed on those who lingered out the most wretched of lives, a life without hope, in the most miserable of prisons. It is painful to behold a man employing his talents to corrupt himself. Nature has been kinder to Mr. Burke than he is to her. He is not affected by the reality of distress touching upon his heart, but by the showy resemblance of it striking his

[1] See the volume in this series by Max Beloff: *The Debate on the American Revolution.*

imagination. He pities the plumage, but forgets the dying bird. Accustomed to kiss the aristocratical hand that hath purloined him from himself, he degenerates into a composition of art, and the genuine soul of nature forsakes him. His hero or his heroine must be a tragedy-victim expiring in show, and not the real prisoner of misery, sliding into death in the silence of a dungeon.

22: WILLIAM BELSHAM. *Reflections on the French Revolution*

1791

William Belsham (1752–1827), was a member of a dissenting family and the brother of Thomas Belsham, a well-known Unitarian divine. He was a voluminous writer on politics and history, in support of Whig and Dissenting principles. (*Essays Philosophical and Moral, Historical and Literary*, 1799, II, pp. 258–9.)

WE all know that the English constitution supposes, and wisely supposes, that the King can do no wrong; and it is certain that no government can expressly authorize resistance against itself. Will Mr. Burke pretend that the Revolution in England was an event to be justified by an appeal to the forms of the constitution; which must necessarily regard resistance as rebellion? No; but the public safety required a deviation from forms. And how, in the name of common sense, with which the fine sense of Mr. Burke seems to have very little connection, is that deviation to be vindicated, but by resorting to the original and primary principles of government, as stated and defended by Dr. Price? Almost in the same breath, indeed, in which Dr. Price is impeached for inculcating treasonable doctrines, Mr. Burke himself admits that a tyrant may be deposed, and even punished, " provided it is done with dignity ". But however dignified Mr.

Burke's plan of resistance to tyranny might be, most assuredly in the execution of it, or " in reducing his principles to practice", he would not incur less personal risk from the penalties of the law than Dr. Price; so that his imperious scorn, which knows no distinction between a Cataline and a Cato, a Jack Cade and a Hampden, a Peters and a Price, may be with equal and retorted scorn repaid.

23: SIR BROOKE BOOTHBY. *A Letter to the Rt. Hon. Edmund Burke*

1791

(Pp. 19–20, 21, 26.)

THE question then is reduced to this; Whether the late government of France was such as ought to have been endured. It must I think appear to every man who acknowledges the inestimable value of a free constitution that it was not. A government where the foundation of all law is comprised in one short formula, FOR SUCH IS OUR PLEASURE—CAR TEL EST NOTRE PLAISIR; where the personal liberty, and consequently the property and life of every individual, is held at the absolute will and disposal of one man; is a government shocking to the common sense and common feelings of mankind. . . . Every humane mind will anticipate with heart-felt satisfaction the approach of that day when the race of despots shall have disappeared from the face of the earth; and when, by their rusty coins and mutilated statues, they shall be known to have existed, it shall be said of them as of the giants of old, "in those days there were tyrants in the land". . . . But let us turn . . . to the most magnificent spectacle that has ever presented itself to the human eye. A great and generous nation, animated with one soul, rising up as one man to demand the restitution of their natural rights.

24: JAMES MACKINTOSH. *Vindiciæ Gallicæ*

1791

Sir James Mackintosh (1765–1832) was an unsuccessful physician and journalist, until the *Vindiciæ Gallicæ* made his name. Subsequently he became a successful lawyer. By 1801 he was anxious " to wipe off the disgrace of having been once betrayed into an approbation of that conspiracy against God and man", the French Revolution. The *Vindiciæ Gallicæ* was published as a reply to Burke's *Reflections*. (Pp. 105–9.)

THE three Aristocracies, Military, Sacerdotal, and Judicial, may be considered as having formed the French Government. They have appeared, so far as we have considered them, incorrigible. All attempts to improve them would have been little better than (to use the words of Mr. Burke) " mean reparations on mighty ruins". They were not perverted by the accidental depravity of their members. They were not infected by any transient passion, which new circumstances would extirpate. The fault was in the essence of the institutions themselves, which were irreconcilable with a free Government. But it is objected, these institutions might have been *gradually* reformed. The spirit of Freedom would have silently entered. The progressive wisdom of an enlightened nation would have remedied, in process of time, their defects, without convulsion.

To this argument I confidently answer, *that these institutions would have destroyed LIBERTY, before Liberty had corrected their SPIRIT*. Power vegetates with more vigour after these gentle prunings. A slender reform amuses and lulls the people; the popular enthusiasm subsides, and the moment of effectual reform is irretrievably lost. No important political improvement was ever obtained in a period of tranquillity. The corrupt interest of the Governors is so strong, and the cry of the people so feeble, that it were vain to expect it. If the effervescence of the popular mind is suffered to pass away without effect, it would be absurd to expect from languor what enthusiasm had not obtained. If radical reform is not, at such a moment, procured, all partial changes are evaded and defeated in the tranquillity which succeeds. The gradual reform that arises from the presiding principle exhibited in the specious theory of Mr. Burke, is belied by the experience of all ages. Whatever excellence, whatever freedom is discoverable in Governments, has been infused into them by the shock of a revolution, and their subsequent progress has been only the accumulation of abuse. It is hence that the most enlightened politicians have recognized the necessity of *frequently recalling Governments to their first principles*; a truth equally suggested to the penetrating intellect of Machiavel, by his experience of the Florentine democracy, and by his research into the history of ancient Commonwealths.—Whatever is good ought to be pursued at the moment it is attainable. The public voice, irresistible in a period of convulsion, is contemned with impunity, when dictated by that lethargy into which nations are lulled by the tranquil course of their ordinary affairs. The ardour of reform languishes in unsupported tediousness. It perishes in an impotent struggle with adversaries, who receive new strength from the progress of the day. No hope of great political improvement (let us repeat it) is to be entertained from tranquillity, for its natural operation is to strengthen all those, who are interested in perpetuating abuse. The National Assembly seized the moment of eradicating the corruptions and abuses, which afflicted their country. Their reform was total, that it might be commensurate with the evil, and *no part of it was delayed*, because to spare an abuse at such a period was to consecrate it; because the enthusiasm which carries nations to such enterprises is short-lived, and the opportunity of reform, if once neglected, might be irrevocably fled.

25: THE CONSTITUTIONAL SOCIETY. Declaration proposed and adopted by the Society on 28 May 1791

The famous Society for Promoting Constitutional Information had been founded in April 1780, during the American War. Among its original members were a number of distinguished men of liberal sympathies, including Major John Cartwright and John Horne Tooke, both important figures in eighteenth-century radicalism. The Society, which published pamphlets on the need for parliamentary reform, fell into obscurity after the American War, but was revived in 1792, under much more radical leadership. Among those who attended its meetings was Tom Paine. Several of its leading members were arrested in 1794 and the Society never recovered from this blow. (*Political Papers* of Christopher Wyvill, 1800, V, iv.)

THE Society for Constitutional Information, vigilant to prevent the dangerous Influence of Publications detrimental to Civil and Religious Liberty, think it may be useful to the Public to express their disapprobation of the indecent virulence with which Mr. Edmund Burke has, with deplorable inconsistency to his former professions, censured the illustrious Patriots of a neighbouring Kingdom, for delivering more than twenty-five millions of their Fellow Creatures from a state of abject oppression, and civil bondage.

26: W. A. MILES. Observations on reading the *Reflections on the French Revolution* by Mr. Burke

March 1791

William Augustus Miles (1753 ?–1817) held various minor official or semi-official posts, and was used by Pitt as a confidential agent in France. He has been called a " wearisome busybody ", but his posthumously published *Correspondence on the French Revolution* has historical value and shows considerable insight. (*Correspondence of W. A. Miles on the French Revolution, 1789–1817*, edited by the Rev. C. P. Miles, 1890, I, p. 266–7.)

MR. Paine comes forward with a pamphlet of considerable ingenuity, containing a string of self-evident propositions, abstractedly taken, which are well calculated to act on vulgar minds. . . . But this pamphlet would never have had an existence except for the ill-judged and ill-timed rhapsody of Mr. Burke. The sermon of Dr. Price, against whom this rhapsody is partly levelled, would have been forgotten had it not been for the forward zeal of his officious adversary. . . . By controverting its arguments in print, an appeal was made, as it were, to the nation. The people were called upon to judge between the parties, and thereby the cause of faction was more completely served by the means taken to counteract it than it would have been by fifty discourses from the pulpit of the dissenting minister. Disputes on forms of government, like contests for modes of faith, may be carried on to eternity.

27: THOMAS CHRISTIE. *Letters on the Revolution in France*

1791

Thomas Christie (1761–96), was a Unitarian and son of the Provost of Montrose. He founded the Analytical Review, and visited Paris in 1789 where he met many of the leaders of the Revolution, of which he became an enthusiastic advocate. In his *Letters on the Revolution in France, Part I*, 1791, he emphasized the general tranquillity in Paris and the firm alliance between the Monarch and the people. Part II never appeared. (Pp. 47–8.)

I HAVE heard more talk about government, more *sedition*, in Mr. Burke's sense of the term, since the publication of his book, than ever I heard in all my life before. The people of England had no need of Mr. Burke's book to prejudice them against the French Revolution; they were sufficiently prejudiced before it. Ninety-nine out of a hundred, having access to no better source of information than the newspapers, which in general have been filled with misrepresentations, were persuaded that matters were going on very badly in France; that all was riot, confusion, and bloodshed there; and they would have long continued to hold that notion; for though books had been published to undeceive them, few would have taken the trouble to read them. The affairs of foreign nations have little interesting to the majority of men; and the good people of England, but for Mr. Burke, would have been still going on thanking Heaven, that while there was nothing but war and trouble in France, all was peace and quietness in England. From this state of tranquil unconcern, Mr. Burke has roused them by his ill-judged efforts to plunge them deeper into it. By connecting the affairs of France with matters at home, he has awakened the curiosity of the public, and given to the subject an interest that it never had before.

28: FANNY BURNEY. Entry in her Diary for 18 June 1792

Fanny Burney, Madame d'Arblay (1752–1840) is best known as the author of *Evelina* and *Cecilia*. She was petted by Dr. Johnson, and rewarded for her services to literature and her father's to music by being appointed second keeper of the robes to Queen Charlotte. She resigned before her health was completely undermined and remained devoted to the royal family. She married in 1793 a penniless French emigré, General d'Arblay. (*Diary and Letters of Madame d'Arblay*, edited by C. Barrett (1904) V, pp. 91–3.)

AFTER this my father joined us, and politics took the lead. He (Mr. Burke) spoke then with an eagerness and a vehemence that instantly banished the graces, though it redoubled the energies, of his discourse. " The French Revolution," he said, " which began by authorising and legalising injustice, and which by rapid steps had proceeded to every species of despotism except owning a despot, was now menacing all the universe and all mankind with the most violent concussion of principle and order." My father heartily joined, and I tacitly assented to his doctrines, though I feared not with his fears.

One speech I must repeat, for it is explanatory of his conduct, and nobly explanatory. When he had expatiated upon the present dangers, even to English liberty and property, from the contagion of havoc and novelty, he earnestly exclaimed, " This it is that has made ME an abettor and supporter of Kings! Kings are necessary, and, if we would preserve peace and prosperity, we must preserve THEM. We must all put our shoulders to the work! Ay, and stoutly, too! "

This subject lasted till dinner.

At dinner Mr. Burke sat next Mrs. Crewe, and I had the happiness to be seated next Mr. Burke; and my other neighbour was his amiable son.

The dinner, and the dessert when the servants were removed, were delightful. How I wish my dear Susanna and Fredy could meet this wonderful man when he is easy, happy, and with people he cordially likes! But politics, even on his own side, must always be excluded; his irritability is so terrible on that theme that it gives immediately to his face the expression of a man who is going to defend himself from murderers.

I can give you only a few little detached traits of what passed, as detail would be endless.

Charles Fox being mentioned, Mrs. Crewe told us that he had lately said, upon being shown some passage in Mr. Burke's book which he had warmly opposed, but which had, in the event, made its own justification, very candidly, " Well! Burke is right—but Burke is often right, only he is right too soon".

" Had Fox seen some things in that book," answered Mr. Burke, " as soon, he would at this moment, in all probability, be first minister of this country."

PART II

THE STRUGGLE FOR PARLIAMENTARY REFORM

THE DEBATE IN PARLIAMENT

29: HENRY FLOOD. Speech on his Motion for a Reform in Parliament, House of Commons

4 March 1790

Henry Flood (1732–91) was one of the greatest of Irish leaders in the eighteenth century. Together with Grattan he led the campaign which secured the independence of the Irish Parliament in 1782. In 1783 he was elected a member of the Westminster House of Commons at the same time as he held a seat in the Dublin Parliament. (*Parliamentary History*, *XXVIII*, pp. 455–6.)

THE whole number of electors is infinitely short of what it ought to be, and, what is worse, the majority of the representatives who decide for the whole, are chosen by a number of electors not exceeding six or eight thousand; though these representatives are to act for eight millions of people. A new body of constituents is therefore wanting; and in their appointment two things are to be considered; one, that they should be numerous enough, because numbers are necessary to the spirit of liberty; the other, that they should have a competent degree of property, because that is conducive to the spirit of order. To supply this deficiency, both in the representative and constituent body, my proposition shall be directed.

But I am told this is not the time. And why? because, forsooth, there are disturbances in France. Now first I say, that if those disturbances were ten times greater, than with every exaggeration they are represented to be, yet that mass of confusion and ruin would only render the argument more completely decisive in favour of a timely and temperate reform here. And why? because it is only from want of timely and temperate reform there, that these evils have fallen upon France. They could not begin with reparation in France: there was nothing to repair: they did not begin with ruin, they found ruin accomplished to their hands.

I am no friend to revolutions, because they are an evil: I am, therefore, a friend to timely reform, and for this reason, that it renders revolutions unnecessary; whilst they who oppose such reform, may be enemies to revolution in their hearts, but they are friends to it by their folly.

30: WILLIAM WINDHAM. Speech on Mr. Flood's Motion, House of Commons

4 March 1790

(*Parliamentary History*, *XXVIII*, pp. 467–8.)

BUT, Sir, were I even disposed to approve of the right hon. gentleman's notions of reform, I should still feel it my duty to object in the strongest manner to the time in which he has thought proper to bring them forward. What, would he recommend you to repair your house in the hurricane season? The right hon. gentleman, indeed, professes only to wish to open the door for a change, being perfectly indifferent himself as to what that change might be. Now a change may be good in the abstract, but merely for the sake of a change, I can never consent to pull down the fabric, and take the chance of building it up again. This, to use the language of play (though I am myself no gamester), would not be playing upon velvet, a little only might be gained, and every thing might be lost. As to a love of change generally, this passion is natural to all ages and countries; but men are not more fond of innovation, than they are apt to differ as to the particular schemes of reform that are to be carried into execution. It is not enough to say, that a majority of the people are friendly to reform in general, unless some particular mode of reformation be also agreed upon. But even were this the case, and were any scheme of parliamentary reform generally approved of, I should still think it my duty to oppose the dangerous and progressive spirit of innovation;—I must still enter my protest against the strange mixture of metaphysics with politics, which we are witnessing in the neighbouring country, where it would seem as if the ideal world were about to overrun the real. In that country speculatists and theorists are now *frontibus adversis pugnantia*. Let us, in good time, avoid the infection.

31: DEBATE ON MR. GREY'S NOTICE OF A MOTION RELATIVE TO PARLIAMENTARY REFORM. House of Commons

30 April 1792

William Pitt the Younger (1759–1806), was Chancellor of the Exchequer at 23 and Prime Minister at 25, retaining this office with one brief interval until his death. Coleridge allowed him only a " premature and unnatural dexterity in the combination of words." Certainly he made many errors in the conduct of the war with France, into which he had reluctantly entered, but we can understand also Canning's lines, written after his resignation in 1801:

" And, oh, if again the next tempest should rise,
The dawnings of peace should fresh darkness deform,
When we turn to thy hopeless retirement our eyes,
We shall long for the Pilot who weathered the storm."

Charles James Fox (1749–1806), Pitt's great rival, was the spoilt son of the notorious Henry Fox, Lord Holland. He early distinguished himself as a gambler at Almacks' and Brooks', and as a classical scholar at Oxford. " A libertine in politics", he spent most of his life in opposition, but defended the great English tradition of freedom better than if he had been in office. Brougham said of him, " A life of gambling and intrigue, and faction, left the nature of Charles Fox as little tainted with selfishness or falsehood, and his heart as little hardened, as if he had lived and died in a farm-house; or rather as if he had not outlived his childish years."

Charles Grey, later second Earl Grey (1764–1845), who brought forward this motion, entered parliament in 1786 and attached himself to Fox. He was one of the aristocratic group of reformers and a leading member of the Society of Friends of the People. A fervent advocate of reform in youth, he carried out his principles in old age by passing the Reform Act of 1832.

(*Parliamentary History*, *XXIX*, pp. 1,307–36.)

PITT

He would therefore confess, that, in one respect, he had changed his opinion upon this subject, and he was not afraid to own it. He retained his opinion of the propriety of a reform in parliament, if it could be obtained without danger or mischief, by a general concurrence, pointing harmlessly at its object. But he confessed he was afraid, at this moment, that if agreed on by that House, the security of all the blessings we enjoyed would be shaken to the foundation. He confessed he was not sanguine enough to hope that a reform at this time could safely be attempted. His object always had been, but now most particularly so, to give permanence to that which we actually enjoy, rather than remove any subsisting grievances. He conceived that the beautiful system of our constitution, and the only security we had for the continuance of it, was in the House of Commons; but he was sorry to confess, that that security was imperfect, while there were persons who thought that the people were not adequately represented in parliament.

He put it not only to that House, but also to the country at large: and he would ask all moderate men in it, what were their feelings on this subject at this moment? He believed that he could anticipate the answer—" This is not a time to make hazardous experiments."

FOX

In short, upon the word " innovation " he must take the liberty of repeating what he had uttered almost the first time he addressed that House; an observation which some thought quaintly expressed, " That the greatest innovation that could be introduced in the constitution of England was, to come to a vote, that there should be no innovation in it." The greatest beauty of the constitution was, that in its very principle it admitted of perpetual improvement, which time and circumstances rendered necessary. It was a constitution, the chief excellence of which was, that of admitting a perpetual reform.

Burke

Mr. Burke ridiculed the idea of a moderate or temperate reform as impossible, nor could he look upon the present schemes as if there were two parties, one for a temperate reform, and the other for a subversion of the constitution. And he would ask those hon. gentlemen, if they could answer for all who might join them on this occasion, and were sure that they would be satisfied with moderate measures ?

Grey

The fact was, that observing an opinion was rising in the country, that was likely to lead to danger, if means to prevent it were not taken in time, a set of gentlemen, of whom he had the honour to be one, had thought that the best possible means of preventing mischief was, to look into the constitution, and to suggest the correction of such abuses as might be found to exist in its practice, in order to take from its enemies that only great ground of their clamour, that the constitution was beautiful in theory, but corrupt in practice.

32: WILLIAM WINDHAM. Letter to W. J. Gurney

2 May 1792

(*The Windham Papers*, I, pp. 100–3.)

MY mind is so full of the measures which made the subject of our debate on Monday[1] that I can hardly forbear writing or speaking to any friend, who I think likely to have ideas at all similar to my own upon the subject. Though my declaration upon the occasion was not exactly what some of the papers have put in my mouth, that " whenever or in whatever shape a motion for Parliamentary Reform was brought forward, I would oppose it" (such a declaration exceeding even my objections to Parliamentary Reform, and being such as no man hardly would make), yet nothing can be more decided, than my hostility to the measures now pursuing nor than my determination to oppose them to the utmost extremity.

You will not be surprised at this determination, when I tell you, as I did to the House, though they have omitted I see in the papers, that part of what I said, that in my opinion this is little short of the commencement of civil troubles. I can consider it as nothing but the first big drops of that storm, which having already deluged France is driving fast to this country. I have in general been far from adverse to the principles and cause of the French Revolution. So

[1] Debate on Parliamentary Reform. See No. 31.

much otherwise indeed, that from the beginning almost, Mr. Burke and I have never exchanged a word on the subject. But when an attempt is made to bring the same principles home to us, Principles in a great measure extravagant and false and which at best have no practical application here, I shall ever prove myself as violent an opposer of them as Mr. Burke or any one can be.

It is as the commencement of changes similar to those that have taken place in France, that I view the measures now declared. . . .

When the principle of change, such as that now adopted, is once established, of change not founded on a comparison of a specifick grievance with a specifick remedy, but proceeding on a general speculation of benefits to arise from this or that mode of constituting a Parliament, what is there that is to put a stop to it, till we run the full career of all that the speculators of the present day may wish to drive us to ? We must not shut our eyes to the fact, that there is at this time a spirit very generally diffused, as it has been very wickedly excited, of changing the present constitution of things without any distinct view of what is to be substituted in its room. The promotors of this spirit call the means which they apply, an appeal to reason. But to whose reason do they appeal ? To the reason of those, who they know can be no judges of the question. To the reason of the very lower orders of the community, whom it is easy to make discontented, as their situation must ever render them too apt to be, but whom no man, not meaning to betray them would ever erect into judges of the first moral principles of Government, or of the advantages or disadvantages of great political measures.

33: CHARLES JAMES FOX. Speech on the Address of Thanks, House of Commons

13 December 1792

(*Parliamentary History*, XXX, pp. 19–20.)

WELL and nobly and seasonably, has the noble earl said—and I would not weaken the sentiment by repeating it in terms less forcible than his own, but that eternal truth cannot suffer by the feebleness of the terms in which it is conveyed—" There are speculative people in this country, who disapprove of the system of our government, and there must be such men as long as the land is free; for it is of the very essence of freedom for men to differ upon speculative points." Is it possible to conceive, that it should enter into the imaginations of freemen to doubt this truth? The instant that the general sense of the people shall question this truth, and that opinion shall be held dependent on the will of ministers and magistrates, from that moment I date the extinction of our liberties as a people. Our constitution was not made, thank God! in a day. It is the result of gradual and progressive wisdom. Never has the protecting genius of England been either asleep or satisfied.

O but man, proud man!
Drest in a little brief authority,
Plays such fantastic tricks before high heaven,
As make the angels weep.

Now, it seems, the constitution is complete—now we are to stand still. We are to deride the practice and the wisdom of our forefathers: we are to elevate ourselves with the constitution in our hands, and to hold it forth to a wondering world as a model of human perfection. Away with all further improvement, for it is impossible! Away with all further amelioration of the state of man in society, for it is needless! Let no man touch this work of man; it is like the work of heaven, perfect in all its parts, and, unlike every other work of man, it is neither capable of perversion nor subject to decay! Such is the presumptuous language that we hear; and, not content with this haughty tone, they imitate the celebrated anathema of brother Peter in the *Tale of a Tub*, and exclaim, " G–d confound you both eternally if you offer to believe otherwise."

34: DEBATE ON MR. GREY'S MOTION FOR A REFORM OF PARLIAMENT, House of Commons

26 May 1797

Sir Francis Burdett (1770–1844), the fourth baronet, entered Parliament in 1796. He had a long and lively career as M.P. for Westminster (1807–37). He was an ardent supporter of all reforms, until after the passage of the Reform Bill. (*Parliamentary History XXXIII*, pp. 644, 673, 782, 714–5.)

GREY

They would do him the justice, however, to allow that, in his propositions for a reform in parliament, he had never proceeded on any speculation of natural and imprescriptible rights. The measures which he had the honour to bring forward were founded, not on speculative, but on practical grounds. Both the speculative and the practical defects of the present system had been so largely discussed and so often repeated, that his labour on the present occasion was much abated without injury to the cause. His views, he repeated, had proceeded on practical grounds, and not on grounds of right; because no man could claim any particular form of government upon a ground of right.

PITT

The utmost point of difference, indeed, that ever subsisted between those who supported, and those who opposed the question of reform, previous to the French revolution, which forms a new era in politics, and in the history of the world, was union and concert in comparison with the views of those who maintained that question upon grounds of expediency, and those who assert it as a matter of right. The question with those who contended for reform on grounds of expediency, then was, whether the means proposed were calculated to infuse new vigour into the constitution? The object with those who affect a parliamentary reform upon French principles, is the shortest way to compass its utter destruction. From the period when the new and alarming era of the French revolution broke in upon the world, and the doctrines which it ushered into light laid hold of the minds of men, I found that the grounds upon which the question rested were essentially and fundamentally altered. Whatever may have been my former opinion, am I to be told that I am inconsistent, if I feel that it is expedient to forego the advantage which any alteration may be calculated to produce, rather than afford an inlet to principles with which no compromise can be made: rather than hazard the utter annihilation of a system under which this country has flourished in its prosperity, by which it has been supported in its adversity, and by the energy and vigour of which it has been enabled to recover from the difficulties with which it has had to contend?

SIR FRANCIS BURDETT

It is not my intention to follow the chancellor of the exchequer through all his turnings and windings: that would be an Herculean labour, to which I do not pretend to be equal. I state, therefore, in the first place, that endeavours to encroach upon the liberties of the people characterized an early part of the present reign, and that, of late years, efforts directed to that end have been much too successful, and that we are going rapidly on towards an arbitrary government. Good God! when shall we lay aside that humiliating confidence which has enabled the minister to bring us into so deplorable a condition, and which confidence this minister has this day laid claim to, by the advancing of principles that lead directly to slavery?

Fox

If it is clearly demonstrated, that genuine representation alone can give solid power, and that in order to make government strong, the people must make the government; you ought to act on this grand maxim of political wisdom thus demonstrated, and call in the people, according to the original principles of your system, to the strength of your government. In doing this you will not innovate, you will not imitate. In making the people of England a constituent part of the government of England, you do no more than restore the genuine edifice designed and framed by our ancestors.

The Agitation for Parliamentary Reform in the Country

35: THE LONDON CORRESPONDING SOCIETY
Address and Resolutions

24 May 1792

The London Corresponding Society, the most famous of eighteenth-century reform societies, was founded on the night of 25 January 1792, at the Bell Tavern, Exeter Street, Strand. Its treasurer and secretary was Thomas Hardy (see note to No. 58). The Society was a poor man's club and its penny a week subscription was modelled on the journeymen's clubs of the time. Its fame is partly due to the State trials of 1794, partly also to the fact that it was the first working-class political organization. The Society rapidly acquired a large membership and was soon in correspondence with similar societies in the provinces. It organized a number of big open-air demonstrations and was the heart and soul of the agitation against the Government until its suppression. (*State Trials*, *XXIV*, pp. 377–8.)

ASSURED that man, individual man, may justly claim liberty as his birthright, we naturally conclude that, as a member of society, it becomes his indispensable duty to preserve inviolate that liberty for the benefit of his fellow citizens, and of his and their posterity.

For, as in associating, he gave up certain of his rights, in order to secure the possession of the remainder, and *voluntarily* yielded up only as much as was necessary for the general good—so he may not barter away the liberties of his posterity, nor desert the common cause by *tamely* and *supinely* suffering to be purloined from the people of whom he makes a part, their natural and unalienable RIGHTS OF RESISTANCE TO OPPRESSION, and of SHARING IN THE GOVERNMENT OF THEIR COUNTRY; without the full and uninterrupted exercise of which RIGHTS, no man can with truth call himself or his country free.

Yet of late, the very men who have dared to oppress the nation, have also dared to advance, that *all resistance to their oppression is illegal*; while on the other hand, FRAUD OR FORCE, sanctioned by custom and blind submission, has withdrawn, and now withholds, from a very great majority of the tax-paying, industrious, and useful inhabitants of Great Britain, the RIGHT of sharing in the government of *their own* commonwealth, and in the management of *their own* interests.

The *few* who are now permitted to elect representatives, and those who are chosen by this *small number of electors*, disgrace the country at large by *buying* and *selling* votes, by *corrupting* and being *corrupted*—the former by their behaviour at elections, and the latter by their conduct in the senate—more than sufficient to prove that THE NATION IS UNREPRESENTED, and that THE PRESENT SYSTEM IS TOTALLY UNCONSTITUTIONAL—if by the word constitutional, any thing is meant.

Roused at last from their torpor, and eager to remedy the evil,—various, numerous, and respectable societies have been formed by the people, in different parts of the kingdom, several have also arisen in the metropolis; and among them *the London Corresponding Society*, with modesty, but with firmness, claim the attention of their country to the following resolutions:

Resolved,

I. That every individual has a right to share in the government of that society of which he is a member—unless incapacitated.

II. That nothing but nonage, privation of reason, or an offence against the general laws of society, can incapacitate him.

III. That it is no less the RIGHT than the DUTY of every citizen to keep a watchful eye on the government of his country, that the laws by being multiplied do not degenerate into *oppression*; and that those who are entrusted with the government, do not substitute *private interest* for *public advantage*.

IV. That the people of Great Britain are not *effectually* represented in parliament.

V. That in consequence of a *partial*, *unequal*, and therefore *inadequate representation*, together with the corrupt method in which representatives are elected; *oppressive taxes*, *unjust laws*, *restrictions of liberty*, and *wasting of the public money*, have ensued.

VI. That the only remedy to those evils, is a fair, equal, and impartial representation of the people in parliament.

VII. That a fair, equal, and impartial representation can never take place until *all partial privileges* are abolished.

VIII. That this society do express their abhorrence of tumult and violence—aiming at reform, not anarchy—reason, firmness, and unanimity, are the only arms they themselves will employ, or persuade their fellow citizens to exert, against ABUSE OF POWER.—Signed by order of the committee,

T. HARDY, secretary.

April 2nd, 1792.

36: THE FRIENDS OF THE PEOPLE IN THE BOROUGH. Foundation Resolution

19 April 1792

(Trial of John Horne Tooke, 17–22 November 1794. *State Trials, XXV*, pp. 139–40.)

AT a Meeting at the Three Tuns tavern, Southwark, April 19th, 1792,

Mr. Samuel Favell in the chair,

Resolved, That we do now form ourselves into a society for the diffusion of political knowledge.

Resolved, That the society be denominated THE FRIENDS OF THE PEOPLE.

Resolved, That the following be the declaration of this society:

" CONSIDERING that ignorance, forgetfulness, or contempt of the RIGHTS OF MEN are the sole causes of public grievances, and of the corruption of government; the society, formed for the purpose of investigating and asserting those rights, and of uniting their efforts, with those of their fellow-citizens, for correcting national abuses, and restraining exorbitant and unnecessary taxation, do hereby declare—

1st. That the great end of civil society is GENERAL HAPPINESS.

2nd. That NO FORM OF GOVERNMENT is good, any farther than it secures that object.

3rd. That all civil and political authority is derived from the people.

4th. That equal active citizenship is the unalienable right of all men; minors, criminals, and insane persons excepted.

5th. That the exercise of that right in appointing an adequate REPRESENTATIVE GOVERNMENT is the wisest device of human policy, and the only security of NATIONAL FREEDOM.

We also declare, that we are wearied with the unmeaning names of WHIG and TORY, and of MINISTERIAL and OPPOSITIONAL parties, and having often—too often, been deceived by both, we can no longer implicitly confide in either. We will THINK for ourselves; we will study our own rights; and we leave to the INS and the OUTS all that idle quibble of debate which only serves to amuse and deceive the nation, and to hold it alternately the prey of COURT and PARTY INTRIGUES.

We have beheld corruption generated upon corruption under the auspices of every administration; from whence we have reason to infer, that some RADICAL DEFECT exists in the system of government, that admits of no cure but from the united efforts of the nation.

37: REV. CHRISTOPHER WYVILL. Letter to James Martin

28 April 1792

Rev. Christopher Wyvill (1740–1822), a Yorkshire country gentleman of ancient lineage, became secretary of the Yorkshire Association for Parliamentary Reform in 1779. He took a leading part in drawing up the Yorkshire Petition for Reform, presented to Parliament in 1780. An early supporter of Pitt, he ceased later to believe in his sincerity in the cause of parliamentary reform. The very important "Wyvill Papers" are practically a documentary history of the early agitation for Reform. (Wyvill: *Political Papers*, 1800, V, pp. 22–5.)

As Mr. Paine endeavours to put the People upon somewhat very different from mere Reformation, and backs his proposal by holding out to the Poor annuities to be had out of the superfluous wealth of the Rich, I thought the extremely dangerous tendency of his licentious doctrines required opposition, as much perhaps as the slavish tendency of the Publications of his Right Hon. Antagonist. I own I should be extremely concerned indeed to find that any considerable body was formed on principles and with views which I think unjustifiable and pernicious in the extreme; and it seems clearly to be the interest of the real Friends of the Constitution to endeavour that some substantial improvement may be soon obtained, though far short of what we may think our due, lest in the progess of a few years, or even months, events may occur which may prevent the possibility of any thing being done by quiet and orderly means. If Mr. Paine should be able to rouze up the lower classes, their interference will probably be marked by wild work, and all we now possess, whether in private property or public liberty, will be at the mercy of a lawless and furious rabble. I am struck more forcibly with these ideas from almost every letter I receive, having now no doubt that Mr. Paine's Pamphlets have been circulated more attentively and more successfully in Yorkshire and other parts of this kingdom than I was aware of when I wrote the Defence of Dr. Price; and in Ireland matters, I believe, are drawing very fast towards a crisis, from the impulse of the same writings. Whether Government, or the Opposition Aristocracy are duly apprised of these threatening circumstances, I know not, nor whether any serious intention has yet been adopted on either side to take the matter up; but it behoves the People, and particularly those who are at their head, to consider the best means to prevent danger from the extreme doctrines of Paine, and yet to avail themselves of the fermentation produced by them to effect some rational and substantial improvement of the Constitution.

In my situation here, as one of the Yorkshire Association, I think it material to the general success of the Cause not to take fresh ground, or to adopt more extensive principles of Parliamentary Reformation, without evidence (which I have not) that the County of York probably would go that length. In what I have stated in the Defence, I think I have reason to assert that the Associated Body in this County, at a proper season, will join; but I do not believe they will go farther. I wish therefore to submit to you, whether the London Reformers will not do well to draw some line that may be exclusive of Paine's projects, and not so greatly different from what the Associations formerly supported as to endanger their not acting together.

38: REV. CHRISTOPHER WYVILL. Letter to the Rev. Dr. Towers

18 May 1793

For Dr. Towers, see note to No. 164. (Wyvill: *Political Papers*, V, p. 138.)

SOME years ago, the business of Political Reformation threw me into a pretty close connection with the Minister, whose sincerity, at that time, I saw no reason to distrust. Since that, my confidence in him, as a Patriot disposed to make sacrifices in favour of Public Liberty, and to run risques to effect a Reformation of Parliament, has been gradually weakened, till at last his conduct in the late great debate on Mr. Grey's Motion on that subject has fully satisfied me that Mr. Pitt is not the person to whom the Nation will owe, in any great degree, the renovation of its Constitution; that he will run no risque to preserve his consistency; that his principal object is not to improve the Constitution, and meliorate the condition of his Countrymen, but to secure the permanence of his power, the duration of which, for a single day, he seems unwilling to hazard for the attainment of that Political Reformation he formerly thought of such mighty importance.

39: JOSEPH GERRALD. *A Convention the only means of saving us from Ruin*

1793

Joseph Gerrald (1763–1796), was a pupil of Dr. Parr at Stanmore, and by profession a barrister. He became involved in radical politics and was a delegate of the London Corresponding Society, together with Margarot, at the Edinburgh Convention of 1793. Arrested by the authorities, he refused to take an opportunity to escape and stood his trial before the notorious Braxfield (see note to No. 107).

He was sentenced to fourteen years' transportation and died soon after his arrival in New South Wales.

Two Conventions were held at Edinburgh. The first, representing eighty Scottish reform societies, was held in December 1792: it was followed by the trials of Muir and Palmer in 1793. The second, " The British Convention of the Delegates of the Friends of the People associated to obtain Universal Suffrage and Annual Parliaments," was held at Edinburgh in November–December 1793. The two delegates from the London Corresponding Society, Joseph Gerrald and Maurice Margarot, were both arrested at this Convention. (pp. 85, 105–6.)

IN this awful season of national calamity I see no other resource, than the interposition of the great body of the people themselves, electing deputies in whom they can confide, and imparting instructions which they must injoin to be executed . . . I shall, now, lay before you the following plan of a convention. By this plan it will appear, that the *majority of wills*, will be, as it ought to be, the legitimate rule of government. . . .

Though a majority of wills is not infallible, and therefore may sometimes produce, in government, a violation of *right*, yet it is the best mode of ascertaining *right* which human ingenuity can devise; for the question will perpetually recur, who are the best judges of the proper mode of conducting their own affairs. No particular set of men hold any particular charter of exemption from the frailties of human nature, and therefore, the people, if they are not governed by a majority of their own wills, can have no other alternative than to be governed by *force.*

40: REV. CHRISTOPHER WYVILL. Letter to Thomas Brand Hollis

19 February 1794

(Wyvill: *Political Papers*, V, pp. 228–9.)

WE have seen bad times before; we have seen other Ministers supported in the most pernicious measures by great majorities in Parliament, while the People were too supine and indifferent to support with effect that radical Reform which alone can secure us from the influence of the Crown. But we never before have seen the People or any great proportion of the People, adverse to Liberty, countenancing by their verdicts and their resolutions the most violent prosecutions, and apparently ready to surrender their most important privileges. The People, however, still love Liberty, though for the present their fear of Anarchy predominates. But never shall we succeed to obtain any substantial Reformation in the only way in which it ought to be attempted, viz. by pacific and legal efforts, unless that fear of Anarchy can be shown to be a groundless fear. To show *that*, and to bring over to the Cause of Liberty and Reform the great multitude of worthy men who shrink from the very name of either one or the other, it seems high time that the popular party should define their intentions more particularly than they yet have done, for while they rest in generalities prudent people will be fearful of joining, and the Minister will have every advantage against them.

Such Papers as those of the London Corresponding Society go so much too far for the Country, that they visibly do much more harm than good. I have waited some posts in anxious expectation of seeing the lately announced address of your Society. I expect much from it; if I do not misunderstand your intention, that will counteract the bad effects of Citizen Martin's Resolutions, and lessen the alarm of the Country, without which it is my firm opinion no good can be done.

41: HENRY YORKE. Speech to a General Meeting of the *Friends of Justice, Liberty and Humanity*, on the Castle Hill, Sheffield

7 April 1794

Henry Yorke, or Henry Redhead (1772–1813), revolutionary orator, was tried for sedition at York in 1795 and sentenced to two years' imprisonment. He married the daughter of the prison governor, became strongly anti-French and was subsequently associated with the journal, the *True Briton*. Sheffield was an important centre of the Reform movement and a Reform Society was founded there in 1791. Its first address was published in December 1791, and one of their early enterprises was to publish a cheap edition of Tom Paine's *Rights of Man*. (Trial of John Horne Tooke, 17–23 November 1794. *State Trials*, *XXV*, pp. 671–6.)

IT was now high time that the people should lay aside leaders, discard factions and *act for themselves*. He strongly inforced these principles, and then entered into a complete detail of the ancient constitution as established by Alfred, which he proved to be at this time totally defaced, if not lost. He then pursued the gradual decline of popular liberty in England, from the anarchy which was the consequence of Danish and Norman invasion; and taking a general sketch of our history, so far as it was connected with the subject of popular representation, he made some strong and pointed remarks on the Revolution in 1688, the object of which, he said, was not, could not be answered, unless annual parliaments and general suffrage were restored.

To effect this just and useful purpose, *revolution of sentiment* must precede revolution of government and manners. The popular energies must be excited, that the popular voice may be felt and heard. The people must grow wise, in order that the people may rule. It is said we preach anarchy, but what is anarchy but the establishment of confusion on the wreck of popular opinion? It is said we are levellers; but those are levellers who would wish to reduce man to the condition of the brute, guided by passion, and uninfluenced by reason. Those are levellers whose hands are dipped in the public spoils; who assert impunity for crimes, and inviolability of persons; who would make humanity take a retrograde motion; who would palsy the arm of justice, and defeat the end of equal laws. We have ever disclaimed the foolish idea of *levelling property*; because our own property, the fruit of our labour, or of our talents, might, by the example, be exposed to the invasion of the first intruder. It were well, if those who confound justice with crimes, would consider that the poor man's property, little as it is, is as precious to him, as is the wealthy stock of the rich man. It were well, if feeling the force of this principle, the aristocracy would unite with us in the cause in which we are embarked.

When such a revolution of sentiment shall have dispersed the mists of prejudice; when by the incessant thunderings from the press, the meanest cottager of our country shall be enlightened and the sun of reason shall shine in its fullest meridian over us; then the commanding voice of the whole people shall *recommend* the five hundred and fifty-eight gentlemen in St. Stephen's Chapel, to go about their business.

After having concluded the above speech, Henry Yorke observed, that as there might be many persons present who came from motives of curiosity, and others who came for a more criminal purpose, he should adduce in justification of the reasoning he had employed, the writings of a man who was the first to reduce into a system, the study of human understanding, and the principles of government—he meant John Locke; whose excellent discourse on civil government he then held in his hand, and from which he read the following extracts.

42: THE FRIENDS OF THE PEOPLE. Address and Resolution agreed to

9 April 1794

The Society of the Friends of the People was a Reform Society founded by the more radical Whigs in April 1792, after dinner at Lord Porchester's house. Fox himself held aloof, but many of his followers joined. Amongst Foxite members of Parliament who belonged to the Society were Grey, Francis, Sheridan, Lambton, Whitbread and Erskine. The Friends of the People were the aristocratic (and very moderate) counterpart of the working class London Corresponding Society: the subscription was a guinea and a half. They lasted little more than two years and the Society seems to have broken up, or fallen away, soon after the 1794 Trials. It was, however, one of the founders of the Friends of the People, Charles Grey, who passed the Reform Act of 1832. (Wyvill: *Political Papers*, V, pp. x–xi.)

LET what will have been the motives of the House of Commons for the conduct they pursued, there is, however, unfortunately no reason to presume that they have, as yet, ceased to operate, and consequently the Society have no inducement again to apply to Parliament. To question the consistency and sincerity of the House, would, perhaps, on any occasion be indecorous; but, on the subject of Parliamentary Reform, it would be even absurd. The situation of the Honourable Members being the same, it is not reasonably to be presumed that their sense of the advantages annexed to it will have changed; and their votes are much too intimately blended with their interests, to admit a doubt that they are sincere.

Under these circumstances, the Society determine for the present not to renew their Petition; but, tho' they will not address the House of Commons, they earnestly appeal to the good sense, the integrity, and the independent spirit of the People of England.—To them the Society cheerfully submit their past conduct, and from the construction which any Friend to the Constitution can put upon it, confidently look for their future character. They trust they have in no instance been betrayed into intemperate warmth; and they are sure no menaces will awe them into dishonourable submission. Whatever they have seen, or heard, or read, since the first period of their institution, has more and more convinced them, that a speedy Reform in the Representation is necessary, and strengthened them in their resolution to persevere and to proceed. They are confident that the time is not far distant, when men will be compelled to feel that Liberty and Property are best secured under the guardianship of independence; and that a corrupt system, under whatever disguise it may be concealed, or by whatever abilities it may be supported, will be found to have consulted only the gratification and advancement of interested individuals at the expence of the public good.

43: REV. CHRISTOPHER WYVILL. Letter to Philip Francis

20 December 1794

Sir Philip Francis (1740–1818), moved from officialdom in India to politics in England. He was an ambitious, disappointed and vindictive figure. His supposed authorship of the *Letters of Junius* has been much discussed. Besides being the chief instigator of the trial of Warren Hastings he was also one of the founders of the Friends of the People. (Wyvill: *Political Papers*, V, pp. 250–2.)

UNIVERSAL Suffrage, as a principle of Reform, in the present state of the Country, seems to be neither attainable by any peaceful efforts, nor desirable, if it were possible to be attained. It is a principle so odious to the Great Body of men of Property and Power, that no Reform is likely to be effected while any suspicion remains that the real intention of the popular party is to conduct the business of Reformation to that extent.

But another material question should be well examined, namely, by what means are the changes proposed likely to be effected, or what prospect is there, that a sufficiently respectable Body of Petitioners can be united, to influence Parliament in the ordinary way of application to yield their unwilling consent. Considering the plan of Mr. Francis in this view, he fears that the very circumstances which are its praise in speculation, form in practice an insuperable objection to it. It is a plan of great simplicity, but it is a plan of great extent; it alters almost every thing in our Representative system, and affects the present state of every community in the Kingdom. In all probability, therefore, the Counties and great Corporations in England would oppose it, as offensive to their local prejudices, and injurious to their long-established privileges; the Boroughs would oppose it, as an arbitrary disfranchisement, without conviction or compensation; and Parliament would gladly avail itself of these objections and would reject the proposal probably not without the applause of a great part of the Public, as being a destructive plan, which would leave not one stone of the fabric of Representation standing on another.

44: REV. CHRISTOPHER WYVILL. Letter to Philip Francis

7 January 1795

(Wyvill: *Political Papers*, V, pp. 262–8.)

IT appears to me then that the Members of the House of Commons, who contend so honourably for Political Reformation, never can overcome their more numerous opponents, and induce Parliament to confess and correct its own abuses, but by the assistance of a great majority of the People. Not of that class at the lower end of society, many of whom wish for Universal Suffrage only to abuse it, but of those middle classes, who have had some education, who have some property and some character to preserve, and who probably would prefer some limitation of the Right of Suffrage, as more friendly to peace, to order, and even to rational liberty.

The great body of Reformers in this County has pledged itself to support a limited disfranchisement of Boroughs, by purchasing the consent of the persons interested; and if those terms should be adopted by your Society, I think it extremely probable, but I say it on no express authority, that the Yorkshire Gentlemen might be induced to pledge themselves to support

Annual Parliaments, an extension of the Right of Suffrage to all taxed Householders, and a Reform on similar principles in Scotland, with the other articles mentioned in the Paper of November 29th. An attempt to go beyond this line, to effect a compulsive disfranchisement of the Boroughs, to set aside all the existing Rights of Election, and to divide the Kingdom into new Districts, to return each a single Member, if made in Yorkshire, or in many other Counties less zealous for Reformation, I think, could not succeed, because it is considered as hardly possible to effect a Reform by peaceful means, if those conciliating limitations be not adhered to. It is for this reason, therefore, that I, who own my individual wish that so extensive a Reform might be established, do yet recommend, for the sake of peace, a less extensive scheme, in favour of which there seems good grounds to hope a sufficient union of the County Associations, and other considerable Bodies of Men in London, Manchester, &c. may be effected with the Friends of the People.

It may be thought that holding a model of Reform more perfect than is expected to be carried will excite a greater degree of popular support; but then it is to be feared it may also excite in a still greater proportion the alarms of quiet men, and the opposition of a powerful Aristocracy; and then by what peaceful means can any Reformation be effected? While a hope of peaceful Reformation is left, and at present that hope is by no means a faint one, the utmost caution should be observed not to lessen the prospect of success by adopting measures whose tendency is unpacific. Should the Country be driven to a state of distraction, should revolt unhappily break out, other measures in that terrible crisis may be expedient; but I doubt not you concur with me in thinking it is our duty to avert that crisis, if it be possible, and to propose, at present, such a moderate change as we have reason to hope our united application may obtain.

45: PHILIP FRANCIS. Letter to the Rev. Christopher Wyvill

20 January 1795

(Wyvill: *Political Papers*, V, pp. 280–1.)

WHEN I say generally that the power and the property of the Country ought never to be separated, I think I go as far as a reasonable Proprietor can ask of me. To those who would place power in the hands of indigence, I say that power and property cannot be separated long. Sooner or later the power will take the property, and then what will they have gained but a temporary shifting of possession? At the same time we are not to forget that the little Proprietor is as much to be considered in the distribution of power as the greatest; perhaps more, because, individually, he is less able to defend himself. These are the principles on which I have acted. At first sight, it looks like bravery to run into extremes; but I am sure that to keep the middle path, and to be ready to encounter the violence of either side, or of both, when they unite, as they very often do, is the surest proof of political courage, as well as of public virtue.

46: THE FRIENDS OF THE PEOPLE. Declaration of the Principles and Plan of Parliamentary Reform, recommended by the Society

30 May 1795

(Wyvill: *Political Papers*, V, pp. xix–xxiii.)

OUR object is to obtain and secure to the Commons of Great Britain, a real Representation in Parliament, freely chosen by themselves, independent of the Nobility and the Crown, and amenable at short intervals to the judgment of their Constituents. If it were possible to obtain and secure this object, by any means, in which the interests and powers, at present in possession of the Elections were likely to concur, and if it belonged to *us* to arbitrate between the right of the Commons at large, and the personal claims of purchase, possession, or prescription, we might be content to yield to measures of accommodation, and endeavour to compound, in the first instance, with the actual occupants of the common property, on reasonable terms of concession. But, since it is evidently impracticable at once to satisfy the interest and to remove the abuse, we shall not waste our thoughts in attempting to reconcile contradictions, but proceed to deliver the positive principles on which we act, and the plan we have in view, without considering any difficulties but those which belong to the operation in itself, and leave the compensations, which may be claimed by individuals, to be considered by the prudence, and measured by the equity of a future independent House of Commons.

Admitting the general right of voting at Elections to be common and personal, the exercise of it, on the principle we have stated, must be subject to a qualification; so moderate, however, that there may be no condition of life in which it may not be acquired, by labour, by industry, or by talents. If, in the end, it should furnish an Election, as we believe it would do, for the whole united Kingdom, by nearly a million and a half of heads of families, enough would be done to guard the rights of property on one side, and to satisfy the rational claims of personal representation on the other; and if a constituent power, so formed, so extended, and so limited, be not sufficient to create a free and independent House of Commons, the case is desperate; the object can never be obtained.

On these principles we say,

1st. That every householder in Great Britain, *paying parish taxes*, except Peers, should have a vote in the Election of one Member of Parliament.

The species of property, which constitutes this qualification has the advantage of being open, ostensible, and incapable of being disputed. It indicates a real residence, and implies a stationary interest in the place for which the vote is given, and the Representative chosen. But, besides the possession of a competent property, of which the occupation of a house paying taxes is a sufficient presumption, a householder has other qualities, which ought to recommend him to a favourable distinction, and particularly to the trust in question. He is necessarily the master, and probably the father of a family. In the first character, he has a personal credit and respect to maintain; in the second he has given hostages to Society. He is the natural guardian and virtual Representative, not only of his family and servants, but of all those who depend upon him for support, protection, or employment. Such a station deserves confidence, and should be made respectable, that all men may be prompted and encouraged to rise to it. The relations and duties that belong to it, are antecedent to positive institutions, and constitute at once the basis and security of civil society.

2d. The Election of the whole Representation of the Kingdom should be made at the same hour, and on the same day.

4th. That wages should be paid to Members serving in Parliament, and not holding offices under the Crown, not by the particular division for which they are elected, but out of the revenue of the Public, for the general interest of which the Constitution intends them to serve.

5th. Supposing all the preceding measures to be adopted, *and not otherwise*, we then are of opinion, that a General Election for the whole Kingdom might be conducted without tumult or expence, and completed in a few hours; that every fair and honest objection to shortening the Duration of Parliaments would be removed, and that in future the Elections might be triennial, biennial, or even annual, as they were in former times. Members of Parliament, who acted faithfully, would generally be re-chosen; but it is neither safe nor constitutional to leave any Representative very long out of the reach of his Constituents.

47: JOHN THELWALL. *Speech at the General Meeting of the Friends of Parliamentary Reform, called by the London Corresponding Society*

26 October 1795

John Thelwall (1764–1834), the friend of Coleridge, abandoned business and the Law for literature. Swept away by revolutionary doctrines, he became a professional lecturer, and a favourite orator of the radical societies in London. Thelwall was arrested with Hardy and Horne Tooke in 1794, but acquitted. Later he abandoned politics in turn and became a lecturer and writer on elocution and the treatment of defective speech. (Pp. 9–11.)

I CANNOT but feel for the misery of those who are insolently called the lower orders of society, because oppression has made them the basis and foundation upon which the luxury and splendour of political plunderers have been erected. . . . Thus convinced, and thus feeling for the miseries of my fellow beings; perceiving, as I think I do, the political sources of these calamities, and convinced of the necessity of speedy and effectual redress, believe me I do not mean to damp the ardour with which you pursue that object; but I will tell you, according to my judgment, what is the line of conduct by which we may obtain it. It is not by tumult. It is not by violence. It is by reason. . . . Adhere then to reason and to the principles of truth and justice; for these are the principles of Liberty: and be well assured, that when the principles of Liberty shall be well understood throughout the country—when facts shall be known, and causes properly investigated, it will be no longer in the power of tyrannical ministers to oppress you under the semblance of Liberty; or in the words of the Poet to "Make us slaves and tell us 'tis our charter."

48: REV. CHRISTOPHER WYVILL. Letter to John Cartwright

16 December 1797

(Wyvill: *Political Papers*, V, pp. 381–2.)

I HAVE read your Appeal with much approbation of your reasoning in many parts of it, and with a perfect conviction of your good intention. Your petition, I observe with pleasure, is for a Reform on the principle of extending Suffrage to Taxed Householders: On that ground I could cordially agree with you; but to the reasoning which I find directed in some parts of the Appeal to recommend Universal Suffrage, I really could not give my approbation. It is introduced there, as I think, without necessity; and intends, I conceive, to confirm in many minds that apprehension which seems the principal impediment to any Reform, viz. that no encouragement can be given to the most moderate Reformers, without risquing the total ruin of the Country, by bringing on a Reform on the principle of Universal Suffrage. Many there are, and I am myself of that number, who think a Reform on this principle of Universal Suffrage could not be effected without a Civil War: and therefore, that it ought not to be attempted to carry such a Reform, even if on its establishment after a Civil War, it might be expected to produce a peaceful and permanently happy settlement of the State. But that is more than we expect. We think that in times of warm political debate, the Right of Suffrage communicated to an ignorant and ferocious Populace would lead to tumult and confusion: In more quiet times it might be peaceably, but it would be corruptly exercised. On either supposition Rational Liberty would not be improved by the change; and after a series of Elections disgraced by the most shameful corruption, or disturbed by the most furious commotion, we expect that the turbulence or venality of the English Populace would at last disgust the Nation so greatly, that to get rid of the intolerable evils of a profligate Democracy, they would take refuge, as the Romans did, under the protection of Despotic Power. I am far from hoping that you will accede to opinions thus hastily sketched, and contrary to your long habit of thinking; but I state them to you, because I consider you as a sincere well-wisher to your Country; and I flatter myself the statement may induce you to exert your argumentative talents, and great they certainly are, to press for Political Reformation on the more moderate principle of your petition, viz. the giving of the Right of Suffrage to Taxed Householders.

49: JOHN CARTWRIGHT. Letter to the Rev. Christopher Wyvill

25 December 1797

(Wyvill: *Political Papers*, V, pp. 389–91.)

I SHALL now shortly say that my apology for introducing the subject of Universal Suffrage into my late Pamphlet is therein given, and indeed I incline to think it a sufficient one. From the supposed obnoxiousness of this principle, our insidious adversaries artfully attack Reform in such a mode that it cannot on any other ground be completely defended. I see no cause to decline such a defence, although I may perhaps, in some degree, accord with those who think a part of the Community too ignorant and vicious to make a right use of Political Liberty. I hope, however, that such would make but a small number, *provided the exercise of that Liberty were but under wise regulations*. In arguing for a principle, I have a right to presume that it is to be accompanied with suitable laws for giving it its proper effect, and for preventing its abuse. So guarded, I can scarcely, even in the present state of Society, imagine the adoption of the principle into practice really dangerous. But to detail those laws would require some time and thought.

On the old maxim of teaching a young archer to shoot at the moon, in order that he may acquire the power of throwing his arrow far enough for practical purposes, I have always thought that a free discussion of the principle of Universal Suffrage the most likely means of obtaining any Reform at all worth contending for. And I request you to observe in what quarter, and from what exertions in the Cause of Reform have there been made any decided and steady Converts to the Cause. Had not the principle of Universal Suffrage been freely discussed, I believe we should even now have had to begin again where we took up the business at the end of the American War. Instead of which, I trust we have now a solid foundation laid in a knowledge of the true principles of Political Liberty; and I am perfectly convinced that we are in no sort of danger, if a danger it be, of an adoption of the dreaded principle. It is, however, the fear of that principle that must produce us the concession of the Taxed Householders; was there nothing behind to excite that fear, we should be treated to the end with that contempt we have too often experienced. Perhaps few will be thought more strenuous than myself in favour of the extended system. If then I join in petitioning for the limited system, and am ready to declare that I believe the Country would be safe if so much could be obtained, can more be expected? In support of a plan, having in it the limitation alluded to, I am desirous of giving my most hearty concurrence. On the other point respecting *duration*, I own my mind goes decidedly to Annual in preference to Triennial Parliaments, and for many strong reasons which have for a course of years occupied my mind, and against which I see none but what appear to me to originate either in a corrupt principle on the part of the Objecters, or in a most unnecessary fear on the part of the

Reformers. I am for holding to the *safe* point with inflexible steadiness. It must in time be conceded to us. The argument touching those who are unfit for Political Power, by reason of their ignorance and ferocity, is here altogether out of the question. The question is simply which duration of Parliaments bids fairest to preserve their purity, and is most consistent with the National Rights and the principles of free Government. The arguments in favour of Annual are in my estimation unanswerable.

In favour of a plan for Annual Elections, and including the Taxed Householders, no exertion of mine shall ever be wanting; and I am well convinced that even a vast majority of those Societies that have distinguished themselves by asserting the doctrine of Universal Suffrage, would cheerfully and gladly acquiesce, so that no fear whatever could remain of any future attempts to push matters further. I speak this from conversations I have had with men who have influence amongst them.

Reformers. I am for holding to the *age* point with inflexible steadiness. It must in time be conceded to us. The argument touching those who are unfit for Political Power, by reason of their ignorance and ferocity, is here altogether out of the question. The question is simply which duration of Parliaments bids fairest to preserve their purity, and is most consistent with the National Rights and the principles of free Government. The arguments in favour of Annual are in my estimation unanswerable.

In favour of a plan for Annual Elections, and including the Taxed Householders, no exertion of mine shall ever be wanting; and I am well convinced that even a vast majority of those Societies that have distinguished themselves by asserting the doctrine of Universal Suffrage, would cheerfully and gladly acquiesce, so that no fear whatever could remain of any future attempts to push matters further. I speak this from conversations I have had with men who have influence amongst them.

PART III

NATURAL RIGHTS AND SOVEREIGNTY

The Rights of Man

50: EARL STANHOPE. *A Letter from Earl Stanhope to the right honourable Edmund Burke*

1790

Charles Stanhope (1753–1816), the third Earl, was the brother-in-law and political ally of Pitt, but broke with him over the French Revolution. Stanhope became Chairman of the Revolution Society, and a strong opponent of the war with France. He was called " Citizen " Stanhope. Besides politics, Stanhope had extensive scientific interests, and was an indefatigable and often successful inventor. Among his inventions were a process of stereotyping, adopted by the Clarendon Press, the Stanhope microscopic lens, and the Stanhope Demonstrator, an instrument for performing logical operations. (Pp. 26–7, 34.)

ALL warrantable political Power is derived, either mediately, or immediately, from the *People*. All political Authority is a TRUST; and every wilful act of abuse of that Authority, is a *Breach of Trust*. The natural RIGHTS of the PEOPLE are sacred and *inalienable*.—*Rights*, of which Despotism may *rob* them for a time, but, which it is not in the Power of Tyranny to *annihilate*. We, therefore, commemorate with rapture, the glorious Æra, when the *Army of England* nobly refused to overturn our *free* Constitution and had the virtue to join the Standard of King William. And we exult (with Mr. Fox) that the *Army of France*, last year, followed that glorious example, by refusing to become the Instruments of the servitude of their Fellow Citizens. . . .

The Revolution in France is one of the most striking and memorable pages in History; and no political event was, perhaps, ever more pregnant with good consequences to future ages. That great and glorious Revolution will, in time, disseminate throughout Europe, liberality of sentiment, and a just regard for Political, Civil, and Religious Liberty. It will, in all probability, make the World, for Centuries, prosperous, free, and happy, when the Author of the *Sublime and Beautiful* shall be no more, and the WHIG Principles from St. Omers[1] be forgotten.

[1] This is a hit at Burke, who was often accused of Catholic sympathies and caricatured as a Jesuit.

51: JAMES MACKINTOSH. *Vindiciæ Gallicæ*

1791

(P. 113.)

THE rights and the nature of man are to the Legislator what the general properties of matter are to the Mechanic, the first guide, because they are founded on the widest experience. In the second class are to be ranked observations on the excellencies and defects of those Governments which have existed, that teach the constructions of a more perfect machine. BUT EXPERIENCE IS THE BASIS OF ALL. Not the puny and trammelled experience of a *Statesman by trade*, who trembles at any change in the *tricks* which he has been taught, or the *routine* in which he has been accustomed to move, but an experience liberal and enlightened, which hears the testimony of ages and nations, and collects from it the general principles which regulate the mechanism of society.

52: JAMES MACKINTOSH. *Vindiciæ Gallicæ*

1791

(Pp. 216–8.)

JUSTICE is expediency, but it is expediency, speaking by general maxims, into which reason has concentrated the experience of mankind. Every general principle of justice is demonstrably expedient, and it is this utility alone that confers on it a moral obligation. But it would be fatal to the existence of morality, if the utility of every *particular act* were to be the subject of deliberation in the mind of every moral agent. A general moral maxim is to be obeyed, even if the inutility is evident, because the precedent of deviating more than balances any utility that may exist in the particular deviation. Political first principles are of this description. They are only moral principles adapted to the civil union of men. When I assert that a man has a right to life, liberty, &c. I only mean to enunciate a MORAL MAXIM founded on *general interest*, which prohibits any attack on these possessions. In this primary and radical sense, all rights, natural as well as civil, arise from expediency. But the moment the moral edifice is reared, its basis is hid from the eye for ever. The moment these maxims, which are founded on an utility that is paramount and perpetual, are embodied and consecrated, they cease to yield to partial and subordinate expediency. It then becomes the perfection of virtue to consider, not whether an action be useful, but whether it be right.

The same necessity for the substitution of general maxims exists in politics as in morals. These precise and inflexible principles, which yield neither to the seduction of passion, nor the suggestions of interest, ought to be the guide of Public as well as private morals.—Acting according to the natural rights of men, is only another expression for acting according to those GENERAL MAXIMS of *social morals* which prescribe what is *right and fit* in human intercourse. We have proved that the social compact does not alter these maxims, or destroy these rights, and it incontestibly follows, from the same principles which guide all morality, that no expediency can justify their infraction.

53: JAMES MACKINTOSH. *Vindiciæ Gallicæ*

1791

(Pp. 306–8.)

BUT, says Mr. Burke, we do not contend that right is created by antiquarian research. We are far from contending that possession legitimates tyranny, or that fact ought to be confounded with right. But, (to strip Mr. Burke's eulogies on English wisdom of their declamatory appendage) the impression of antiquity endears and ennobles freedom, and fortifies it by rendering it august and venerable in the popular mind. The illusion is useful. The expediency of *political imposture* is the whole force of the argument. A principle odious and suspected to the friends of freedom, as the grand bulwark of secular and spiritual despotism in the world. To pronounce that men are only to be governed by delusion is to libel the human understanding, and to consecrate the frauds that have elevated Despots and Muftis, Pontiffs and Sultans, on the ruin of degraded and oppressed humanity. But the doctrine is as false as it is odious. Primary political truths are few and simple. It is easy to make them understood, and to transfer to Government the same enlightened self-interest that presides in the other concerns of life. It may be made to be respected, not because it is ancient, or because it is sacred, not because it has been established by Barons, or applauded by Priests, but because it is useful. Men may easily be instructed to maintain rights which it is their *interest* to maintain, and duties which it is their *interest* to perform. This is the only principle of authority that does not violate justice and insult humanity. It is also the only one which can possess stability. The various fashions of prejudice and factitious sentiment which have been the basis of Governments, are short-lived things. The illusions of chivalry, and the illusions of superstition, which give splendor or sanctity to Government, are in their turn succeeded by new modes of opinion and new systems of manners. Reason alone, and natural sentiment, are the denizens of every nation, and the cotemporaries of every age.

54: JAMES MACKINTOSH. *Vindiciæ Gallicæ*

1791

Pp. 115–22.

ALL the Governments that now exist in the world, (except the United States of America) have been fortuitously formed. They are the produce of chance, not the work of art. They have been altered, impaired, improved and destroyed by accidental circumstances, beyond the foresight or controul of wisdom. Their parts thrown up against present emergencies formed no systematic whole. It was certainly not to have been presumed, that these *fortuitous Governments* should have surpassed the works of intellect, and precluded all nearer approaches to perfection. Their origin without doubt furnishes a strong presumption of an opposite nature. It might teach us to expect in them many discordant principles, many jarring forms, much unmixed evil, and much imperfect good, many institutions which had long survived their motive, and many of which reason had never been the author, nor utility the object. Experience, *even in the best of these Governments*, accords with such expectations.

A Government of *art*, the work of legislative intellect, reared on the immutable basis of natural right and general happiness, which should combine the excellencies, and exclude the defects of the various constitutions which chance has scattered over the world, instead of being precluded by the perfection of any of those forms, was loudly demanded by the injustice and absurdity of them all. It was time that men should learn to tolerate nothing ancient that reason does not respect, and to shrink from no novelty to which reason may conduct. It was time that the human powers, so long occupied by subordinate objects, and inferior arts, should mark the commencement of a new æra in history, by giving birth to the art of improving government, and increasing the civil happiness of man. It was time, as it has been wisely and eloquently said, that Legislators, instead of that narrow and dastardly *coasting* which never ventures to lose sight of usage and precedent, should, guided by the *polarity* of reason, hazard a bolder navigation, and discover, in unexplored regions, the treasure of public felicity.

The task of the French Legislators was, however, less hazardous. The philosophers of Europe had for a century discussed all objects of public œconomy. The conviction of a great majority of enlightened men had, after many controversies, become on most questions of general politics, uniform. A degree of certainty, perhaps nearly equal to that which such topics will admit, had been attained. The National Assembly were therefore not called on to make discoveries. It was sufficient if they were not uninfluenced by the opinions, nor exempt from the spirit of their age. They were fortunate enough to live in a period when it was only necessary to affix the stamp of laws to what had been prepared by the research of philosophy. They will here, however, be attacked by a futile commonplace. The most specious *theory*, it will be said, is often impracticable, and any attempt to transfer speculative doctrines into the practice of States is chimerical and frantic. If by theory be understood vague conjecture, the objection is not worth discussion; but if by theory be meant inference from the moral nature and political state of man, then I assert, that whatever such theory pronounces to be true, must be practicable, and that whatever on the subject is impracticable, must be false. To resume the illustration from the mechanical arts—Geometry, it may be justly said, bears nearly the same relation to mechanics that abstract reasoning does to politics. The *moral forces* which are employed in politics are the passions and interests of men, of which it is the province of metaphysics to teach the nature and calculate the strength, as mathematics do those of the mechanical powers. Now suppose it had been mathematically proved, that by a certain alteration in the structure of a machine, its effect would be increased *four-fold*, would an instructed mechanic hesitate about the change? Would he be deterred, because he was the *first* to discover it? Would he thus sacrifice his own advantage to the blindness of his predecessors, and the obstinacy of his cotemporaries? —Let us suppose a whole nation, of which the artizans thus rejected theoretical improvement—Mechanics might there, as a *science*, be most profoundly understood, while as an *art*, it exhibited nothing but rudeness and barbarism. The principles of Newton and Archimedes might be taught in the schools, while the architecture of the people might not have reached beyond the cabins of New Holland, or the shipbuilding of the Esquimaux. In a state somewhat similar regarding political science has Europe continued for a great part of the eighteenth century.[1] All the great questions of general politics had, as we have remarked, been nearly decided, and almost all the decision had been hostile to established institutions—yet these institutions still flourished in all their vigor. The same man who cultivated liberal science in his cabinet, was compelled to administer a barbarous jurisprudence on the bench. The same MONTESQUIEU, who thought as a philosopher of the eighteenth, was compelled to decide as a magistrate of the fourteenth century. The apostles of toleration, and the ministers of the Inquisition, were cotemporaries. The torture continued to be practised in the age of Beccaria. The Bastile devoured its victims in the country of Turgot. The criminal code, even of those nations in which it was the mildest, was oppressive and savage. The laws respecting religious opinion, even where there was a *pretended* toleration, outraged the most evident deductions of reason. The true principles of commercial policy, though they had been reduced to demonstration, influenced the councils of no State. Such was the fantastic spectacle presented by the European nations, who, philosophers in theory, and barbarous in practice, exhibited to the observing eye two opposite and inconsistent aspects of manners and opinions. But such a State carried in itself the seeds of its own destruction. Men will not long dwell in hovels, with the model of a palace before their eyes.

[1] Mechanics, because no passion or interest is concerned in the perpetuity of abuse, always yield to scientific improvement. Politics, for the contrary reason, always resist it. It was the remark of Hobbes, that if any interest or passion were concerned in disputing the theorems of geometry, different opinions would be maintained regarding them. It has actually happened (to justify the remark of that great man) that under the administration of TURGOT *a financial reform, grounded on a mathematical demonstration, was derided as visionary nonsense!* So much for the sage preference of practice to theory.

55: CAPEL LOFFT. *Remarks on the Letter of the Rt. Hon. Edmund Burke*

1791

Capel Lofft (1751–1824), a country gentleman, was the author of many works on literature, politics and law. By conviction a Foxite and a reformer, he enthusiastically defended Rousseau against Burke. (2nd edition, 1791, pp. 21, 26, 28–9, 31–2.)

If MR. BURKE views the REVOLUTION in this country in 1688 rightly, it was an exertion of public authority to establish freedom for the People of that age, in so far as their leaders thought proper to establish it: but to perpetuate *slavery* on their posterity for ever: since if the stipulations which they chose at that time to make were to be for ever binding on their descendants by an irrepealable law, whatever defects or mischiefs time and experience might discover, the Law, which derives its force in every free state from being an expression of the will of the state, might act in the most perfect contrariety to their will. . . . I feel very different emotions from those of pleasure, in being obliged to dissent from MR. BURKE; but I find another point which compels me to express my dissent: his denial of the *responsibility* of the *King* to the Public. . . . A King, or Governors of any designation, irresponsible to the community in cases which exclude all other means of redress, would be as monstrous an incongruity, compared with the universal principles and necessary end of government, as a King in the ordinary state of the *British* government, responsible for measures, which, in such state, must always have been resolved and executed by ministers in their known departments. . . . Whatever privileges, whatever glory, are inheritable from civil institution, the rights of men, the honour of intellectual and moral agents, the illustrious rank of men determined to be free, is of date far higher, and of origin transcendently more venerable. It is an inheritance coeval with the commencement of humanity; its ensigns are the countenance impressed with the divine character of Reason; its gallery the extent of the habitable earth; its monuments, the imperishable memory of the wisest, best, and bravest of the species of every age and country; its evidence, the voice of Nature; its title, our equal relation to the Deity: from whom we derive in common, the powers, the obligations, and the correspondent Rights of man; Reason, Conscience, and Freedom.

56: THOMAS PAINE. *The Rights of Man*

1791

(Part I, pp. 8–14.)

As Mr. Burke occasionally applies the poison drawn from his horrid principles (if it is not prophanation to call them by the name of principles) not only to the English nation, but to the French Revolution and the National Assembly, and charges that august, illuminated and illuminating body of men with the epithet of *usurpers*, I shall, *sans ceremonie*, place another system of principles in opposition to his.

The English Parliament of 1688 did a certain thing, which, for themselves and their constituents, they had a right to do, and which it appeared right should be done: but, in addition to this right, which they possessed by delegation, *they set ub another right by assumption*, that of binding and controuling posterity to the end of time. The case, therefore, divides itself into two parts; the right which they possessed by delegation, and the right which they set up by assumption. The first is admitted; but with respect to the second, I reply—

There never did, there never will, and there never can exist a parliament, or any description of men, or any generation of men, in any country, possessed of the right or the power of binding and controuling posterity to the "*end of time*," or of commanding for ever how the world shall be governed, or who shall govern it: and therefore all such clauses, acts or declarations, by which the makers of them attempt to do what they have neither the right nor the power to do, nor the power to execute, are in themselves null and void. Every age and generation must be as free to act for itself, *in all cases*, as the ages and generations which preceded it. The vanity and presumption of governing beyond the grave is the most ridiculous and insolent of all tyrannies. Man has no property in man; neither has any generation a property in the generations which are to follow. The parliament or the people of 1688, or of any other period, had no more right to dispose of the people of the present day, or to bind or to controul them *in any shape whatever*, than the parliament or the people of the present day have to dispose of, bind or controul those who are to live a hundred or a thousand years hence. Every generation is and must be competent to all the purposes which its occasions require. It is the living, and not the dead, that are to be accommodated. When man ceases to be, his power and his wants cease with him; and having no longer any participation in the concerns of this world, he has no longer any authority in directing who shall be its governors, or how its government shall be organized, or how administered.

I am not contending for, nor against, any form of government, nor for, nor against, any party, here or elsewhere. That which a whole nation chooses to do, it has a right to do. Mr. Burke says, No. Where, then, *does* the right exist? I am contending for the rights of the *living*, and against their being willed away, and controuled and contracted for, by the manuscript assumed authority of the dead; and Mr. Burke is contending for the authority of the dead over the rights and freedom of the living.

Those who have quitted the world, and those who have not yet arrived at it, are as remote from each other as the utmost stretch of mortal imagination can conceive. What possible obligation then can exist between them; what rule or principle can be laid down, that two non-entities, the one out of existence and the other not in, and who never can meet in this world, that the one should controul the other to the end of time?

From what, or from whence, does Mr. Burke prove the right of any human power to bind posterity for ever? He has produced his clauses, but he must produce also his proofs, that such a rightexisted, and shew how it existed. If it ever existed, it must now exist, for whatever appertains to the nature of man cannot be annihilated by man. It is the nature of man to die, and he will continue to die as long as he continues to be born. But Mr. Burke has set up a sort of political Adam, in whom all posterity are bound for ever; he must therefore prove that his Adam possessed such a power, or such a right.

The circumstances of the world are continually changing, and the opinions of men change also; and as government is for the living, and not for the dead, it is the living only that has any right in it. That which may be thought right and found convenient in one age may be thought wrong and found inconvenient in another. In such cases, Who is to decide, the living, or the dead?

As almost one hundred pages of Mr. Burke's book are employed upon these clauses, it will consequently follow, that if the clauses themselves, so far as they set up an *assumed*, *usurped* dominion over posterity for ever, are unauthoritative, and in their nature null and void; that all his voluminous inferences, and declamation drawn therefrom, or founded thereon, are null and void also; and on this ground I rest the matter.

57: THOMAS PAINE. *The Rights of Man*

1791

(Part I, pp. 43–52.)

BEFORE anything can be reasoned upon to a conclusion, certain facts, principles, or data, to reason from, must be established, admitted, or denied. Mr. Burke, with his usual outrage, abuses the *Declaration of the rights of Man*, published by the National Assembly of France as the basis on which the constitution of France is built. This he calls "paltry and blurred sheets of paper about the rights of man."—Does Mr. Burke mean to deny that *man* has any rights? If he does, then he must mean that there are no such things as rights anywhere, and that he has none himself; for who is there in the world but man? But if Mr. Burke means to admit that man has rights, the question then will be: What are those rights, and how came man by them originally?

The error of those who reason by precedents drawn from antiquity, respecting the rights of man, is, that they do not go far enough into antiquity. They do not go the whole way. They stop in some of the intermediate stages of an hundred or a thousand years, and produce what was then done as a rule for the present day. This is no authority at all. If we travel still farther into antiquity, we shall find a direct contrary opinion and practice prevailing; and if antiquity is to be authority, a thousand such authorities may be produced, successively contradicting each other; but if we proceed on, we shall at last come out right; we shall come to the time when man came from the hand of his Maker. What was he then? Man. Man was his high and only title, and a higher cannot be given him.—But of titles I shall speak hereafter.

If any generation of men ever possessed the right of dictating the mode by which the world should be governed for ever, it was the first generation that existed; and if that generation did not do it, no succeeding generation can shew any authority for doing it, nor set any up. The illuminating and divine principle of the equal rights of man (for it has its origin from the Maker of man) relates, not only to the living individuals, but to generations of men succeeding each other. Every generation is equal in rights to the generations which preceded it, by the same rule that every individual is born equal in rights with his contemporary.

Every history of the creation, and every traditionary account, whether from the lettered or unlettered world, however they may vary in their opinion or belief of certain particulars, all agree in establishing one point, *the unity of man*; by which I mean that man is all of *one degree*, and consequently that all men are born equal, and with equal natural rights, in the same manner as if posterity had been continued by *creation* instead of *generation*, the latter being only the mode by which the former is carried forward; and consequently, every child born into the world must be considered as deriving its existence from God. The world is as new to him as it was to the first man that existed, and his natural right in it is of the same kind.

Hitherto we have spoken only (and that but in part) of the natural rights of man. We have now to consider the civil rights of man, and to show how the one originates out of the other. Man did not enter into society to become *worse* than he was before, nor to have less rights than he had before, but to have those rights better secured. His natural rights are the foundation of all his civil rights. But in order to pursue this distinction with more precision, it will be necessary to mark the different qualities of natural and civil rights.

A few words will explain this. Natural rights are those which appertain to man in right of his existence. Of this kind are all the intellectual rights, or rights of the mind, and also all those rights of acting as an individual for his own comfort and happiness, which are not injurious to the natural rights of others. Civil rights are those which appertain to man in right of his being a member of society. Every civil right has for its foundation some natural right pre-existing in the individual, but to which his individual power is not, in all cases, sufficiently competent. Of this kind are all those which relate to security and protection.

From this short review, it will be easy to distinguish between that class of natural rights which man retains after entering into society, and those which he throws into the common stock as a member of society.

The natural rights which he retains, are all those in which the *power* to execute is as perfect in the individual as the right itself. Among this class, as is before mentioned, are all the intellectual rights, or rights of the mind; consequently, religion is one of those rights. The natural rights which are not retained, are all those in which, though the right is perfect in the individual, the power to execute them is defective. They answer not his purpose. A man, by natural right, has a right to judge in his own cause; and so far as the right of the mind is concerned, he never surrenders it. But what availeth it him to judge, if he has not power to redress? He therefore deposits this right in the common stock of society, and takes the arm of society, of which he is a part, in preference and in addition to his own. Society *grants* him nothing. Every man is a proprietor in society, and draws on the capital as a matter of right.

It has been thought a considerable advance towards establishing the principles of Freedom, to say, that government is a compact between those who govern and those who are governed: but this cannot be true, because it is putting the effect before the cause; for as man must have existed before governments existed, there necessarily was a time when governments did not exist, and consequently there could originally exist no governors to form such a compact with. The fact therefore must be, that the *individuals themselves*, each in his own personal and sovereign right, *entered into a compact with each other* to produce a government: and this is the only mode in which governments have a right to arise, and the only principle on which they have a right to exist.

58: THOMAS ERSKINE. Speech for the Defence at the Trial of Thomas Hardy for Treason

28 October–5 November 1794

Thomas Erskine (1750–1823) was never a brilliant lawyer, but he was unquestionably the greatest advocate of his day. The friend of Fox and Sheridan, he failed to make much impression in Parliament, but won a great reputation as counsel for the defence in the trials of Tom Paine, Walker, Thomas Hardy and Horne Tooke. To the end of his life he remained liberal in his sympathies, opposing the Six Acts of 1819–20 and working for the cause of Greek independence. He was made Lord Chancellor in 1806 and a baron the same year.

Thomas Hardy (1752–1832), a Scottish shoemaker who lived at No. 9 Piccadilly, became Secretary of the London Corresponding Society. Hardy was exceptional among the English Jacobins by being an organizer, rather than an orator or pamphleteer. He may indeed be regarded as one of the founders of working-class politics in Great Britain. Arrested in 1794 with Horne Tooke, and others who had taken part in the activities of the London Corresponding Society, Hardy was defended by Erskine and acquitted. He was subsequently pensioned by Sir Francis Burdett.

(*State Trials*, *XXIV*, pp. 930–1.)

THE rights of man are the foundation of all government, and to secure them is the only reason of men's submitting to be governed;—it shall not be fastened upon the unfortunate prisoner at the bar, nor upon any other man, that because these natural rights were asserted in France, by the destruction of a government which oppressed and subverted them, a process happily effected here by slow and imperceptible improvements, that therefore they can only be so asserted in England, where the government, through a gradation of improvement, is well calculated to protect them. We are, fortunately, not driven in this country to the terrible alternatives which were the unhappy lot of France, because we have had a happier destiny in the forms of a free constitution; this, indeed, is the express language of many of the papers before you, that have been complained of; particularly in one alluded to by the Attorney General, as having been written by a gentleman with whom I am particularly acquainted; and though in that spirited composition there are, perhaps, some expressions proceeding from warmth which he may not desire me critically to justify, yet I will venture to affirm, from my own personal knowledge, that there is not a man in Court more honestly public-spirited and zealously devoted to the constitution of King, Lords, and Commons, than the honourable gentleman I allude to (Felix Vaughan, esq. barrister at law[1]). It is the phrase, therefore, and not the sentiment expressed by it, that can alone give justifiable offence;—it is, it seems, a *new* phrase commencing in revolutions, and never used before in discussing the rights of British subjects, and therefore can only be applied in the sense of those who framed it;—but this is so far from being the truth, that the very phrase sticks in my memory, from the repeated application of it to the rights of subjects, under this and every other establishment, by a gentleman whom you will not suspect of using it in any other sense. The rights of man were considered by Mr. Burke, at the time that the great uproar was made

[1] Assistant Counsel to the prisoners.

upon a supposed invasion of the East India Company's charter, to be the foundation of, and paramount to all, the laws and ordinances of a state:—the ministry, you may remember, were turned out for Mr. Fox's India Bill, which their opponents termed an attack upon the chartered rights of man, or, in other words, upon the abuses supported by a monopoly in trade. Hear the sentiments of Mr. Burke, when the NATURAL and CHARTERED rights of men are brought into contest. Mr. Burke, in his speech in the House of Commons, expressed himself thus: "The first objection is, that the bill is an attack on the chartered rights of men. As to this objection, I must observe that the phrase of 'the chartered *rights of men*,' is full of affectation; and very unusual in the discussion of privileges conferred by charters of the present description. But it is not difficult to discover what end that ambiguous mode of expression, so often reiterated, is meant to answer.

The rights of *men*, that is to say, the *natural rights of mankind*, are indeed sacred things; and if any public measure is proved mischievously to affect them, the objection ought to be fatal to that measure, even if no charter at all could be set up against it".

59: EDMUND BURKE. *Reflections on the Revolution in France*

1790

(*Works*, II, pp. 330–6.)

IT is no wonder therefore, that with these ideas of everything in their constitution and government at home, either in church or state, as illegitimate and usurped, or at best as a vain mockery, they look abroad with an eager and passionate enthusiasm. Whilst they are possessed by these notions, it is vain to talk to them of the practice of their ancestors, the fundamental laws of their country, the fixed form of a constitution, whose merits are confirmed by the solid test of long experience, and an increasing public strength and national prosperity. They despise experience as the wisdom of unlettered men; and as for the rest, they have wrought under-ground a mine that will blow up, at one grand explosion, all examples of antiquity, all precedents, charters, and acts of parliament. They have " the rights of men." Against these there can be no prescription; against these no agreement is binding: these admit no temperament, and no compromise: anything withheld from their full demand is so much of fraud and injustice. Against these their rights of men let no government look for security in the length of its continuance, or in the justice and lenity of its administration. The objections of these speculatists, if its forms do not quadrate with their theories, are as valid against such an old and beneficent government, as against the most violent tyranny, or the greenest usurpation. They are always at issue with governments, not on a question of abuse, but a question of competency, and a question of title. I have nothing to say to the clumsy subtilty of their political metaphysics. Let them be their amusement in the schools.—" *Illa se jactat in aula —Æolus, et clauso ventorum carcere regnet.*"—But let them not break prison to burst like a *Levanter*, to sweep the earth with their hurricane, and to break up the fountains of the great deep to overwhelm us.

Far am I from denying in theory, full as far is my heart from withholding in practice, (if I were of power to give or to withhold,) the *real* rights of men. In denying their false claims of right, I do not mean to injure those which are real, and are such as their pretended rights would totally destroy. If civil society be made for the advantage of man, all the advantages for which it is made become his right. It is an institution of beneficence; and law itself is only beneficence acting by a rule. Men have a right to live by that rule; they have a right to do justice, as between their fellows, whether their fellows are in public function or in ordinary occupation. They have a right to the fruits of their industry; and to the means of making their industry fruitful. They have a right to the acquisitions of their parents; to the nourishment and improvement of their offspring; to instruction in life, and to consolation in death. Whatever each man can separately do, without trespassing upon others, he has a right to do for himself; and he has a right to a fair portion of all which society, with all its combinations of skill and force, can do in his favour. In this partnership all men have equal rights; but not to equal things.

He that has but five shillings in the partnership, has as good a right to it, as he that has five hundred pounds has to his larger proportion. But he has not a right to an equal dividend in the product of the joint stock; and as to the share of power, authority, and direction which each individual ought to have in the management of the state, that I must deny to be amongst the direct original rights of man in civil society; for I have in my contemplation the civil social man, and no other. It is a thing to be settled by convention.

If civil society be the offspring of convention, that convention must be its law. That convention must limit and modify all the descriptions of constitution which are formed under it. Every sort of legislative, judicial, or executory power are its creatures. They can have no being in any other state of things; and how can any man claim under the conventions of civil society, rights which do not so much as suppose its existence? rights which are absolutely repugnant to it? One of the first motives to civil society, and which becomes one of its fundamental rules, is, *that no man should be judge in his own cause*. By this each person has at once divested himself of the first fundamental right of uncovenanted man, that is, to judge for himself, and to assert his own cause. He abdicates all right to be his own governor. He inclusively, in a great measure, abandons the right of self-defence, the first law of nature. Men cannot enjoy the rights of an uncivil and of a civil state together. That he may obtain justice, he gives up his right of determining what it is in points the most essential to him. That he may secure some liberty, he makes a surrender in trust of the whole of it.

Government is not made in virtue of natural rights, which may and do exist in total independence of it;

and exist in much greater clearness, and in a much greater degree of abstract perfection: but their abstract perfection is their practical defect. By having a right to everything they want everything. Government is a contrivance of human wisdom to provide for human *wants*. Men have a right that these wants should be provided for by this wisdom. Among these wants is to be reckoned the want, out of civil society, of a sufficient restraint upon their passions. Society requires not only that the passions of individuals should be subjected, but that even in the mass and body, as well as in the individuals, the inclinations of men should frequently be thwarted, their will controlled, and their passions brought into subjection. This can only be done *by a power out of themselves*; and not, in the exercise of its function, subject to that will and to those passions which it is its office to bridle and subdue. In this sense the restraints on men, as well as their liberties, are to be reckoned among their rights. But as the liberties and the restrictions vary with times and circumstances, and admit of infinite modifications, they cannot be settled upon any abstract rule; and nothing is so foolish as to discuss them upon that principle.

The moment you abate anything from the full rights of men, each to govern himself, and suffer any artificial, positive limitation upon those rights, from that moment the whole organization of government becomes a consideration of convenience. This it is which makes the constitution of a state, and the due distribution of its powers, a matter of the most delicate and complicated skill. It requires a deep knowledge of human nature and human necessities, and of the things which facilitate or obstruct the various ends, which are to be pursued by the mechanism of civil institutions. The state is to have recruits to its strength, and remedies to its distempers. What is the use of discussing a man's abstract right to food or medicine? The question is upon the method of procuring and administering them. In that deliberation I shall always advise to call in the aid of the farmer and the physician, rather than the professor of metaphysics.

The science of constructing a commonwealth, or renovating it, or reforming it, is, like every other experimental science, not to be taught *a priori*. Nor is it a short experience that can instruct us in that practical science; because the real effects of moral causes are not always immediate; but that which in the first instance is prejudicial may be excellent in its remoter operation; and its excellence may arise even from the ill effects it produces in the beginning. The reverse also happens: and very plausible schemes, with very pleasing commencements, have often shameful and lamentable conclusions. In states there are often some obscure and almost latent causes, things which appear at first view of little moment, on which a very great part of its prosperity or adversity may most essentially depend. The science of government being therefore so practical in itself, and intended for such practical purposes, a matter which requires experience, and even more experience than any person can gain in his whole life, however sagacious and observing he may be, it is with infinite caution that any man ought to venture upon pulling down an edifice, which has answered in any tolerable degree for ages the common purposes of society, or on building it up again, without having models and patterns of approved utility before his eyes.

These metaphysic rights entering into common life,

like rays of light which pierce into a dense medium, are, by the laws of nature, refracted from their straight line. Indeed in the gross and complicated mass of human passions and concerns, the primitive rights of men undergo such a variety of refractions and reflections, that it becomes absurd to talk of them as if they continued in the simplicity of their original direction. The nature of man is intricate; the objects of society are of the greatest possible complexity: and therefore no simple disposition or direction of power can be suitable either to man's nature, or to the quality of his affairs. When I hear the simplicity of contrivance aimed at and boasted of in any new political constitutions, I am at no loss to decide that the artificers are grossly ignorant of their trade, or totally negligent of their duty. The simple governments are fundamentally defective, to say no worse of them. If you were to contemplate society in but one point of view, all these simple modes of polity are infinitely captivating. In effect each would answer its single end much more perfectly than the more complex is able to attain all its complex purposes. But it is better that the whole should be imperfectly and anomalously answered, than that, while some parts are provided for with great exactness, others might be totally neglected, or perhaps materially injured, by the over-care of a favourite member.

The pretended rights of these theorists are all extremes: and in proportion as they are metaphysically true, they are morally and politically false. The rights of men are in a sort of *middle*, incapable of definition, but not impossible to be discerned. The rights of men in governments are their advantages; and these are often in balances between differences of good; in compromises sometimes between good and evil, and some times between evil and evil. Political reason is a computing principle; adding, subtracting, multiplying, and dividing, morally and not metaphysically, or mathematically, true moral denominations.

By these theorists the right of the people is almost always sophistically confounded with their power. The body of the community, whenever it can come to act, can meet with no effectual resistance; but till power and right are the same, the whole body of them has no right inconsistent with virtue, and the first of all virtues, prudence. Men have no right to what is not reasonable, and to what is not for their benefit; for though a pleasant writer said, *Liceat perire poetis*, when one of them, in cold blood, is said to have leaped into the flames of a volcanic revolution, *Ardentem frigidus Ætnam insiluit*, I consider such a frolic rather as an unjustifiable poetic licence, than as one of the franchises of Parnassus; and whether he were poet, or divine, or politician, that chose to exercise this kind of right, I think that more wise, because more charitable, thoughts would urge me rather to save the man, than to preserve his brazen slippers as the monuments of his folly.

The kind of anniversary sermons to which a great part of what I write refers, if men are not shamed out of their present course, in commemorating the fact, will cheat many out of the principles, and deprive them of the benefits, of the revolution they commemorate. I confess to you, Sir, I never liked this continual talk of resistance, and revolution, or the practice of making the extreme medicine of the constitution its daily bread. It renders the habit of society dangerously valetudinary: it is taking periodical doses of mercury sublimate, and swallowing down repeated provocatives of cantharides to our love of liberty.

60: EDMUND BURKE. Speech on the Petition of the Unitarians, House of Commons

11 May 1792

(*Works*, VI, pp. 113–4.)

I NEVER govern myself, no rational man ever did govern himself, by abstractions and universals. I do not put abstract ideas wholly out of any question, because I well know that under that name I should dismiss principles; and that without the guide and light of sound, well-understood principles, all reasonings in politics, as in everything else, would be only a confused jumble of particular facts and details, without the means of drawing out any sort of theoretical or practical conclusion. A statesman differs from a professor in an university; the latter has only the general view of society; the former, the statesman, has a number of circumstances to combine with those general ideas, and to take into his consideration. Circumstances are infinite, are infinitely combined; are variable and transient; he who does not take them into consideration is not erroneous, but stark mad,—*dat operam ut cum ratione insaniat*,—he is metaphysically mad. A statesman, never losing sight of principles, is to be guided by circumstances; and, judging contrary to the exigencies of the moment, he may ruin his country for ever.

I go on this ground, that government, representing the society, has a general superintending control over all the actions, and over all the publicly propagated doctrines, of men, without which it never could provide adequately for all the wants of society; but then it is to use this power with an equitable discretion, the only bond of sovereign authority. For it is not, perhaps, so much by the assumption of unlawful powers, as by the unwise or unwarrantable use of those which are most legal, that governments oppose their true end and object; for there is such a thing as tyranny as well as usurpation. You can hardly state to me a case, to which legislature is the most confessedly competent, in which, if the rules of benignity and prudence are not observed, the most mischievous and oppressive things may not be done. So that after all it is a moral and virtuous discretion, and not any abstract theory of right, which keeps governments faithful to their ends. Crude, unconnected truths are in the world of practice what falsehoods are in theory.

61: ARTHUR YOUNG. *The Example of France a Warning to Britain*

1793

(2nd edition, 1793, pp. 2–4.)

I AM inclined to think the application of theory to matters of government, a surprising imbecility in the human mind; for men to be ready to trust to reason in inquiries, where experiment is equally at hand for their guide, has been pronounced, by various great authorities, to be, in every other science, the grossest folly—why the observation should not equally extend to the science of legislation, will not easily appear.

I have been too long a farmer to be governed by any thing but events; I have a constitutional abhorrence of theory, of all trust in abstract reasoning; and consequently I have a reliance merely on experience, in other words, on events, the only principle worthy of an experimenter.

Sovereignty of the People

62: MRS. MACAULAY GRAHAM. *Observations on the Reflections of the Right Hon. Edmund Burke on the Revolution in France, in a letter to Earl Stanhope*

1790

Mrs. Macaulay Graham, Catharine Macaulay (1731–1791), was described by Mary Wollstonecraft as "the woman of the greatest abilities that this country has ever produced." She wrote the history of England in eight volumes, and many controversial works. Her life was as controversial as her writings.

THE liberty that was taken in the year 1688, by a Convention of Lords and Commons, to depose King James, the reigning sovereign, from the throne, and to vest the sovereignty of the realm in his daughter Mary, and her husband, the Prince of Orange . . . and this to the prejudice not only of King James but of his son, who had been acknowledged as the lawful heir of his throne; and also to the prejudice of the House of Savoy, who by lineal descent were the next in regular succession; are indeed facts which *might warrant a plain-thinking man* in the opinion, that the present reigning family owe their succession to the choice or assent of the people.

However strongly the warm friends of freedom might wish that this abstract right of the people, of chusing their own magistrates, and deposing them for ill conduct, had been laid open to the publick by a formal declaration of such a right in the act of succession, this certainly was not a period of time for carrying these wishes into execution. The whole body of the people had swallowed deeply of the *poison* of church policy; *passive obedience*, by their means, had so entirely supplanted the *abstract notion* of the *rights of men*, which prevailed in the opposition to Charles the First; and so desirous were the triumphant party to prevent the revival of such a principle, by which their interests had been affected, that they took care to confound the *only just authority* they had for their conduct in as great *a mist of words and tenses as possible*. . . . Instead of thinking with Mr. Burke, that such a plain declaration of the rights of men would have tended to disturb the quiet of the nation, I firmly believe that it would have had a contrary effect; for, in that case, these endless disputes between the Tories, and Whigs, would soon have had an end.

63: JAMES MACKINTOSH. *Vindiciæ Gallicæ*

1791

(Pp. 323–4.)

THUS evidently has it appeared, from the conduct and language of the leaders of the Revolution, that it was a *deposition* and an *election*; and that all language of a contrary tendency, which is to be found in their acts, arose from the remnant of their own prejudice, or from concession to the prejudice of others, or from the superficial and presumptuous policy of imposing august illusions on mankind. The same spirit regulated, the same prejudices impeded their progress in every department. "They acted," says Mr. Burke, "by their ancient States." They did not—Were the Peers, and the members of a dissolved House of Commons, with the Lord-Mayor of London, &c. convoked by a summons from the Prince of Orange, the Parliament of England? No. They were neither lawfully elected nor lawfully assembled. But they affected a semblance of a Parliament in their convention, and a semblance of hereditary right in their election. The subsequent act of Parliament is nugatory; for as that Legislature derived its whole existence and authority from the Convention, it could not return more than it had received, and could not therefore *legalize* the acts of the body which created it. If they were not previously legal, the Parliament itself was without *legal* authority, and could therefore give no legal sanction. It is therefore without any view to a prior, or allusion to a posterior Revolution, that Dr. Price, and the Revolution Society of London, think themselves entitled to conclude, that abused power is revocable, and corrupt Governments ought to be reformed.

64: CHARLES JAMES FOX. Speech on the King's Message for an Augmentation of the Forces, House of Commons

1 February 1793

(*Parliamentary History*, XXX, p. 310.)

MR. FOX said he had already differed sufficiently with a right hon. gentleman (Mr. Burke) on this subject, to wish to provoke any fresh difference; but even against so great an authority he must say, that the people are the sovereign in every state; that they have a right to change the form of their government, and a right to cashier their governors for misconduct, as the people of this country cashiered James II, not by a parliament, or any regular form known to the constitution, but by a convention speaking the sense of the people; that convention produced a parliament and a king. They elected William to a vacant throne, not only setting aside James whom they had just cashiered for misconduct, but his innocent son. Again, they elected the House of Brunswick, not individually, but by dynasty; and that dynasty to continue while the terms and conditions on which it was elected were fulfilled, and no longer. He could not admit the right to do all this but by acknowledging the sovereignty of the people as paramount to all other laws.

But it was said, that although we had once exercised this power, we had in the very act of exercising it, renounced it for ever. We had neither renounced it, nor, if we had been so disposed, was such a renunciation in our power. We elected first an individual, then a dynasty, and lastly passed an act of parliament in the reign of Queen Anne, declaring it to be the right of the people of this realm to do so again without even assigning a reason. If there were any persons among us, who doubted the superior wisdom of our monarchical form of government, their error was owing to those who changed its strong and irrefragable foundation in the right and choice of the people to a more flimsy ground of title.

65: JAMES MACKINTOSH. *Vindiciæ Gallicæ*

1791

(Pp. 337–8.)

THE criterion that distinguishes *laws* from *dictates*, freedom from servitude, rightful Government from usurpation, *the law being an expression of the general will*, is wanting. This is the grievance which the admirers of the Revolution in 1688 desire to remedy according to its *principles*. This is that perennial source of corruption which has increased, is increasing, and ought to be diminished. If the general interest is not the object of our Government, it is, it must be, because the general will does not govern.

66: THOMAS PAINE. *The Rights of Man*

1791

(Part I, pp. 152–3, 156–8.)

REASON and Ignorance, the opposites of each other, influence the great bulk of mankind. If either of these can be rendered sufficiently extensive in a country, the machinery of Government goes easily on. Reason obeys itself; and Ignorance submits to whatever is dictated to it.

The two modes of Government which prevail in the world, are, *first*, Government by election and representation; *secondly*, Government by hereditary succession. The former is generally known by the name of republic; the latter by that of monarchy and aristocracy.

Those distinct and opposite forms, erect themselves on the two distinct and opposite bases of Reason and Ignorance.—As the exercise of government requires talents and abilities, and as talents and abilities cannot have hereditary descent, it is evident that hereditary succession requires a belief from man, to which his reason cannot subscribe, and which can only be established upon his ignorance; and the more ignorant any country is, the better it is fitted for this species of Government.

On the contrary, Government, in a well constituted republic, requires no belief from man beyond what his reason can give. He sees the *rationale* of the system, its origin and its operation; and as it is best supported when best understood, the human faculties act with boldness, and acquire, under this form of Government, a gigantic manliness.

As, therefore, each of those forms acts on a different base, the one moving freely by the aid of reason, the other by ignorance, we have next to consider, what it is that gives motion to that species of Government which is called mixed Government, or, as it is sometimes ludicrously stiled, a Government of *this*, *that* and *t'other*.

The moving power in this species of Government, is of necessity, Corruption. However imperfect election and representation may be in mixed Governments, they still give exercise to a greater portion of reason than is convenient to the hereditary Part; and therefore it becomes necessary to buy the reason up. A mixed Government is an imperfect everything, cementing and soldering the discordant parts together by corruption, to act as a whole. Mr. Burke appears highly disgusted that France, since she had resolved on a revolution, did not adopt what he calls "*A British Constitution*"; and the regretful manner in which he expresses himself on this occasion, implies a suspicion that the British Constitution needed something to keep its defects in countenance.

In mixed governments there is no responsibility; the parts cover each other till responsibility is lost; and the corruption which moves the machine, contrives at the same time its own escape.

When we survey the wretched condition of man

under the monarchical and hereditary systems of Government, dragged from his home by one power, or driven by another, and impoverished by taxes more than by enemies, it becomes evident that those systems are bad, and that a general revolution in the principle and construction of Governments is necessary.

What is Government more than the management of the affairs of a Nation? It is not, and from its nature cannot be, the property of any particular man or family, but of the whole community, at whose expence it is supported; and though by force and contrivance it has been usurped into an inheritance, the usurpation cannot alter the right of things. Sovereignty, as a matter of right, appertains to the Nation only, and not to any individual; and a Nation has at all times an inherent indefeasible right to abolish any form of government it finds inconvenient, and establish such as accords with its interest, disposition, and happiness. The romantic and barbarous distinction of men into Kings and subjects, though it may suit the condition of courtiers, cannot that of citizens; and is exploded by the principle upon which Governments are now founded. Every citizen is a member of the Sovereignty, and as such, can acknowledge no personal subjection; and his obedience can be only to the laws.

What were formerly called Revolutions, were little more than a change of persons, or an alteration of local circumstances. They rose and fell like things of course, and had nothing in their existence or their fate that could influence beyond the spot that produced them. But what we now see in the world, from the Revolutions of America and France, are a renovation of the natural orders of things, a system of principles as universal as truth and the existence of man, and combining moral with political happiness and national prosperity.

"I. *Men are born and always continue free, and equal in respect of their rights. Civil distinctions, therefore, can be founded only on public utility.*

"II. *The end of all political associations is the preservation of the natural and imprescriptible rights of man; and these rights are liberty, property, security, and resistance of oppression.*

"III. *The Nation is essentially the source of all Sovereignty; nor can ANY INDIVIDUAL, or ANY BODY OF MEN, be entitled to any authority which is not expressly derived from it.*"

67: JAMES MACKINTOSH. *Vindiciæ Gallicæ*

1791

(Pp. 263–4.)

IT will not be controverted, that the object of a representative Legislature is to collect the general will. To accord with this principle, there must be the same unity in the *representative* as in the *original* WILL.—That will is ONE. It cannot therefore, without solecism, be *doubly* represented. The social body supposes a perfect unity, and no man's will can have TWO discordant organs. Any *absolute* negative opposed to the national will, decisively spoken by its Representatives, is radically null, as an usurpation of popular sovereignty. Thus far does the abstract principle of a Representative Government condemn the division of the Legislature.

68: CHARLES JAMES FOX. Speech on Mr. Grey's Motion for a Reform in Parliament, House of Commons

6–7 May 1793

(*Parliamentary History*, XXX, pp. 922–3.)

HE was ready to say with Locke, that government originated not only for, but from the people, and that the people were the legitimate sovereign in every community. If such writings as were now branded as subversive of all government had not been read and studied, would the parliament of 1640 have done those great and glorious things, but for which we might be now receiving the mandates of a despot, like Germans, or any other slaves. A noble lord [Mornington] had discovered that Rousseau, in his Social Contract, had said a very extravagant thing. He was not very well qualified to judge, for he had found the beginning of the Social Contract so extravagant, that he could not read it through, but he believed it was one of the most extravagant of that author's works. He did not mean to say that the noble lord had produced an extravagant saying from Rousseau as a novelty; but it was somewhat remarkable, that an extravagant thing, from the most extravagant work of an extravagant foreign author, should be produced as an argument against a reform in the representation of the people of Great Britain.

69: THE LONDON CORRESPONDING SOCIETY
Address to the Inhabitants of Great Britain, on the Subject of Parliamentary Reform

6 August 1792

(Trial of John Horne Tooke, 17–22 November 1794. *State Trials*, XXV, pp. 590–2.)

LET no man imagine himself unconcerned in the proposed reform—let no one think so meanly of his situation or abilities as to suppose his coming forward will be of no service to the cause of liberty! numbers, union, and perseverance must in the end be crowned with success, while compared with the small efforts of each individual associating and thereby countenancing the demand of the nation to be restored to its constitutional rights! how great will appear the advantages resulting therefrom!——

An HONEST PARLIAMENT!

An ANNUAL PARLIAMENT!

A PARLIAMENT wherein EACH INDIVIDUAL WILL HAVE HIS REPRESENTATIVE.

Soon then we should see our liberties restored, the press free, the laws simplified, judges unbiassed, juries independent, needless places and pensions retrenched, immoderate salaries reduced, the public better served, taxes diminished, and the necessaries of life more within the reach of the poor, youth better educated, prisons less crowded, old age better provided for, and sumptuous feasts, at the expense of the starving poor, less frequent. Look not upon this, dear countrymen, as an enthusiastic vision; but rather let us together take a calm and reasonable review of such an honest parliament assembled—let us in idea, curtail their session unto even the short duration of three months in one year, or sixty-four meetings for doing the annual business of the nation. Still five hundred honest men, meeting sixty-four times, with both intention and capacity to serve their country, must do *something*—must employ their time somehow. Contested elections, none or very few, and soon determined; party debates, none, the interest of the people being one; long speeches much diminished, honest men seeking reason, not oratory; no placemen in the senate, corrupt influence dies away, and with it all tedious, obstinate, ministerial opposition to measures calculated for the public good.

M. MARGAROT, chairman.
T. HARDY, secretary.

70: THOMAS ERSKINE. Speech for the Defence at the Trial of John Horne Tooke

17–22 November 1794

John Horne Tooke (1736–1812) was ordained priest in 1760 and began his duties at Brentford. He rapidly deserted religion for politics, and was involved in the thick of the Wilkes agitation. In 1771 he quarrelled with Wilkes, founded the independent Constitutional Society and joined the Society for Constitutional Information, founded in 1780. He was an argumentative, pugnacious, quarrelsome, original character who kept house with two illegitimate daughters, first in Soho, later in Wimbledon, and who was mixed up in most of the radical campaigns in the last thirty odd years of the eighteenth century. He was contemptuous of the Whigs (in 1790 he opposed Fox at the Westminster election) but disliked Paine and the more extreme radicals, and exercised a moderating influence in the reforming societies during the revolutionary decade. Arrested with Hardy in May 1794, he was tried for treason in November and promptly acquitted. The verdict was popular, for despite his peculiarities he was widely esteemed. He was a man of considerable intellectual power with original ideas on philology and philosophy. (*State Trials*, XXV, pp. 279–80.)

THE House of Commons is perpetually talked of as if it were a self-existing body, independent of the people; whereas it is their mere agent; the organ by which they speak and act; and which betrays and abdicates its trust the moment that it assumes a language of its own, which the people do not auspicate and approve. Take away *such* a House of Commons from the British government—remove the control which the people have in it upon the executive authority by the free choice of their representatives, and then tell me how it differs from the most despotic establishments, which are the just detestation of the world. Yet how can it be asserted that the people of England have that control, if they have not the free choice which bestows it? The Society of the Friends of the People, part of whose proceedings the crown has thought fit to make evidence, and to speak of with respect, have placed upon the Journal of the House of Commons, and demonstrated by positive evidence, this fallen, humiliated condition of the country.

I do not mean, therefore, to say (and let it be understood that I have not said), that my clients would not be equally guilty, and equally subject to capital punishment, if, under the irritation of this or any other grievance, they had said—Let us supersede this surreptitious parliament, and hold a convention to assume its functions.—When I asserted that the people in this, and in every country, had a right to change their government, I never meant—what must have been supposed by the Court, from the indulgent interruption I received—I never meant that each individual, choosing for himself, might rise in arms to overturn, by force, an established constitution—Far from it, gentlemen—I meant to say—what the people of England will be the last to misunderstand, as they were the first to practise—that all governments stand upon the public will, and ought to endure only for the public benefit; and that when this sacred maxim is forgotten, or trampled upon, a nation, without the conspiracy of individuals, which criminal law can act upon, will, sooner or later, *do itself justice*.

71: EDMUND BURKE. *An Appeal from the New to the Old Whigs*

1791

(*Works*, III, pp. 76–8.)

BUT there is one topic upon which I hope I shall be excused in going a little beyond my design. The factions, now so busy amongst us, in order to divest men of all love for their country, and to remove from their minds all duty with regard to the state, endeavour to propagate an opinion, that the *people*, in forming their commonwealth, have by no means parted with their power over it. This is an impregnable citadel, to which these gentlemen retreat whenever they are pushed by the battery of laws and usages, and positive conventions. Indeed it is such and of so great force, that all they have done, in defending their outworks, is so much time and labour thrown away. Discuss any of their schemes—their answer is—It is the act of the *people*, and that is sufficient. Are we to deny to a *majority* of the people the right of altering even the whole frame of their society, if such should be their pleasure? They may change it, say they, from a monarchy to a republic to-day, and tomorrow back again from a republic to a monarchy; and so backward and forward as often as they like. They are masters of the commonwealth; because in substance they are themselves the commonwealth. The French Revolution, say they, was the act of the majority of the people; and if the majority of any other people, the people of England for instance, wish to make the same change, they have the same right.

Just the same undoubtedly. That is, none at all. Neither the few nor the many have a right to act merely by their will, in any matter connected with duty, trust, engagement, or obligation. The constitution of a country being once settled upon some compact, tacit or expressed, there is no power existing of force to alter it, without the breach of the covenant, or the consent of all the parties. Such is the nature of a contract. And the votes of a majority of the people, whatever their infamous flatterers may teach in order to corrupt their minds, cannot alter the moral any more than they can alter the physical essence of things. The people are not to be taught to think lightly of their engagements to their governors; else they teach governors to think lightly of their engagements towards them. In that kind of game in the end the people are sure to be losers. To flatter them into a contempt of faith, truth, and justice, is to ruin them; for in these virtues consist their whole safety— To flatter any man, or any part of mankind, in any description, by asserting, that in engagements he or they are free, whilst any other human creature is bound, is ultimately to vest the rule of morality in the pleasure of those who ought to be rigidly submitted to it; to subject the sovereign reason of the world to the caprices of weak and giddy men.

But, as no one of us men can dispense with public or private faith, or with any other tie of moral obligation, so neither can any number of us. The number engaged in crimes, instead of turning them into laudable acts, only augments the quantity and intensity of the guilt. I am well aware, that men love to hear of their power, but have an extreme disrelish to be told of their duty. This is of course; because every duty is a limitation of some power. Indeed arbitrary power is so much to the depraved taste of the vulgar, of the vulgar of every description, that almost all the dissensions, which lacerate the commonwealth, are not concerning the manner in which it is to be exercised, but concerning the hands in which it is to be placed. Somewhere they are resolved to have it. Whether they desire it to be vested in the many or the few, depends with most men upon the chance which they imagine they themselves may have of partaking in the exercise of that arbitrary sway, in the one mode or in the other.

It is not necessary to teach men to thirst after power. But it is very expedient that by moral instruction they should be taught, and by their civil constitutions they should be compelled, to put many restrictions upon the immoderate exercise of it, and the inordinate desire. The best method of obtaining these two great points forms the important, but at the same time the difficult, problem to the true statesman. He thinks of the place in which political power is to be lodged, with no other attention, than as it may render the more or the less practicable its salutary restraint, and its prudent direction. For this reason no legislator, at any period of the world, has willingly placed the seat of active power in the hands of the multitude; because there it admits of no control, no regulation, no steady direction whatsoever. The people are the natural control on authority; but to exercise and to control together is contradictory and impossible.

72: EDMUND BURKE. *An Appeal from the New to the Old Whigs*

1791

(*Works*, III, pp. 82–4.)

WHEN the supreme authority of the people is in question, before we attempt to extend or to confine it, we ought to fix in our minds, with some degree of distinctness, an idea of what it is we mean, when we say the PEOPLE.

In a state of *rude* nature there is no such thing as a people. A number of men in themselves have no collective capacity. The idea of a people is the idea of a corporation. It is wholly artificial; and made, like all other legal fictions, by common agreement. What the particular nature of that agreement was, is collected from the form into which the particular society has been cast. Any other is not *their* covenant. When men, therefore, break up the original compact or agreement which gives its corporate form and capacity to a state, they are no longer a people; they have no longer a corporate existence; they have no longer a legal, coactive force to bind within, nor a claim to be recognised abroad. They are a number of vague, loose individuals, and nothing more. With them all is to begin again. Alas! they little know how many a weary step is to be taken before they can form themselves into a mass, which has a true, politic personality.

We hear much from men, who have not acquired their hardness of assertion from the profundity of their thinking, about the omnipotence of a *majority*, in such a dissolution of an ancient society as hath taken place in France. But amongst men so disbanded, there can be no such thing as majority or minority; or power in any one person to bind another. The power of acting by a majority, which the gentlemen theorists seem to assume so readily, after they have violated the contract out of which it has arisen, (if at all it existed,) must be grounded on two assumptions; first, that of an incorporation produced by unanimity; and secondly, an unanimous agreement, that the act of a mere majority (say of one) shall pass with them and with others as the act of the whole.

We are so little affected by things which are habitual, that we consider this idea of the decision of a *majority* as if it were a law of our original nature: but such constructive whole, residing in a part only, is one of the most violent fictions of positive law, that ever has been or can be made on the principles of artificial incorporation. Out of civil society nature knows nothing of it; nor are men, even when arranged according to civil order, otherwise than by very long training, brought at all to submit to it. The mind is brought far more easily to acquiesce in the proceedings of one man, or a few, who act under a general procuration for the state, than in the vote of a victorious majority in councils, in which every man has his share in the deliberation. For there the beaten party are exasperated and soured by the previous contention, and mortified by the conclusive defeat. This mode of decision, where wills may be so nearly equal, where, according to circumstances, the smaller number may be the stronger force, and where apparent reason may be all upon one side, and on the other little else than impetuous appetite; all this must be the result of a very particular and special convention, confirmed afterwards by long habits of obedience, by a sort of discipline in society, and by a strong hand, vested with stationary, permanent power, to enforce this sort of constructive general will. What organ it is that shall declare the corporate mind is so much a matter of positive arrangement, that several states, for the validity of several of their acts, have required a proportion of voices much greater than that of a mere majority. These proportions are so entirely governed by convention, that in some cases the minority decides. The laws in many countries to *condemn* require more than a mere majority; less than an equal number to *acquit*. In our judicial trials we require unanimity either to condemn or to absolve. In some incorporations one man speaks for the whole; in others, a few. Until the other day, in the constitution of Poland, unanimity was required to give validity to any act of their great national council or diet. This approaches much more nearly to rude nature than the institutions of any other country. Such, indeed, every commonwealth must be, without a positive law to recognise in a certain number the will of the entire body.

If men dissolve their ancient incorporation, in order to regenerate their community, in that state of things each man has a right, if he pleases, to remain an individual. Any number of individuals, who can agree upon it, have an undoubted right to form themselves into a state apart, and wholly independent. If any of these is forced into the fellowship of another, this is conquest, and not compact. On every principle, which supposes society to be in virtue of a free covenant, this compulsive incorporation must be null and void.

73: SIR BROOKE BOOTHBY. *Observations on the Appeal from the New to the Old Whigs and on Mr. Paine's* Rights of Man

1792

(Pp. 115–6.)

FOR a nation to love liberty it is sufficient that she knows it, and to be free it is sufficient that she wills it.

In the first of these aphorisms whether the modern Lycurgus means to speak of a practical or a theoretical acquaintance with civil liberty; whether of a love created by the habitual experience of its excellence, or by the attraction of its abstract beauty; of American or French liberty; we are left to discover. If he had said that a government resting on laws, by which personal liberty and property are equally secured to all, and which no man has the power to dispense with or control is the best foundation for national happiness, he would have repeated an intelligible truth, confirmed by the experience and consent of ages. But this could not have been reduced to the quintessence of a philosophical maxim, nor have hitched into the antithesis which follows—*and to be free it is sufficient that she wills it*. Nothing can be more vague than the sense of abstract terms when used by confused minds. Supposing the adverse interests and passions of men to be united in one volition, a supposition not very easy to make, civil liberty is an extremely complicated idea, and men must differ from each other widely in their conception of it. National freedom depends upon the action and re-action of a thousand springs. It is not only the result of great wisdom, but of great good fortune; it must be the work of time and experience, and supported by a combination of circumstances, which from the few free states recorded in the annals of mankind we must suppose to be extremely rare.

74: RICHARD HEY. *Happiness and Rights*

1792

Richard Hey (1745–1835), was a mathematician, Fellow and tutor of Magdalene College, Cambridge. Among other works, he published dissertations on gaming, duelling and suicide. (p. 65.)

FOR these Arguments prove that a number much less than half of a Society may, in many cases, command the Remainder. At the same time, they allow, in some cases, that even a Majority is not sufficient. France and Spain may, if you please, be taken as one region. Now, if, by some abstract Theory, a Majority is to govern universally, and France is allowed to have more Inhabitants than Spain, the French (when unanimous) might make laws for the region consisting of France and Spain, and, as a Majority, might rightfully compel the obedience of the Spaniards.

Those who plead for supreme Liberty and equal Rights, would (I apprehend) find it difficult to shew, on the one hand, that any Authority not derived originally from *unanimous* consent can bind the dissentient Part of a Community in any proposed case: and, if the same persons take for granted that a Majority is to bind the Whole, they would, on the other hand, find a difficulty in proving that France has not a right to command Spain, the Southern half of Britain, as more populous, to command the Northern half, or the like in other countries. They have set up two Principles which agree but ill together. The equalising Principle destroys the Principle which supports the right of a Majority *as* a Majority. Yet these Theorists find they are run so hard, when they attempt to maintain the beloved independency of every Individual, that they are driven to adopt the scheme of a Majority. And as (I believe) they would find a great difficulty in supporting the scheme of a Majority, upon such equalising and independent principles as they profess; their best way, clearly, is not to attempt to prove it at all, but to take it for granted.

75: WILLIAM PITT. Speech on Mr. Grey's Motion for a Reform in Parliament, House of Commons

6–7 May 1793

(*Parliamentary History*, XXX, pp. 892–3, 901–2.)

THE conduct of the French, in all its circumstances, bore a peculiar application to this country; it presented the fruits opening, in due season, the legitimate offspring of those trees, under the specious pretext of liberty, planted against this country and its allies The French had disclosed a system of disseminating their principles, and procuring proselytes in every part of Europe—a system which they had particularly followed up with respect to this country. Such was the case without—what was the situation of affairs within? Societies had been formed in this country, affiliated with the Jacobin clubs in France, and though they had since assumed a different shape, were then employed for the purpose of spreading Jacobin principles. In this object they proceeded with a degree of boldness and confidence, proportioned to the success of the French arms. We thus beheld the scheme which we had anticipated as the result of the new constitutions in France opening upon us. We had more immediately an opportunity of seeing what were the views of the legislators in France with respect to this country, and what their instruments in England were endeavouring to effect. For while in France they always mentioned the pretext of a parliamentary reform, as the medium by which they were to introduce their principles, their instruments here always took care to connect the system of parliamentary reform with all those delusive doctrines upon which was founded the newly raised fabric of French freedom—Nothing less than a National Convention was held out as a sufficient remedy for the abuses which prevailed in the representation, and the sole organ through which a more perfect form of government was to be obtained; namely, such a government as should acknowledge no other source of authority and no other rule of conduct, than the will of the majority. In short, French principles were inculcated as the true standard of political belief, and the example of the French government proposed as a worthy object of imitation.

In what is called the government of the multitude, they are not the many who govern the few, but the few who govern the many. It is a species of tyranny, which adds insult to the wretchedness of its subjects, by styling its own arbitrary decrees the voice of the people, and sanctioning its acts of oppression and cruelty under the pretence of the national will. Such is the nature of those principles connected with the right of individual suffrage; and how far you are prepared to give countenance to that measure, by referring it to a committee as a subject of deliberation, you are now called to determine.

WILLIAM GODWIN AND *Political Justice*

76: THOMAS PAINE. *The Rights of Man*

1792

(Part II, pp. 8–11.)

GOVERNMENT is no farther necessary than to supply the few cases to which society and civilization are not conveniently competent; and instances are not wanting to show, that everything which government can usefully add thereto, has been performed by the common consent of society, without government.

So far is it from being true, as has been pretended, that the abolition of any formal government is the dissolution of society, that it acts by a contrary impulse, and brings the latter the closer together. All that part of its organization which it had committed to its government, devolves again upon itself, and acts through its medium. When men, as well from natural instinct as from reciprocal benefits, have habituated themselves to social and civilized life, there is always enough of its principles in practice to carry them through any changes they may find necessary or convenient to make in their government. In short, man is so naturally a creature of society that it is almost impossible to put him out of it.

Formal government makes but a small part of civilized life; and when even the best that human wisdom can devise is established, it is a thing more in name and idea, than in fact. It is to the great and fundamental principles of society and civilization—to the common usage universally consented to, and mutually and reciprocally maintained—to the unceasing circulation of interest which, passing through its million channels, invigorates the whole mass of civilized man—it is to these things, infinitely more than to any thing which even the best instituted government can perform, that the safety and prosperity of the individual and of the whole depends.

The more perfect civilization is, the less occasion has it for government, because the more does it regulate its own affairs, and govern itself; but so contrary is the practice of old governments to the reason of the case, that the expences of them increase in the proportion they ought to diminish. It is but few general laws that civilized life requires, and those of such common usefulness, that whether they are enforced by the forms of governments or not, the effect will be nearly the same. If we consider what the principles are that first condense men into society, and what the motives that regulate their mutual intercourse afterwards, we shall find, by the time we arrive at what is called government, that nearly the whole of the business is performed by the natural operation of the parts upon each other.

Man, with respect to all those matters, is more a creature of consistency than he is aware, or than governments would wish him to believe. All the great laws of society are laws of nature. Those of trade and commerce, whether with respect to the intercourse of individuals, or of nations, are laws of mutual and reciprocal interests. They are followed and obeyed, because it is the interest of the parties so to do, and not on account of any formal laws their governments may impose or interpose.

But how often is the natural propensity to society disturbed or destroyed by the operations of government! When the latter, instead of being ingrafted on the principles of the former, assumes to exist for itself, and acts by partialities of favour and oppression, it becomes the cause of the mischiefs it ought to prevent.

77: WILLIAM GODWIN. *Political Justice*

1793

William Godwin (1756–1836), was educated as a Sandemanian on such works as *An Account of the Pious Deaths of Many Godly Children.* Dissenting minister (for four years), then a Grub Street writer, he preached universal benevolence, especially towards himself. The revolutionary decade was the period in which his life was at its zenith, when he sold over 4,000 copies of *Political Justice* and knew real happiness with Mary Wollstonecraft. After her death he married, in 1801, a handsome widow, and the rest of his life is a story of family misfortune, bankruptcy, borrowing, seduction and suicide. The father of Mary Shelley and inspirer of *Queen Mab*, he ended his life in the receipt of Whig charity as Yeoman Usher of the Exchequer. (Book II, Chapter V.)

POLITICAL society, as has already been observed, is founded in the principles of morality and justice. It is impossible for intellectual beings to be brought into coalition and intercourse without a certain mode of conduct, adapted to their nature and connection, immediately becoming a duty incumbent on the parties concerned. Men would never have associated if they had not imagined that in consequence of that association they would mutually conduce to the advantage and happiness of each other. This is the real purpose, the genuine basis of their intercourse; and as far as this purpose is answered, so far does society answer the end of its institution.

There is only one postulate more that is necessary to

bring us to a conclusive mode of reasoning upon this subject. Whatever is meant by the term "right"—for it will presently appear that the sense of the term itself has never been clearly understood—there can neither be opposite rights, nor rights and duties hostile to each other. The rights of one man cannot clash with or be destructive of the rights of another; for this, instead of rendering the subject an important branch of truth and morality, as the advocates of the rights of man certainly understand it to be, would be to reduce it to a heap of unintelligible jargon and inconsistency. If one man have a right to be free, another man cannot have a right to make him a slave; if one man have a right to inflict chastisement upon me, I cannot have a right to withdraw myself from chastisement; if my neighbour have a right to a sum of money in my possession, I cannot have a right to retain it in my pocket. —It cannot be less incontrovertible that I have no right to omit what my duty prescribes.

From hence it inevitably follows that men have no rights. By right, as the word is employed in this subject, has always been understood discretion; that is, a full and complete power of either doing a thing or omitting it without the person's becoming liable to animadversion or censure from another; that it, in other words, without his incurring any degree of turpitude or guilt. Now in this sense I affirm that man has no rights, no discretionary power whatever.

It is commonly said that a man has a right to the disposal of his fortune, a right to the employment of his time, a right to the uncontrolled choice of his profession or pursuits. But this can never be consistently affirmed till it can be shown that he has no duties prescribing and limiting his mode of proceeding in all these respects. My neighbour has just as much right to put an end to my existence with dagger or poison as to deny me that pecuniary assistance without which I must starve, or as to deny me that assistance without which my intellectual attainments or my moral exertions will be materially injured. He has just as much right to amuse himself with burning my house or torturing my children upon the rack as to shut himself up in a cell careless about his fellow men and to hide his talent in a napkin.

It is scarcely necessary to add that if individuals have no rights, neither has society, which possesses nothing but what individuals have brought into a common stock. The absurdity of the common opinion, as applied to this subject, is still more glaring, if possible, than in the view in which we have already considered it.

78: WILLIAM GODWIN. *Political Justice*

1793

(Book III, Chapter II.)

IF government be founded in the consent of the people, it can have no power over any individual by whom that consent is refused. If a tacit consent be not sufficient, still less can I be deemed to have consented to a measure upon which I put an express negative. This immediately follows from the observations of Rousseau. If the people, or the individuals of whom the people is constituted, cannot delegate their authority to a representative, neither can any individual delegate his authority to a majority in an assembly of which he is himself a member. The rules by which my actions shall be directed are matters of a consideration entirely personal, and no man can transfer to another the keeping of his conscience and the judging of his duties. But this brings us back to the point from which we set out. No consent of ours can divest us of our moral capacity. This is a species of property which we can neither barter nor resign, and of consequence it is impossible for any government to derive its authority from an original contract.

79: WILLIAM GODWIN. *Political Justice*

1793

(Book V, Chapters XXII, XXIII.)

THE only legitimate object of political institution is the advantage of individuals. All that cannot be brought home to them, national wealth, prosperity and glory, can be advantageous only to those self-interested impostors who, from the earliest accounts of time, have confounded the understandings of mankind the more securely to sink them in debasement and misery.

National assemblies will by no means be thought to deserve our direct approbation if we recollect for a moment the absurdity of that fiction by which society is considered, as it has been termed, as a moral individual. It is in vain that we endeavour to counteract the immutable laws of necessity. A multitude of men after all our ingenuity will still remain no more than a multitude of men. Nothing can intellectually unite them short of equal capacity and identical perception. So long as the varieties of mind shall remain, the force of society can no otherwise be concentrated than by one man for a shorter or a longer term taking the lead of the rest and employing their force, whether material or dependent on the weight of their character, in a mechanical manner, just as he would employ the force of a tool or a machine. All government corresponds in a certain degree to what the Greeks denominated a tyranny. The difference is that in despotic countries mind is depressed by an uniform usurpation, while in republics it preserves a greater portion of its activity, and the usurpation more easily conforms itself to the fluctuations of opinion.

80: WILLIAM GODWIN. *Political Justice*

1793

(Book VIII, Chapter VI.)

TO return to the subject of cooperation. It may be a curious speculation to attend to the progressive steps by which this feature of human society may be expected to decline. For example: shall we have concerts of music? The miserable state of mechanism of the majority of the performers is so conspicuous as to be even at this day a topic of mortification and ridicule. Will it not be practicable hereafter for one man to perform the whole? Shall we have theatrical exhibitions? This seems to include an absurd and vicious cooperation. It may be doubted whether men will hereafter come forward in any mode gravely to repeat words and ideas not their own! It may be doubted whether any musical performer will habitually execute the compositions of others! We yield supinely to the superior merit of our predecessors because we are accustomed to indulge the inactivity of our own faculties. All formal repetition of other men's ideas seems to be a scheme for imprisoning for so long a time the operations of our own mind. It borders perhaps in this respect upon a breach of sincerity, which requires that we should give immediate utterance to every useful and valuable idea that occurs to our thoughts.

81: WILLIAM GODWIN. *Political Justice*

1793

(Book VI, Chapters III, VIII.)

It is a mistake to suppose that speculative differences of opinion threaten materially to disturb the peace of society. It is only when they are enabled to arm themselves with the authority of government, to form parties in the state, and to struggle for that political ascendancy which is too frequently exerted in support of or in opposition to some particular creed that they become dangerous. Wherever government is wise enough to maintain an inflexible neutrality these jarring sects are always found to live together with sufficient harmony. The very means that have been employed for the preservation of order have been the only means that have led to its disturbance. The moment government resolves to admit of no regulations oppressive to either party, controversy finds its level, and appeals to argument and reason instead of appealing to the sword or the stake. The moment government descends to wear the badge of a sect, religious war is commenced, the world is disgraced with inexpiable broils and deluged with blood.

The injuries that result from a system of national education are, in the first place, that all public establishments include in them the idea of permanence. They endeavour it may be to secure and to diffuse whatever of advantageous to society is already known, but they forget that more remains to be known. If they realised the most substantial benefits at the time of their introduction, they must inevitably become less and less useful as they increased in duration. But to describe them as useless is a very feeble expression of their demerits. They actively restrain the flights of mind and fix it in the belief of exploded errors. It has commonly been observed of universities and extensive establishments for the purpose of education that the knowledge taught there is a century behind the knowledge which exists among the unshackled and unprejudiced members of the same political community. The moment any scheme of proceeding gains a permanent establishment it becomes impressed as one of its characteristic features with an aversion to change. Some violent concussion may oblige its conductors to change an old system of philosophy for a system less obsolete; and they are then as pertinaciously attached to this second doctrine as they were to the first. Real intellectual improvement demands that mind should as speedily as possible be advanced to the height of knowledge already existing among the enlightened members of the community and start from thence in the pursuit of farther acquisitions. But public education has always expended its energies in the support of prejudice; it teaches its pupils not the fortitude that shall bring every proposition to the test of examination, but the art of vindicating such tenets as may chance to be previously established.

The project of a national education ought uniformly to be discouraged on account of its obvious alliance with national government. This is an alliance of a more formidable nature than the old and much contested alliance of church and state. Before we put so powerful a machine under the direction of so ambiguous an agent, it behooves us to consider well what it is that we do. Government will not fail to employ it to strengthen its hands and perpetuate its institutions. If we could even suppose the agents of government not to propose to themselves an object which will be apt to appear in their eyes not merely innocent but meritorious, the evil would not the less happen. Their views as institutors of a system of education will not fail to be analogous to their views in their political capacity: the data upon which their conduct as statesmen is vindicated will be the data upon which their instructions are founded. It is not true that our youth ought to be instructed to venerate the constitution, however excellent; they should be instructed to venerate truth, and the constitution only so far as it corresponded with their independent deductions of truth. Had the scheme of a national education been adopted when despotism was most triumphant, it is not to be believed that it could have forever stifled the voice of truth. But it would have been the most formidable and profound contrivance for that purpose that imagination can suggest. Still, in the countries where liberty chiefly prevails, it is reasonably to be assumed that there are important errors, and a national education has the most direct tendency to perpetuate those errors and to form all minds upon one model.

82: WILLIAM GODWIN. *Political Justice*

1793

(Book III, Chapters IV, V; Book IV, Chapters I, II, Section II.)

NO individual can arrive at any degree of moral or intellectual improvement unless in the use of an independent judgment. No state can be well or happily administered unless in the perpetual use of common deliberation respecting the measures it may be requisite to adopt. But though the general exercise of these faculties be founded in immutable justice, justice will by no means uniformly vindicate the particular application of them. Private judgment and public deliberation are not themselves the standard of moral right and wrong; they are only the means of discovering right and wrong, and of comparing particular propositions with the standard of eternal truth.

Too much stress has undoubtedly been laid upon the idea, as of a grand and magnificent spectacle, of a nation deciding for itself upon some great public principle, and of the highest magistracy yielding its claims when the general voice has pronounced. The value of the whole must at last depend upon the quality of their decision. Truth cannot be made more true by the number of its votaries. Nor is the spectacle much less interesting of a solitary individual bearing his undaunted testimony in favour of justice, though opposed by misguided millions.

Legislation, as it has been usually understood, is not an affair of human competence. Reason is the only legislator, and her decrees are irrevocable and uniform. The functions of society extend, not to the making, but the interpreting of law; it cannot decree, it can only declare that which the nature of things has already decreed, and the propriety of which irresistibly flows from the circumstances of the case.

All political power is strictly speaking executive. It has appeared to be necessary, with respect to men as we at present find them, that force should sometimes be employed in repressing injustice; and for the same reasons it appears that this force should as far as possible be vested in the community. To the public support of justice therefore the authority of the community extends. But no sooner does it wander in the smallest degree from the great line of justice than its authority is at an end; it stands upon a level with the obscurest individual, and every man is bound to resist its decisions.

Force has already appeared to be an odious weapon; and if the use of it be to be regretted in the hands of government, it does not change its nature though wielded by a band of patriots. If the cause we plead be the cause of truth, there is no doubt that by our reasonings, if sufficiently zealous and constant, the same purpose may be effected in a milder and more liberal way.

In a word, it is proper to recollect here what has been established as to the doctrine of force in general, that it is in no case to be employed but where every other means is ineffectual. In the question therefore of resistance to government, force ought never to be introduced without the most imminent necessity; never but in circumstances similar to those of defending my life from a ruffian, where time can by no means be gained, and the consequences instantly to ensue are unquestionably fatal.

But since force is scarcely under any circumstances to be employed, of what nature is that resistance which ought constantly to be given to every instance of injustice? The resistance I am bound to employ is that of uttering the truth, of censuring in the most explicit manner every proceeding that I perceive to be adverse to the true interests of mankind. I am bound to disseminate without reserve all the principles with which I am acquainted and which it may be of importance to mankind to know, and this duty it behooves me to practise upon every occasion and with the most persevering constancy. I must disclose the whole system of moral and political truth, without suppressing any part under the idea of its being too bold and paradoxical, and thus depriving the whole of that complete and irresistible evidence without which its effects must always be feeble, partial and uncertain.

The revolutions of states which a philanthropist would desire to witness, or in which he would willingly cooperate, consist principally in a change of sentiments and dispositions in the members of those states. The true instruments for changing the opinions of men are argument and persuasion. The best security for an advantageous issue is free and unrestricted discussion. In that field truth must always prove the successful champion. If then we would improve the social institutions of mankind, we must write, we must argue, we must converse. To this business there is no close; in this pursuit there should be no pause. Every method should be employed—not so much positively to allure the attention of mankind, or persuasively to invite them to the adoption of our opinions, as to remove every restraint upon thought and to throw open the temple of science and the field of enquiry to all the world.

Those instruments will always be regarded by the discerning mind as suspicious which may be employed with equal prospect of success on both sides of every question. This consideration should make us look with aversion upon all resources of violence. When we descend into the listed field, we of course desert the vantage ground of truth and commit the decision to uncertainty and caprice. The phalanx of reason is invulnerable; it advances with deliberate and determined pace; and nothing is able to resist it. But when we lay down our arguments and take up our swords, the case is altered. Amidst the barbarous pomp of war and the clamorous din of civil brawls, who can tell whether the event shall be prosperous or miserable?

We must therefore carefully distinguish between informing the people and inflaming them. Indignation, resentment and fury are to be deprecated; and all we should ask is sober thought, clear discernment and intrepid discussion.

83: WILLIAM GODWIN. *Political Justice*

1793

(Book V, Chapter XIV.)

NOTHING can be more certain than the omnipotence of truth, or, in other words, than the connection between the judgment and the outward behaviour. If science be capable of perpetual improvement, men will also be capable of perpetually advancing in practical wisdom and justice. Once establish the perfectibility of man and it will inevitably follow that we are advancing to a state in which truth will be too well known to be easily mistaken, and justice too habitually practised to be voluntarily counteracted. Nor shall we see reason to think upon severe reflection that this state is so distant as we might at first be inclined to imagine. Error is principally indebted for its permanence to social institution. Did we leave individuals to the progress of their own minds, without endeavouring to regulate them by any species of public foundation, mankind would in no very long period convert to the obedience of truth. The contest between truth and falsehood is of itself too unequal for the former to stand in need of support from any political ally. The more it be discovered, especially that part of it which relates to man in society, the more simple and self-evident will it appear; and it will be found impossible any otherwise to account for its having been so long concealed than from the pernicious influence of positive institution.

BURKE'S THEORY OF THE STATE

84: EDMUND BURKE. *Reflections on the Revolution in France*

1790

(*Works*, II, pp. 357–9.)

THE vanity, restlessness, petulance, and spirit of intrigue, of several petty cabals, who attempt to hide their total want of consequence in bustle and noise, and puffing, and mutual quotation of each other, makes you imagine that our contemptuous neglect of their abilities is a mark of general acquiescence in their opinions. No such thing, I assure you. Because half a dozen grasshoppers under a fern make the field ring with their importunate chink, whilst thousands of great cattle, reposed beneath the shadow of the British oak, chew the cud and are silent, pray do not imagine that those who make the noise are the only inhabitants of the field; that, of course, they are many in number; or that, after all, they are other than the little, shrivelled, meagre, hopping, though loud and troublesome, insects of the hour.

I almost venture to affirm, that not one in a hundred amongst us participates in the "triumph" of the Revolution Society. If the king and queen of France, and their children, were to fall into our hands by the chance of war, in the most acrimonious of all hostilities, (I deprecate such an event, I deprecate such hostility,) they would be treated with another sort of triumphal entry into London. We formerly have had a king of France in that situation; you have read how he was treated by the victor in the field; and in what manner he was afterwards received in England. Four hundred years have gone over us; but I believe we are not materially changed since that period. Thanks to our sullen resistance to innovation, thanks to the cold sluggishness of our national character, we still bear the stamp of our forefathers. We have not (as I conceive) lost the generosity and dignity of thinking of the fourteenth century; nor as yet have we subtilized ourselves into savages. We are not the converts of Rousseau; we are not the disciples of Voltaire; Helvetius has made no progress amongst us. Atheists are not our preachers; madmen are not our lawgivers. We know that *we* have made no discoveries, and we think that no discoveries are to be made, in morality; nor many in the great principles of government, nor in the ideas of liberty, which were understood long before we were born, altogether as well as they will be after the grave has heaped its mould upon our presumption, and the silent tomb shall have imposed its law on our pert loquacity. In England we have not yet been completely embowelled of our natural entrails; we still feel within us, and we cherish and cultivate, those inbred sentiments which are the faithful guardians, the active monitors of our duty, the true supporters of all liberal and manly morals. We have not been drawn and trussed, in order that we may be filled, like stuffed birds in a museum, with chaff and rags and paltry blurred shreds of paper about the rights of man. We preserve the whole of our feelings still native and entire, unsophisticated by pedantry and infidelity. We have real hearts of flesh and blood beating in our bosoms. We fear God; we look up with awe to kings; with affection to parliaments; with duty to magistrates; with reverence to priests; and with respect to nobility.[1] Why? Because when such ideas are brought before our minds, it is *natural* to be so affected; because all other feelings are false and spurious, and tend to corrupt our minds, to vitiate our primary morals, to render us unfit for rational liberty; and by teaching us a servile, licentious, and abandoned insolence, to be our low sport for a few holidays, to make us perfectly fit for, and justly deserving of, slavery, through the whole course of our lives.

You see, Sir, that in this enlightened age I am bold enough to confess, that we are generally men of untaught feelings; that instead of casting away all our old prejudices, we cherish them to a very considerable degree, and, to take more shame to ourselves, we cherish them because they are prejudices; and the longer they have lasted, and the more generally they have prevailed, the more we cherish them. We are afraid to put men to live and trade each on his own private stock of reason; because we suspect that this stock in each man is small, and that the individuals would do better to avail themselves of the general bank and capital of nations and of ages. Many of our men of speculation, instead of exploding general prejudices, employ their sagacity to discover the latent wisdom which prevails in them. If they find what they seek,

[1] The English are, I conceive, misrepresented in a letter published in one of the papers, by a gentleman thought to be a dissenting minister. When writing to Dr. Price of the spirit which prevails at Paris, he says, "The spirit of the people in this place has abolished all the proud *distinctions* which the *king* and *nobles* had usurped in their minds; whether they talk of *the king, the noble, or the priest*, their whole language is that of the most *enlightened and liberal amongst the English*." If this gentleman means to confine the terms *enlightened and liberal* to one set of men in England, it may be true. It is not generally so.

and they seldom fail, they think it more wise to continue the prejudice, with the reason involved, than to cast away the coat of prejudice, and to leave nothing but the naked reason; because prejudice, with its reason, has a motive to give action to that reason, and an affection which will give it permanence. Prejudice is of ready application in the emergency; it previously engages the mind in a steady course of wisdom and virtue, and does not leave the man hesitating in the moment of decision, sceptical, puzzled, and unresolved. Prejudice renders a man's virtue his habit; and not a series of unconnected acts. Through just prejudice, his duty becomes a part of his nature.

85: EDMUND BURKE. *Reflections on the Revolution in France*

1790

(*Works*, II, pp. 306–9.)

YOU will observe, that from Magna Charta to the Declaration of Right, it has been the uniform policy of our constitution to claim and assert our liberties, as an *entailed inheritance* derived to us from our forefathers, and to be transmitted to our posterity; as an estate specially belonging to the people of this kingdom, without any reference whatever to any other more general or prior right. By this means our constitution preserves a unity in so great a diversity of its parts. We have an inheritable crown; an inheritable peerage; and a House of Commons and a people inheriting privileges, franchises, and liberties, from a long line of ancestors.

This policy appears to me to be the result of profound reflection; of rather the happy effect of following nature, which is wisdom without reflection, and above it. A spirit of innovation is generally the result of a selfish temper, and confined views. People will not look forward to posterity, who never look backward to their ancestors. Besides, the people of England well know, that the idea of inheritance furnishes a sure principle of conservation, and a sure principle of transmission; without at all excluding a principle of improvement. It leaves acquisition free; but it secures what it acquires. Whatever advantages are obtained by a state proceeding on these maxims, are locked fast as in a sort of family settlement; grasped as in a kind of mortmain for ever. By a constitutional policy, working after the pattern of nature, we receive, we hold, we transmit our government and our privileges, in the same manner in which we enjoy and transmit our property and our lives. The institutions of policy, the goods of fortune, the gifts of providence, are handed down to us, and from us, in the same course and order. Our political system is placed in a just correspondence and symmetry with the order of the world, and with the mode of existence decreed to a permanent body composed of transitory parts; wherein, by the disposition of a stupendous wisdom, moulding together the great mysterious incorporation of the human race, the whole, at one time, is never old, or middle-aged, or young, but, in a condition of unchangeable constancy, moves on through the varied tenor of perpetual decay, fall, renovation, and progression. Thus, by preserving the method of nature in the conduct of the state, in what we improve, we are never wholly new; in what we retain, we are never wholly obsolete. By adhering in this manner and on those principles to our forefathers, we are guided not by the superstition of antiquarians, but by the spirit of philosophic analogy. In this choice of inheritance we have given to our frame of polity the image of a relation in blood; binding up the constitution of our country with our dearest domestic ties; adopting our fundamental laws into the bosom of our family affections; keeping inseparable, and cherishing with the warmth of all their combined and mutually reflected charities, our state, our hearths, our sepulchres, and our altars.

Through the same plan of a conformity to nature in our artificial institutions, and by calling in the aid of her unerring and powerful instincts, to fortify the fallible and feeble contrivances of our reason, we have derived several other, and those no small benefits, from considering our liberties in the light of an inheritance. Always acting as if in the presence of canonized forefathers, the spirit of freedom, leading in itself to misrule and excess, is tempered with an awful gravity. This idea of a liberal descent inspires us with a sense of habitual native dignity, which prevents that upstart insolence almost inevitably adhering to and disgracing those who are the first acquirers of any distinction. By this means our liberty becomes a noble freedom. It carries an imposing and majestic aspect. It has a pedigree and illustrating ancestors. It has its bearings and its ensigns armorial. It has its gallery of portraits; its monumental inscriptions; its records, evidences, and titles. We procure reverence to our civil institutions on the principle upon which nature teaches us to revere individual men; on account of their age, and on account of those from whom they are descended. All your sophisters cannot produce anything better adapted to preserve a rational and manly freedom than the course that we have pursued, who have chosen our nature rather than our speculations, our breasts rather than our inventions, for the great conservatories and magazines of our rights and privileges.

You might, if you pleased, have profited of our example, and have given to your recovered freedom a correspondent dignity. Your privileges, though discontinued, were not lost to memory. Your constitution, it is true, whilst you were out of possession, suffered waste and dilapidation; but you possessed in some parts the walls, and, in all, the foundations, of a noble and venerable castle. You might have repaired those walls; you might have built on those old foundations. Your constitution was suspended before it was perfected; but you had the elements of a constitution very nearly as good as could be wished. In your old states you possessed that variety of parts corresponding with the various descriptions of which your community was happily composed; you had all that combination, and all that opposition of interests, you had that action and counteraction, which, in the natural and in the political world, from the reciprocal struggle of discordant powers, draws out the harmony of the universe. These opposed and conflicting interests, which you considered as so great a blemish in your old and in our present constitution, interpose a salutary check to all precipitate resolutions. They render deliberation a matter not of choice, but of necessity; they make all change a subject of *compromise*, which naturally begets moderation; they produce *temperaments* preventing the sore evil of harsh, crude, unqualified reformations, and rendering all the headlong exertions of arbitrary power, in the few or in the many, for ever impracticable. Through that diversity of members and interests, general liberty had as many securities as there were separate views in the several orders; whilst by pressing down the whole by the weight of a real monarchy, the separate parts would have been prevented from warping, and starting from their allotted places.

86: EDMUND BURKE. *An Appeal from the New to the Old Whigs*

1791

(*Works*, III, pp. 79–80.)

TAKING it for granted that I do not write to the disciples of the Parisian philosophy, I may assume, that the awful Author of our being is the Author of our place in the order of existence; and that having disposed and marshalled us by a divine tactic, not according to our will, but according to his, he has, in and by that disposition, virtually subjected us to act the part which belongs to the place assigned us. We have obligations to mankind at large, which are not in consequence of any special voluntary pact. They arise from the relation of man to man, and the relation of man to God, which relations are not matters of choice. On the contrary, the force of all the pacts which we enter into with any particular person, or number of persons amongst mankind, depends upon those prior obligations. In some cases the subordinate relations are voluntary, in others they are necessary—but the duties are all compulsive. When we marry, the choice is voluntary, but the duties are not matter of choice. They are dictated by the nature of the situation. Dark and inscrutable are the ways by which we come into the world. The instincts which give rise to this mysterious process of nature are not of our making. But out of physical causes, unknown to us, perhaps unknowable, arise moral duties, which, as we are able perfectly to comprehend, we are bound indispensably to perform. Parents may not be consenting to their moral relation; but consenting or not, they are bound to a long train of burthensome duties towards those with whom they have never made a convention of any sort. Children are not consenting to their relation, but their relation, without their actual consent, binds them to its duties; or rather it implies their consent, because the presumed consent of every rational creature is in unison with the predisposed order of things. Men come in that manner into a community with the social state of their parents, endowed with all the benefits, loaded with all the duties, of their situation. If the social ties and ligaments, spun out of those physical relations which are the elements of the commonwealth, in most cases begin, and alway continue, independently of our will; so, without any stipulation on our own part, are we bound by that relation called our country, which comprehends (as it has been well said) "all the charities of all." Nor are we left without powerful instincts to make this duty as dear and grateful to us, as it is awful and coercive. Our country is not a thing of mere physical locality. It consists, in a great measure, in the ancient order into which we are born. We may have the same geographical situation, but another country; as we may have the same country in another soil. The place that determines our duty to our country is a social, civil relation.

87: EDMUND BURKE. *An Appeal from the New to the Old Whigs*

1791

(*Works*, III, pp. 85–7.)

TO enable men to act with the weight and character of a people, and to answer the ends for which they are incorporated into that capacity, we must suppose them (by means immediate or consequential) to be in that state of habitual social discipline, in which the wiser, the more expert, and the more opulent conduct, and by conducting enlighten and protect, the weaker, the less knowing, and the less provided with the goods of fortune. When the multitude are not under this discipline, they can scarcely be said to be in civil society. Give once a certain constitution of things, which produces a variety of conditions and circumstances in a state, and there is in nature and reason a principle which, for their own benefit, postpones, not the interest, but the judgment, of those who are *numero plures*, to those who are *virtute et honore majores*. Numbers in a state (supposing, which is not the case in France, that a state does exist) are always of consideration—but they are not the whole consideration. It is in things more serious than a play, that it may be truly said, *satis est equitem mihi plaudere*.

A true natural aristocracy is not a separate interest in the state, or separable from it. It is an essential integrant part of any large body rightly constituted. It is formed out of a class of legitimate presumptions, which, taken as generalities, must be admitted for actual truths. To be bred in a place of estimation; to see nothing low and sordid from one's infancy; to be taught to respect one's self; to be habituated to the censorial inspection of the public eye; to look early to public opinion; to stand upon such elevated ground as to be enabled to take a large view of the wide-spread and infinitely diversified combinations of men and affairs in a large society; to have leisure to read, to reflect, to converse; to be enabled to draw the court and attention of the wise and learned wherever they are to be found;—to be habituated in armies to command and to obey; to be taught to despise danger in the pursuit of honour and duty; to be formed to the greatest degree of vigilance, foresight, and circumspection, in a state of things in which no fault is committed with impunity, and the slightest mistakes draw on the most ruinous consequences—to be led to a guarded and regulated conduct, from a sense that you are considered as an instructor of your fellow-citizens in their highest concerns, and that you act as a reconciler between God and man—to be employed as an administrator of law and justice, and to be thereby amongst the first benefactors to mankind—to be a professor of high science, or of liberal and ingenuous art—to be amongst rich traders, who from their success are presumed to have sharp and vigorous understandings, and to possess the virtues of diligence, order, constancy, and regularity, and to have cultivated an habitual regard to commutative justice—these are the circumstances of men, that form what I should call a *natural* aristocracy, without which there is no nation.

The state of civil society, which necessarily generates this aristocracy, is a state of nature; and much more truly so than a savage and incoherent mode of life. For man is by nature reasonable; and he is never perfectly in his natural state, but when he is placed where reason may be best cultivated, and most predominates. Art is man's nature. We are as much, at least, in a state of nature in formed manhood, as in immature and helpless infancy. Men, qualified in the manner I have just described, form in nature, as she operates in the common modification of society, the leading, guiding, and governing part. It is the soul to the body, without which the man does not exist. To give therefore no more importance, in the social order, to such descriptions of men, than that of so many units, is a horrible usurpation.

When great multitudes act together, under that discipline of nature, I recognise the PEOPLE. I acknowledge something that perhaps equals, and ought always to guide, the sovereignty of convention. In all things the voice of this grand chorus of national harmony ought to have a mighty and decisive influence. But when you disturb this harmony; when you break up this beautiful order, this array of truth and nature, as well as of habit and prejudice; when you separate the common sort of men from their proper chieftains, so as to form them into an adverse army, I no longer know that venerable object called the People in such a disbanded race of deserters and vagabonds. For a while they may be terrible indeed; but in such a manner as wild beasts are terrible. The mind owes to them no sort of submission. They are, as they have always been reputed, rebels. They may lawfully be fought with, and brought under, whenever an advantage offers. Those who attempt by outrage and violence to deprive men of any advantage which they hold under the laws, and to destroy the natural order of life, proclaim war against them.

88: EDMUND BURKE. *Reflections on the Revolution in France*

1790

(*Works*, II, pp. 368–9.)

SOCIETY is indeed a contract. Subordinate contracts for objects of mere occasional interest may be dissolved at pleasure—but the state ought not to be considered as nothing better than a partnership agreement in a trade of pepper and coffee, calico or tobacco, or some other such low concern, to be taken up for a little temporary interest, and to be dissolved by the fancy of the parties. It is to be looked on with other reverence; because it is not a partnership in things subservient only to the gross animal existence of a temporary and perishable nature. It is a partnership in all science; a partnership in all art; a partnership in every virtue, and in all perfection. As the ends of such a partnership cannot be obtained in many generations, it becomes a partnership not only between those who are living, but between those who are living, those who are dead, and those who are to be born. Each contract of each particular state is but a clause in the great primæval contract of eternal society, linking the lower with the higher natures, connecting the visible and invisible world, according to a fixed compact sanctioned by the inviolable oath which holds all physical and all moral natures, each in their appointed place.

This law is not subject to the will of those, who by an obligation above them, and infinitely superior, are bound to submit their will to that law. The municipal corporations of that universal kingdom are not morally at liberty at their pleasure, and on their speculations of a contingent improvement, wholly to separate and tear asunder the bands of their subordinate community, and to dissolve it into an unsocial, uncivil, unconnected chaos of elementary principles. It is the first and supreme necessity only, a necessity that is not chosen, but chooses, a necessity paramount to deliberation, that admits no discussion, and demands no evidence, which alone can justify a resort to anarchy. This necessity is no exception to the rule; because this necessity itself is a part too of that moral and physical disposition of things, to which man must be obedient by consent or force: but if that which is only submission to necessity should be made the object of choice, the law is broken, nature is disobeyed, and the rebellious are outlawed, cast forth, and exiled, from this world of reason, and order, and peace, and virtue, and fruitful penitence, into the antagonist world of madness, discord, vice, confusion, and unavailing sorrow.

PART IV

FREEDOM OF OPINION

Fox's Libel Act

89: AN ACT TO REMOVE DOUBTS RESPECTING THE FUNCTIONS OF JURIES IN CASES OF LIBEL

1792

(*Statutes at Large*, 32 Geo. III, cap. 60.)

WHEREAS Doubts have arisen whether on the trial of an Indictment or Information for the making or publishing any Libel, . . . it be competent to the Jury impannelled to try the same to give their Verdict upon the whole Matter in Issue: Be it therefore declared and enacted, . . .

That, on every such Trial, the Jury sworn to try the Issue may give a General Verdict of Guilty or Not Guilty upon the whole matter put in Issue upon such Indictment or Information; and shall not be required or directed by the Court or Judge before whom such Indictment or Information shall be tried, to find the Defendant or Defendants Guilty, merely on the Proof of the Publication by such Defendant or Defendants of the Paper charged to be a Libel, and of the Sense ascribed to the same in such Indictment or Information.

90: EARL OF ABINGDON. Speech on Mr. Fox's Libel Bill, House of Lords

11 May 1792

Willoughby Bertie (1740–99), fourth Earl of Abingdon, was a supporter of Wilkes and an opponent of the North Ministry. An advocate of peace with America and the conciliation of Ireland, he supported the French Revolution and opposed the war with France. His views, however, appear to have been rather erratic. Horace Walpole described him as " a singular young man . . . extremely underbred but warmly honest." He was noted for his skill in playing the flute. (*Parliamentary History*, XXIX, p. 1371.)

NOT to mention the libellous pamphlets that have of late been published, who is it that can see the libellous prints that are daily exhibited in every print-shop of this city, and not shudder at the atrocity of their authors ? Instead, therefore, of giving a check to the law concerning libels, as it now stood, its observance should be more rigidly enforced: and in doing this, he had no apprehensions for the loss of English liberty; for his maxim was, that in the English constitution there was liberty enough; and that, Cromwell like, he that seeks for more, means to have less. Let him, therefore, in the fashionable cant of the times, leave with the right reverend bench of bishops, that little canticle of the once thought wise man Soloman, who said, " remove not the ancient land-marks which thy fathers have set," and with the rest of your lordships, as the bar to this madness of innovation that is now let loose upon us, that noble exclamation of our ancestors, "Nolumus leges Angliæ mutari!"

91: LORD CAMDEN. Speech on Mr. Fox's Libel Bill, House of Lords

8 June 1792

Charles Pratt, Earl of Camden (1714–94), was a briefless barrister when he made his reputation in a trial of 1752, in which he successfully asserted the competence of the jury to determine the entire question in cases of seditious libel. He gave the famous decision on general warrants in 1763, and became Lord Chancellor in the Chatham Administration of 1766. His last speeches were in defence of the principle he had asserted at the outset of his career, and his authority did much to carry Fox's Libel Act in 1792. (*Parliamentary History*, XXIX, pp. 729–32.)

WITH regard to those papers, called seditious libels, there had been a variety of opinions, and his lordship said, that as a matter of delicacy, he should not then enter into those opinions: but, he conceived, that the principal cause of complaint respecting libels, had been owing to the directions of some judges: who had told juries, if they found the publication and innuendos, they must find the defendant guilty. Some judges had told the jury " you have nothing to try but the publication and innuendos." But his lordship conceived that the right of juries to decide the whole matter in cases of libels, was, by the present law, clear and unequivocal; and he pledged himself to the House to prove that if the twelve judges, nay, if twenty-four judges, declared on any given case, put to them on this subject, that juries had not a right to decide upon the criminality, upon the law and upon any fact stated in the record, they were wrong; they acted against the statutes; they acted against the known and positive law of the land.

Some would say, that the question was, what was, and what was not a seditious libel? Who were capable of judging of the seditious tendency? The jury ought to be, and the jury were by the law of England; but although he had no doubts on this point, others had, and therefore it was necessary to remove those doubts. He would not venture to say what had generally been the direction of judges, but he knew what it ought to be. Some judges had summed up, and given direction to the juries in this manner; "Gentlemen, if the publication is proved to your satisfaction, and the innuendoes apply to the subject as they profess to do, that is, if the words have the meaning ascribed to them in the indictment or information, then you must find the defendant guilty." "What! the jury might answer, are we to find the defendant guilty, even although we are of opinion no tumult could be occasioned by the publication, or that none was intended by it?" To which the judge might reply, "Yes, you are." This he did not hesitate to say, was a wrong direction, and a verdict so obtained, was not the verdict of a jury.

All the difference on this subject between the judges and the jury, had arisen in cases of public and seditious libels. In matters of private libel, the good sense and honest meaning of both commonly met, and were agreed. It was only in cases of seditious libels, that there had arisen any difficulty or ground of contention. He had long endeavoured to define what a seditious libel was, but had not been able to find any definition, which either met the approbation of his own mind, or could be deemed satisfactory to others. Some would have every censure on the measures of government considered as a libel. If this was the case, every channel of public information would be converted into a mere vehicle of panegyric. The voice of truth would cease to be heard amidst the notes of adulation. Others again, would have only groundless calumnies on government regarded as libels. But who were then to decide? to whom was it left to pronounce, whether what was called calumny, was well or ill-founded? It was of consequence that this power should be placed in hands where it was neither liable to abuse, nor open to corruption. By being placed in the hands of juries, it afforded the most probable means of safety, and became the best instrument of justice.—" My lords," said he, " give to the jury or to the judge the right of trial of the subjects of this country; you must give it to one of them, and I think you can have no difficulty which to prefer: place the press under the power of the jury, where it ought to be."

92: DEBATE IN THE HOUSE OF LORDS ON MR. FOX'S LIBEL BILL

1 June 1792

(*Parliamentary History*, XXIX, pp. 1,536–7.)

THE *Lord Chancellor*[1] then wished to know whether the learned lord would consent to a clause being inserted in the bill to do justice between the public and defendants prosecuted for libels. This clause was to grant a new trial, if the court should be dissatisfied with a verdict given for the defendant.

Earl *Camden* said, What! after a verdict of acquittal?

The *Lord Chancellor*. Yes.

Earl *Camden*. No, I thank you.

[1] Lord Thurlow.

The Fear of Sedition

93: ROYAL PROCLAMATION AGAINST SEDITIOUS WRITINGS

21 May 1792

(*Parliamentary History*, XXIX, pp. 1,476–7.)

George *R*.

WHEREAS divers wicked and seditious writings have been printed, published, and industriously dispersed, tending to excite tumult and disorder, by endeavouring to raise groundless jealousies and discontents in the minds of our faithful and loving subjects, respecting the laws and happy constitution of government, civil and religious, established in this kingdom; and endeavouring to vilify and bring into contempt the wise and wholesome provisions made at the time of the glorious revolution, and since strengthened and confirmed by subsequent laws for the preservation and security of the rights and liberties of our faithful and loving subjects. And whereas divers writings have also been printed, published, and industriously dispersed, recommending the said wicked and seditious publications to the attention of all our faithful and loving subjects. And whereas we have also reason to believe that correspondences have been entered into with sundry persons in foreign parts, with a view to forward the criminal and wicked purposes above mentioned. . . .

We, therefore, being resolved, as far as in us lies, to repress the wicked and seditious practices aforesaid, and to deter all persons from following so pernicious an example, have thought fit, by the advice of our privy council, to issue this our royal proclamation, solemnly warning all our loving subjects, as they tender their own happiness, and that of their posterity to guard against all such attempts which aim at the subversion of all regular government within this kingdom, and which are inconsistent with the peace and order of society; and earnestly exhorting them at all times, and to the utmost of their power, to avoid and discourage all proceedings, tending to produce riots and tumults; and we do strictly charge and command all our magistrates in and throughout our kingdom of Great Britain, that they do make diligent inquiry in order to discover the authors and printers of such wicked and seditious writings as aforesaid, and all others who shall disperse the same.

It being our determination, for the preservation of the peace and happiness of our faithful and loving subjects, to carry the laws vigorously into execution against such offenders as aforesaid.

Given at our court at the Queen's House, the 21st day of May, 1792 in the 32nd year of our reign.

94: *THE TIMES*

5 December 1792

LET seditious Men look to their conduct! The strong arm of CONSTITUTIONAL JUSTICE is now uplifted, and those who offend against the Law, may now expect its utmost rigour.

But it is not the united force of the Civil and Military, that the disturbers of public peace have now only to dread; another power has manifested its determined resolution to defend our glorious national fabrick, as it now stands—and that power is called the LOYAL ASSOCIATING VOICE OF THE PEOPLE. . . .

One of the great leading features of these associated bodies will be, instantly to deliver over to the law every person that is heard to utter disaffection; or to propagate by writing, printing, or publishing any words or arguments which have the smallest tendency to disturb the public peace, or alienate the affections of the people from their loyalty to their Sovereign, and their veneration for the Constitution of their Country. . . .

All those who pervert the Legal Freedom of the Press into licentious abuse of the Constitution, should be immediately apprehended, brought to instant trial, and in case of being found guilty by their country, directly punished.

95: THE ASSOCIATION FOR PRESERVING LIBERTY AND PROPERTY AGAINST REPUBLICANS AND LEVELLERS. Resolutions of 20 November 1792

This Association was founded by John Reeves (1752 ?–1829), a lawyer and the author of a History of English Law, and Charles Philip Yorke (1764–1834), Member of Parliament for Cambridgeshire. Reeves held various minor official positions and received favours from Pitt. The Association met with great success and rapidly linked up with similar societies throughout the country.

The Association's papers were published in two parts: Part I. *Liberty and Property preserved against Republicans and Levellers, a collection of tracts.*

Part II. *Publications of the Society for preserving Liberty and Property.* At the Crown and Anchor in the Strand, 1793.

(See also Nos. 158, 160, 161.)

At a MEETING OF GENTLEMEN *at the* CROWN AND ANCHOR TAVERN, *in the Strand, November* 20, 1792,
JOHN REEVES, ESQ. *in the Chair.*

The following CONSIDERATIONS *and* RESOLUTIONS *were entered into and agreed upon:*

Considering the danger to which the Publick Peace and Order are exposed by the circulating of mischievous Opinions, founded upon plausible but false reasoning; and that this circulation is principally carried on by the industry of Clubs and Societies of various denominations in many parts of the kingdom:

It appears to us, that it is now become the duty of

all Persons, who wish well to their Native Country, to endeavour, in their several neighbourhoods, to prevent the sad effects of such mischievous industry; and that it would greatly tend to promote these good endeavours, if Societies were formed in different parts of the Kingdom, whose object should be to support the Laws, to suppress seditious Publications, and to defend our Persons and Property against the innovations and depredations that seem to be threatened by those who maintain the mischievous opinions before alluded to.

It appears to us, the tendency of these Opinions is, that we are voluntarily to surrender every thing we now possess; our Religion and our Laws; our civil Government and Civil Society; and that we are to trust to the formation of something New, upon the principles of Equality, and under the auspices of speculative men, who have conceived ideas of perfection that never yet were known in the world.

We do, as private men, unconnected with any Party, . . . think it expedient and necessary to form ourselves into an ASSOCIATION . . . and we do hereby resolve, and declare as follows:

FIRST—That the persons present at this Meeting do become a Society for discouraging and suppressing Seditious Publications, tending to disturb the Peace of this Kingdom, and for supporting a due execution of the Laws made for the protection of persons and property.

96: WILLIAM WINDHAM. Speech in the Debate on the Address of Thanks, House of Commons

13 December 1792

(*Parliamentary History*, XXX, pp. 38–9.)

THE art with which these sentiments were introduced among the lower classes of society was consummate; they pretended that they taught nothing but philosophical truths; but instead of arguing philosophically in their books they made round assertions, and they acted wisely for their purpose by so doing; for the persons to whom they addressed themselves, were incapable of pursuing a subject logically from premises to a conclusion, nor would this mode of reasoning suit their cause. Not even these assertions were made, until they had prepared the mind to receive them; they gained the affections first by flattering the passions, and then they proceeded to instruct, as they termed it. Whether the law, even in the freest country in the world, ought to permit every man to preach what doctrines he thought fit, and gain over as many proselytes as he could, was a question that had often been suggested, and which he should determine in the negative; for these truths as they were termed, would dwindle into nothing, if the sentiment built upon them could be seen, and the consequences of them anticipated; but these poor peasants had not the power of deducing consequences, and therefore they listened to assertion.—Nor could he see the harm there was of preventing all endeavours to explain to a poor illiterate fellow, whose extent of powers was but barely adequate to the task of procuring food for his own subsistence, points which had divided the opinions of the ablest writers. He saw no great loss to society from putting an end to public house political clubs, and alehouse debates on politics; in short, he saw no reason why they should not be altogether suppressed.

97: ARTHUR YOUNG. *The Example of France a Warning to Britain*

1793

(P. 139.)

BUT neither a militia, association, nor any other measure to be devised would yield security were the licentiousness (not the liberty) of the press to be permitted to so shameful and destructive a length, as we have of late years experienced in England. It will probably be found after this period that no constitution, whether good or bad, can possibly exist against a licentious press. The old government of France was ruined unquestionably by inattention to this engine: the new tyranny established there is well aware of that momentous truth, and hath accordingly converted it, like the lanthorn into an engine of government. Where the licentiousness of the press is in any degree allowed, the general instruction of the lower classes must become the seed of revolt, and it is for this reason that the friends of reform, and zealous admirers of French equality, are strenuous for sunday and charity schools.

98: HANNAH MORE: *Modern Politicians: a word to the working classes of Great Britain, by Will Chip, a Country Carpenter*

1797?

JACK. What paper have you got there? What dost look so glum for?

TOM (looking on the paper). Cause enough. Why, the news here tells me that I am very unhappy, and very miserable, which I never should have known hadn't I the luck to light on this paper.

JACK. . . . . What is the matter?

TOM. Matter? Why, I want liberty . . . I want a *general* reform.

JACK. I'll tell you a story. When our Squire married his lady, who is out of the way fine and likes to do every thing like the French, she begged him to pull down the old house, and build it up in her frippery way. "What!" says the Squire, "shall I pull down this fine old house, which has stood firm these many years,—this house in which my fathers have lived comfortable for ages past,—this house too, which has weathered many a stormy war, and only underwent a little needful repair in the Revolution that took place years ago,—this house too, which all my neighbours take pattern by, shall I pull it all down, because may be, there's a bad passage here, and a dark closet there, and an awkward room or two in it? Our forefathers took time for what they did. They understood foundation-work; none of your lath-and-plaster buildings, which are up in a day and down in a night, for me!" My lady mumpt and grumbled, but the old house was let stand, and a glorious one it is; though there may be a little fault or two in it, and though a few decays want stopping; so now and then they mend a little thing, and they'll go on mending, I dare say, as they have leisure, to the end of the chapter, if they are but let alone. But no pull-me-down works. What is it you are crying out for, Tom?

TOM. Why for a perfect government.

JACK. You might as well cry for the moon. There's nothing perfect in this world, take my word for it, though the Squire says we come nearer to it than any country in the world ever did.

99: ANON. *Rights of Swine, An Address to the Poor*

1794

(Trial of Thomas Hardy, 28 October–5 November 1794. *State Trials*, XXIV, pp. 745–8.)

GREAT GOD! What spectacle so affecting to a reflecting mind as Great Britain in her present state! On the one hand, we see the impudent nobles advertising their "*Grand Dinners*," in the very face of the hungry poor, whom they have ruined!! On the other hand, widows, orphans, and others are weeping, and often dying for want of bread! What can be more odious in the sight of heaven, than feast and famine in the same nation? Yet this is literally the case in this kingdom, at this moment, and not only in the nation, but in every town, in every street, yea, often under the very same roof!

Open your eyes, O ye poor of the land!—in vain are your hands and your mouths open! Do you not see how you are cajoled and degraded, by the paltry subscriptions made for you, at different times and in various parts of the nation; which serve only to make your slavery more servile, and your misery of longer duration? I revere generous subscribers and collectors, but I scorn the means! Ye poor, take a farther look into your rights, and you will see, that, upon the principles of reason and justice, every peaceable and useful person has a right, yea, a " *Divine Right* " to be satisfied with the good of the land!

Hearken! O ye poor of the land! Do you fret and whine at oppression —' yes ' — ' Then, as ye do, so did your fathers before you '— and, if you *do no more*, your children may whine after you! Awake! Arise! arm yourselves—with truth, justice and reason—lay siege to corruption; and your unity and invincibility shall teach your oppressors terrible things! Purge the Representation of your Country—claim, as your inalienable right, Universal Suffrage, and Annual Parliaments. And whenever you have the gratification to choose a representative, let him be from among the lower order of men, and he will know how to sympathize with you, and represent you in character. Then, and not till then, shall you experience universal Peace and incessant Plenty.

A FRIEND TO THE POOR.

Stockport, Jan. 5, 1794

100: A PLACARD. For the Benefit of John Bull

1794

(Trial of Thomas Hardy, 1794, *State Trials*, XXIV, pp. 681–3.)

For
The Benefit of JOHN BULL

At the
FEDERATION THEATRE, in EQUALITY SQUARE,
On Thursday, the 1st of April, 4971.
Will be performed,
A new and entertaining Farce, called
LA GUILLOTINE;
or,
GEORGE'S HEAD IN THE BASKET!
Dramatis Personæ.
Numpy the Third, by Mr. GWELP,
(Being the last time of his appearing in that character)
Prince of Leeks, by Mr. GWELP, junior.
Duke of Dice, by Mr. FREDDY,
(from Osnaburgh.)
Duke of Jordan, by Mr. WILLIAM HENRY FLOGGER (from the Creolian Theatre.)
Uncle Toby, Mr. RICHMOND.
Grand Inquisitor, Mr. PENSIONER REEVES.
Don Quixote, Knight of the Dagger,
by Mr. EDMUND CALUMNY.
And Chancellor of the Exchequer, by Mr. BILLY TAXLIGHT.
Municipal Officers, National Guards, &c.
By Citizens Xof, NADIREHS, YERG, ENIKSRE, &c.
Banditti, Assassins, Cut Throats, and Wholesale Dealers in Blood, by THE EMPRESS OF RUFFIANS, THE EMPEROR OF HARM-ANY, THING OF PRUSSIA, PRINCE OF S. CASH-HELL, &c.

Between the Acts,
A new Song, called " Twenty more, kill them! "
by BOBADIL BRUNSWICK.
Tight Rope Dancing, from the Lamp-post,
By Messrs. CANTERBURY, YORK, DURHAM, &c.
In the course of the Evening will be sung, in Full Chorus,
CA IRA.
and
BOB SHAVE GREAT GEORGE OUR——!
The whole to conclude with
A GRAND DECAPITATION
of
PLACEMEN, PENSIONERS AND GERMAN LEECHES.
Admittance, Three-pence each Person.
Vive la Liberte! Vive la Republique!

Mr. Erskine. The paper was fabricated by the spies who support the prosecution.

Mr. Attorney General. You shall not say that, till you prove it.

Mr. Erskine. I shall prove it.[1]

[1] From the report of the trial it does not seem that he did so.

101: THOMAS HOLCROFT: *A Letter to the Right Honourable William Windham, on the Intemperance and Dangerous Tendency of his Public Conduct*

1795

Thomas Holcroft (1745–1809), after early poverty, became a successful dramatist, and author of *The Road to Ruin*, which ran through nine editions in 1792. He was a member of the Society for Constitutional Information. His trial for high treason in 1794 was abandoned by the government, to his disappointment and indignation. He wrote a large number of plays, comic operas, novels, and translated both the *Marriage of Figaro* and Goethe's *Hermann and Dorothea*. He was a friend of William Godwin and of Lamb. His *Memoirs*, published in 1816, were largely compiled by Hazlitt. (pp. 42–3.)

ELECTIONEERING arts, at best, too fatally demonstrate the corruptions of our present system: but even these are odious in degree; and some infinitely more so than others. A loom in mourning was carried in procession, by the friends of your opponent; and the effect it produced, on the distressed manufacturers, was such as might well be expected, but such as you could not endure. You immediately ordered one of the most disgusting spectacles that the human imagination could frame: though I grant that the same detestable artifice had been employed, in every variety, to enflame the populace of London. You went to a carpenter, in person, and directed him to make a guillotine; and to place a female figure, on the platform of the horrid instrument, with its head in the act of being struck off, and bleeding: over which was an inscription, in large letters, THIS IS FRENCH LIBERTY! An artifice, Sir, so full of passion, and of so disgusting and enflaming a nature, was, I believe, never employed before, on such an occasion. Charles Fox, holding the gore dripping head of the late King of France by the hair; Mr. Sheridan feasting with him, at a banquet of decapitated kings; monstrous figures of pretended Frenchmen, devouring the bodies of their murdered fellow citizens; and other infernal devices, had insulted the feelings of the citizens of London, in every print-shop: but no man, perhaps, except yourself, would at a popular election, when party heats and feuds are so violent and so dangerous, thus have been blind to and regardless of their dreadful consequences.

102: WILLIAM WILBERFORCE: Speech in the Debate on the Seditious Meetings Bill, House of Commons

10 November 1795

William Wilberforce (1759–1833), the friend and supporter of Pitt, was converted to religion in the course of a tour in France and Switzerland in 1784. Three years later he founded a society for the suppression of vice, and became the parliamentary leader of the struggle for the abolition of the slave trade. In 1794–95 he temporarily opposed Pitt's policy and advocated peace with France. He was throughout, however, strongly anti-Jacobin in his views. (*Parliamentary History*, XXXII, pp. 292–3.)

HE begged the House to take a considerate review of all that had passed relative to the subject before them for the last three years; so long it was since attempts had been making, by every species of art and industry, to poison the minds of the people of this country, to instil into them jealousies and suspicions, and to excite a contempt for the British constitution and an attachment to those false principles of liberty, which had produced such extensive mischiefs in a neighbouring country; nor was it only French politics which they were importing into this country, but French philosophy also: in the numerous publications by which their opinions were disseminated, there was a marked contempt for every thing sacred, an avowed opposition to the religion, as well as to the constitution of Great Britain. Various means had been taken to put a stop to these proceedings, but in vain; these bad men seemed to redouble their efforts, and to press forward with increased audaciousness. Lectures were given, and harangues delivered, of the most inflammatory nature; hand bills and prints of the most atrocious description were circulated. That all this had not been without effect, was but too manifest from those daring insults on the person of his majesty. What, then, was to be done. Were these men to be suffered to go on without disturbance? It was a question which deserved the rather to be asked, because there were manifestly a systematic principle, a consistency and uniformity in their measures, which plainly evinced a deliberate plan of conduct. Were they to be permitted to pursue in all our great manufacturing towns, what they had begun in more than one of them—that same system of popular assemblies, and debating clubs, and seditious harangues which they had introduced into the capital. Surely it was high time for parliament to stop the progress of this growing mischief: and he thought administration deserved the thanks of the country for making the attempt in spite of all the clamour they must expect to raise amongst those who harboured these bad designs, and amongst others in that House, whom he had observed with sorrow to be but too ready to lend their countenance to them.

103: DEBATE IN THE LORDS ON THE TREASONABLE PRACTICES BILL

13 November 1795

Dr. Samuel Horsley, Bishop of Rochester (1733–1806), early won distinction for his work in astronomy and geometry, and became Secretary of the Royal Society in 1773. He engaged in a long theological controversy with Priestley, and edited the works of Isaac Newton. His sermon of 30 January 1793, before the House of Lords at Westminster Abbey, on the dangers of the spirit of the revolution, brought the congregation to their feet in enthusiasm. He ended his life as Bishop of St. Asaph. (*Parliamentary History*, XXXII, pp. 268–70.)

Bishop of Rochester (Dr. Horsley)

My lords, it is with astonishment I have heard it said, that the various seditious and blasphemous publications of the present day are not likely to produce mischief. What are the springs of human actions? Have the opinions of men no influence upon their actions?—Not their speculative opinions upon mere abstract subjects, but their opinions in morals, religion, and politics,—have these no influence on their actions? Have these publications no tendency to spread opinions? Are they not circulated for that purpose, with great industry, and with too sensible an effect? Have not the minds of the common people been turned by such publications to subjects to which it had been better if their minds never had been turned? Have they not been poisoned with false and pernicious notions? And has not a great change in the demeanour of the lower orders actually been produced?

EARL OF ABINGDON

He wished to ask the reverend prelate, whether *vox populi* was not *vox Dei*? He would prove it was; and that God Almighty always inspired the people upon such occasions, and would do so still: he would prove this by authors as old as Methusalem. If the bill passed, resistance to it might be deemed rebellion, but if the compact settled by the Bill of Rights was broken, the government might happen to be in a state of rebellion against the people. His lordship added, that arguments he had heard that day, appeared to him to be calculated to enforce the exploded principle of passive obedience and non-resistance, and that all who maintained such doctrine, whether bishops or lay peers, were damned beyond all possibility of redemption, by revolutionary principles.

104: MARQUIS OF LANSDOWNE. Speech in the Debate on the Seditious Meetings Bill, House of Lords

9 December 1795

William Petty, Lord Shelburne, first Marquis of Lansdowne (1737–1805), was frequently in office between 1763 and 1783, but usually quarrelled with his colleagues. He regarded himself as a disciple of Chatham, and like him was a bad party man. He opposed the war with France and the laws against sedition, and favoured gradual parliamentary reform. An unpopular politician (" the Jesuit of Berkeley Square "), he was in advance of the time in his views, with more grasp of principles than capacity for managing men. Shelburne was a great patron of literature and the arts: amongst his friends he numbered Bentham. (*Parliamentary History*, XXXII, 534–9.)

HE was of opinion that some precaution was necessary, and these admissions, he trusted, would at least be sufficient to exempt him from the charge of Jacobinism.—But the present bills appeared to him greatly to overshoot the mark. The circumstances did not warrant such an inroad on the constitution. These meetings were of two kinds. Either they were idle in themselves, and might safely be suffered to evaporate; or they were excited by serious grievances. In the latter case, no force could subdue them, and they were to be dispelled only by an adequate redress. An able physician once remarked to him, that it was easy to dispel a local swelling; the only difficulty was to say where it would next make its appearance. No man could deny but that grievances existed, and that the principal one was in the defect of our representation. Our constitution had wonderfully maintained its ground, even after the theory on which it was founded had been given up. He had never been a party man, and therefore was to be understood in all he should say, as expressing merely the sentiments of an individual. He had two objections to party; one was, that, if he attached himself to any set of men, it would necessarily follow that at times he must submit his opinions to theirs, and this he disliked; the other was, that he thought there was a something in the idea of voting with party, naturally and necessarily corrupt. But though no friend to party, as it tended to hamper opinions, he must in justice say, that party had in a great measure supplied the defects of the theory of the constitution, and for two reigns had checked the growing power of the prerogative. A change was now arising, not owing so much to men, as to the perpetual tide in human affairs. In regarding this change, it was necessary for them to take care that one branch of the constitution did not trench on the rights of another.—When he looked at the composition of the legislative powers, he saw them divided, generally speaking, into two bodies; one constantly voting on the side of the minister, and the other as uniformly voting with the party termed the opposition. From hence resulted a false inference, that the act of the minister was the wish of the sovereign, and that he who should oppose any measure of the former was in personal opposition to the latter. But if this was an error on the side of the government, there was an error perfectly correspondent on that of the people; they not unfrequently attributed to the principles and designs of men, what, in fact, were measures attributable only to the state of affairs. In the present criterion, therefore, what was to be done? When the assertion had been made that this was no fit moment to bring forward any such question of grievance as he had described, he agreed to it; but because, by the violence of persons cherishing French principles, the security of the constitution had been menaced—in their care for a particular part, it was not the less incumbent upon their lordships to be watchful that no one branch invaded the rights and privileges of the other—and he could not but see of late many alarming strides of prerogative manifested in the measures submitted to that House. Admitting, as he did, therefore, the expediency of some measure, the query naturally presented itself, whether there might not be found one less violent than that which was now proposed? He had not heard one defender of the present act, who did not confess that it was an invasion of Magna Charta and the Bill of Rights.

What he dreaded was the general gloom which these bills would spread over the people. They would tend more than any thing to destroy that happy union of the lower with the higher classes of society and arm the different orders with animosity against each other. They would destroy that free spirit of Englishmen, which had been the real cause of the energy of our national character, and of our prosperity and wealth. Peace and reform were the only two things which could save the country. He hoped that the country would not be lulled into a false security, and suffer these bills to exist.

105: GEORGE CANNING (with Frere and Ellis). *The Anti-Jacobin*

11 December 1797

George Canning (1770–1827), was the son of a poor barrister and a beautiful girl who went on the stage after her husband's death. Educated at Eton and Christ Church, he was looked down on by the aristocratic Whigs, who might have forgiven him his birth and brilliance if, like Sheridan, he had been on their side. He was an intemperate supporter of Pitt, and one of the chief authors of the witty but cruel *Anti-Jacobin*. In the 1820's, Canning became Foreign Secretary and then Prime Minister. (*The Anti-Jacobin*, No. 5, 11 December, 1797.)

THE SOLDIER'S FRIEND

DACTYLICS

Come, little Drummer Boy, lay down your knapsack here:
I am the soldier's friend—here are some books for you;
Nice clever books by TOM PAINE, the philanthropist.

Here's half-a-crown for you—here are some handbills too—
Go to the barracks, and give all the soldiers some.
Tell them the sailors are all in a mutiny.

(*Exit Drummer Boy, with handbills and half-a-crown*).—*Manet Soldier's Friend.*

Liberty's friends thus all learn to amalgamate,
Freedom's volcanic explosion prepares itself,
Despots shall bow to the fasces of liberty.
  Reason, philosophy, " fiddledum, diddledum,"
  Peace and fraternity, higgledy, piggledy,
  Higgledy, piggledy, " fiddledum diddledum."

Et cætera, et cætera, et cætera.

The Treason Trials

106: THOMAS ERSKINE. Speech for the Defence at the Trial of Thomas Paine

18 December 1792

(*State Trials*, XXII, pp. 414–5, 434, 437.)

THE law of England then, both in its forms and substance, being the only rule by which the author or the work can be justified or condemned, and the charge upon the record being the naked charge of a libel, the cause resolves itself into a question of the deepest importance to us all, THE NATURE AND EXTENT OF THE LIBERTY OF THE ENGLISH PRESS.

The proposition which I mean to maintain as the basis of the liberty of the press, and without which it is an empty sound, is this:—that every man, not intending to mislead, but seeking to enlighten others with what his own reason and conscience, however erroneously, have dictated to him as truth, may address himself to the universal reason of a whole nation, either upon the subject of governments in general, or upon that of our own particular country:—that he may analyze the principles of its constitution,—point out its errors and defects,—examine and publish its corruptions,—warn his fellow-citizens against their ruinous consequences,—and exert his whole faculties in pointing out the most advantageous changes in establishments which he considers to be radically defective, or sliding from their object by abuse.—All this every subject of this country has a right to do, if he contemplates only what he thinks would be for its advantage, and but seeks to change the public mind by the conviction which flows from reasonings dictated by conscience.

The principle is, that every man, while he obeys the laws, is to think for himself, and to communicate what he thinks.—The very ends of society exact this licence, and the policy of the law, in its provisions for its security, has tacitly sanctioned it.—The real fact is, that writings against a free and well-proportioned government, need not be guarded against by laws.—They cannot often exist, and never with effect.—The just and lawful principles of society are rarely brought forward, but when they are insulted and denied, or abused in practice: Mr. Locke's Essay on Government we owe to Sir Robert Filmer, as we owe Mr. Paine's to Mr. Burke;—indeed, between the arguments of Filmer and Burke, I see no essential difference; since it is not worth disputing, whether a king exists by *divine* right, or by *indissoluble human* compact, if he exists whether we will or no.—If his existence be without our consent, and is to continue without benefit, it matters not, whether his title be from God or from man.

Gentlemen, I have insisted, at great length, upon

the origin of governments, and detailed the authorities which you have heard upon the subject, because I consider it to be not only an essential support, but the very foundation of the liberty of the press.—If Mr. Burke be right in HIS principles of government, I admit that the press, in my sense of its freedom, ought not to be free, *nor free in any sense at all*; and that all addresses to the people upon the subject of government,—and all speculations of amendment, of what kind or nature soever, are illegal and criminal;—since, if the people have, without possible recall, delegated all their authorities, they have no jurisdiction to act, and therefore none to think or write upon such subjects;—and it would be a libel to arraign government or any of its acts, before those that have no jurisdiction to correct them.—But on the other hand, as it is a settled rule in the law of England, that the subject may always address a competent jurisdiction; no legal argument can shake the freedom of the press in my sense of it, if I am supported in my doctrines concerning the great unalienable right of the people, to reform or to change their governments.

It is because the liberty of the press resolves itself into this great issue, that it has been, in every country, the last liberty which subjects have been able to wrest from power.—OTHER liberties are held *under* governments, but the liberty of opinion keeps GOVERNMENTS THEMSELVES in due subjection to their duties.

107: LORD JUSTICE BRAXFIELD. Address to the Jury at the Trial of Thomas Muir, Edinburgh

30–31 August, 1793

Robert Macqueen, Lord Braxfield (1722–99), was a Scottish advocate, who became in 1788 Lord Justice Clerk. He presided over the trials of Muir, Margarot and others in Edinburgh in 1793. Cockburn attributes to him the saying, " Bring me the prisoners, and I will find you the law." He is supposed to be the model for Stevenson's " Weir of Hermiston ".

Thomas Muir (1765–98) was a young Scots advocate who played a big part in organizing the Edinburgh Convention of December 1792. He was arrested in 1793 and tried by Braxfield, who sentenced him to fourteen years' transportation. He escaped from Botany Bay in 1796 and died at Chantilly after many adventures.

(*State Trials*, XXIII, p. 229.)

THE question then, gentlemen, for your consideration is simply this: On the whole of the proof led, when taken in connexion, do you think the panel guilty of sedition or not? Now in examining this question, there are two things which you should attend to, which require no proof. The first is, that the British constitution is the best in the world;—for the truth of this, gentlemen, I need only appeal to your own feelings. Is not every man secure in his life, liberty, and property? Is not happiness in the power of every man, except those perhaps, who, from disappointment in their schemes of advancement are discontented?

Does not every man enjoy unmolested the fruits of his industry? And does not every man sit safely under his own vine and his own fig-tree, and none shall make him afraid? The other circumstance, gentlemen, which you have to attend to, is the state of this country during last winter. There was a spirit of sedition and revolt going abroad which made every good subject seriously uneasy.

108: CHARLES JAMES FOX. Letter to Lord Holland

December 1793

(*Memorials and Correspondence of Charles James Fox*, edited by Lord John Russell, 1854, III, pp. 60–2.)

At home we imitate the French as well as we can, and in the trials and sentences of Muir and Palmer in particular, I do not think we fall very far short of our original, excepting inasmuch as transportation to Botany Bay is less severe (and to a gentleman that is not much) than death, I do not think any of the French *soi-disant* judicial proceedings surpass in injustice and contempt of law those in Scotland; and yet I hear from good authority what, till I heard it from authority, I resolutely disbelieved, that not only these proceedings are to be defended in Parliament, but that the sentences are to be executed, and that *sedition*, the most vague and loose in its description of all misdemeanours, is to be considered as punishable, and actually to be punished in Scotland, as a felony. It is evident that those who excute the supposed law in Scotland must *wish* it were law here too, and such are the times that what they wish they may easily obtain if they have the courage to ask it. You will easily believe I shall not acquiesce in this tyranny without an effort, but I am far from sanguine as to success. We live in times of violence and of extremes, and all those who are for creating or even for retaining checks upon power are considered as enemies to order. However, one must do one's duty, and one must endeavour to do it without passion, but everything in Europe appears to my ideas so monstrous that it is difficult to think of things calmly even alone, much more to discuss them so, when heated by dispute. Good God! that a man should be sent to Botany Bay for advising another to read Paine's book, or for reading the Irish address at a public meeting! for these are the *charges* against Muir, and the first of them is I think not satisfactorily proved.

"On tremble en comparant l'offense et le supplice."

109: LORD JUSTICE BRAXFIELD. Address to the Jury at the Trial of William Skirving, Edinburgh

6–7 January 1794

(*State Trials*, XXIII, pp. 590, 592.)

I BELIEVE every one must admit, that of all the nations under the sun, Great Britain is the happiest; and that under all the imperfections that may attend their constitution, it is the most complete system of government that ever existed upon the face of this earth,—with all its imperfections. I am sure, gentlemen, you must all be sensible that you enjoy your lives and your properties, and every thing that is dear to you in perfect security, every man is certain that he will not be deprived of any thing that belongs to him, and there is no man, let him be as great a grumbletonian as he will, if he is asked where he is hurt by the imperfections of the constitution, he cannot tell you, but on the contrary that he is living happily under it. Gentlemen, when that is the case, what construction must you put upon the proceedings of a society, who represent this country as on the very brink of destruction; I submit to you whether that is the work of the people, who have a real regard for society, and if you are of opinion that these meetings are of a seditious nature and of a seditious tendency, when the question comes home to the panel at the bar, you must find him guilty; for, gentlemen, I must observe to you, that it is a rule in law, and a rule in good sense, that if a meeting is illegal, all the members of that meeting are liable for every thing illegal that is done at that meeting, the whole meeting are understood to be guilty, art and part in the crime that is committed, and they are all and each of them amenable to the laws of their country for what they have done.

Gentlemen, they assumed that they wanted merely to obtain a reform in parliament. It is certainly a very lawful thing to apply to parliament, and God forbid it should ever be thought unconstitutional; but it was not a reform in parliament that was their object, but a reform to be brought about by force of arms of their own procuring; for they could not mean to obtain any redress from parliament, when they called themselves the British convention of the delegates of the people, associated to obtain universal suffrage and annual parliaments. It was impossible they could ever obtain from parliament universal suffrage, and for a very good reason, it is a thing that cannot exist; a nation could not subsist under such a government.

110: LORD JUSTICE BRAXFIELD. Address to the Jury at the Trial of Maurice Margarot, Edinburgh

13–14 January 1794

Maurice Margarot, by origin a Frenchman, had settled in London and became a leader of the London Corresponding Society. He was the Society's delegate, with Gerrald, to the Edinburgh Convention of 1793. Arrested and tried before Braxfield, he was sentenced to fourteen years' transportation. He was accused by his fellow victims of appropriating their common relief fund and bringing unjustified charges against them on the voyage out. Even from Botany Bay he managed to make a nuisance of himself to the authorities in London. He returned from transportation in 1812. (*State Trials*, XXIII, p. 766.)

BUT gentlemen, in order to constitute the crime of sedition, it is not necessary that the meeting should have had in view to overturn the constitution by mobs and by violence to overturn the king and parliament. For I apprehend, in some sense, the crime of sedition consists in poisoning the minds of the lieges, which may naturally in the end have a tendency to promote violence against the state; and endeavouring to create a dissatisfaction in the country, which nobody can tell where it will end, it will very naturally end in overt rebellion; and if it has that tendency, though not in the view of the parties at the time, yet if they have been guilty of poisoning the minds of the lieges, I apprehend that that will constitute the crime of sedition to all intents and purposes. Now, gentlemen, take a view of the conduct of this meeting, and attend to the time when all this reform, and all this noise and declamation is made against the constitution. It is at a time when we are at war with a great nation, a cruel ferocious nation, that requires all our strength, and not only our strength, but the strength of all our allies to get the better of them; and the greatest unanimity is necessary. I submit to you whether a man that wishes well to his country, would come forward and insist upon a reform, parliamentary or not parliamentary, at such a crisis; which would create discontent in the minds of the people, when every good subject would promote unanimity among the lieges to meet the common enemy. I say in place of that, to bring forward a great reform in parliament is a thing totally inconsistent with the constitution of this country. I say, bringing it forward at that period is a strong proof that they were not well-wishers to the constitution, but enemies to it. I say that no good member of society would have taken those measures. I appeal to you all, that you are living under a happy government in peace and plenty, in perfect security of your lives and property, the happiest nation upon the face of the earth; and when that is the situation of this country, I appeal to you whether I have not given a fair and just description of it; for a set of men in that situation to raise a faction in the minds of the lower order of the people, and create disaffection to the government, and consequently make a division in that country;—I say, these things appear to be from the very conjuncture at which they are brought forward, sedition of a very high nature.

III: THE TRIAL OF MAURICE MARGAROT. Edinburgh

13–14 January, 1794

(*State Trials*, XXIII, p. 672.)

Mr. *Margarot.*—Now, my lord, comes a very delicate matter indeed. I mean to call upon my lord justice clerk, and I hope that the questions and the answers will be given in the most solemn manner. I have received a piece of information which I shall lay before the Court, in the course of my questions: first, my lord, are you upon oath?

Lord Justice Clerk (Lord Braxfield).—State your questions, and I will tell you whether I will answer them or not; if they are proper questions I will answer them.

Mr. *Margarot.*—Did you dine at Mr. Rochead's at Inverleith in the course of last week?

Lord Justice Clerk.—And what have you to do with that, sir?

Mr. *Margarot.*—Did any conversation take place with regard to my trial?

Lord Justice Clerk.—Go on, sir.

Mr. *Margarot.*—Did you use these words; what should you think of giving him an hundred lashes, together with Botany Bay? or words to that purpose?

Lord Justice Clerk.—Go on; put your questions, if you have any more.

Mr. *Margarot.*—Did any person, did a lady say to you that the mob would not allow you to whip him? and, my lord, did you not say that the mob would be the better for losing a little blood? These are the questions, my lord, that I wish to put to you at present in the presence of the Court: deny them, or acknowledge them.

Lord Justice Clerk.—Do you think I should answer questions of that sort, my lord Henderland?

Lord *Henderland.*[1]—No, my lord, they do not relate to this trial.

[1] Alexander Murray, Lord Henderland (1736–95), Solicitor-General for Scotland, 1775; Lord of Session and a Commissioner of the Court of Justiciary, 1783.

112 : THE LONDON CORRESPONDING SOCIETY. Address to the People of Great Britain and Ireland

20 January 1794

(Trial of John Horne Tooke, November 1794. *State Trials*, XXV, pp. 640–4.)

AT A GENERAL MEETING
of the
LONDON CORRESPONDING SOCIETY
Held at the Globe Tavern, Strand,
On MONDAY, the 20th Day of JANUARY, 1794.
CITIZEN JOHN MARTIN, in the CHAIR.

The following ADDRESS to the PEOPLE of *Great Britain* and *Ireland* was read and agreed to.

CITIZENS;—We have referred to *Magna Charta*, to the *Bill of Rights*, and to the *Revolution* and we certainly do find that our ancestors did establish wise and wholesome laws; but we as certainly find, that, of the venerable Constitution of our ancestors, hardly a vestige remains.

Can you believe that those who send virtuous Irishmen, and Scotchmen fettered with felons to Botany Bay, do not meditate and will not attempt to seize the first moment to send us after them ? Or, if we had not just cause to apprehend the same inhuman treatment; if instead of the most imminent danger, we were in perfect safety from it; should we not disdain to enjoy any liberty or privilege whatever, in which our honest Irish and Scotch brethren did not equally and as fully participate with us? Their cause then and ours is the same. And it is both our duty and our interest to stand or fall together. The Irish parliament and the Scotch judges, actuated by the same English influence, have brought us directly to the point. There is no farther step beyond that which they have taken. We are at issue. We must now choose at once either liberty or slavery for ourselves and our posterity. Will you wait till BARRACKS are erected in every village, and till *subsidized* Hessians and Hanoverians are upon us?

You may ask perhaps, by what means shall we seek redress?

We answer, that men in a state of civilized society are bound to seek redress of the grievances from the laws; as long as any redress can be obtained by the laws. But our common Master whom we serve (whose law is a law of liberty, and whose service is perfect freedom) has taught us not to expect to gather grapes from thorns, nor figs from thistles. We must have redress from our own laws and not from the laws of our plunderers, enemies, and oppressors.

THERE IS NO REDRESS FOR A NATION CIRCUMSTANCED AS WE ARE, BUT IN A FAIR, FREE, AND FULL REPRESENTATION OF THE PEOPLE.

J. MARTIN, CHAIRMAN
T. HARDY, SECRETARY

113: CHARLES JAMES FOX. Speech in the Debate on Mr. Adam's Motion respecting the Trials of Mr. Muir and Mr. Palmer, House of Commons

10 March 1794

For Muir, see the note to Number 107. Thomas Palmer (1747–1802) was a Unitarian minister who had been educated at Eton and Cambridge and had resigned a fellowship at Queens'. He was Minister of Unitarian congregations at Montrose and Dundee from 1783 to 1793. He was arrested and indicted for revising the proofs of a pamphlet for the Dundee Society of the Friends of Liberty. Tried before the notorious Braxfield, he was sentenced to seven years' transportation. He died on the way home from Botany Bay. These protests in Parliament were quite without effect. (*Parliamentary History*, XXX, pp. 1,565–6, 1,571.)

INDEED, Sir, so strikingly disgustful are the whole features of this trial, and so enormous its proceedings, that when I first heard of them, I could not prevail on myself to believe that such proceedings had actually taken place; the charge itself, and the manner in which that charge was exhibited, made my blood run cold within me. I read the first edition, I discredited; I read the second and third editions; I was inclined to disbelieve them all; nor would I even believe it now, but in consequence of what I have heard from this lord advocate himself.

Happy am I to boast, that however I may disapprove of those violent prosecutions which have been conducted in this country against individuals, on charges of sedition, that these, when compared with the trials now before us, are merciful and humane. Happy am I to boast, that it is my fortune to be a subject and an inhabitant of England. Were I a native of Scotland, I would instantly prepare to leave that land of tyranny and of despotism. Until these infamous laws are abrogated, you may talk of justice, you may talk of juries, but all trials are mockeries. Until these infamous laws are abrogated, the liberty of the subject is insecure and unprotected; and Scotland, like France, is a land of despotism and oppression.

114: LORD CHIEF JUSTICE EYRE. Charge to the Middlesex Grand Jury, Trial of Thomas Hardy

2 October 1794

Sir James Eyre (1734–99), was appointed Chief Justice of the Common Pleas in 1793. In contrast with Braxfield he showed great fairness in presiding over the trials of Hardy, Horne Tooke and others. (*State Trials*, XXIV, p. 206.)

THE process is very simple: let us imagine to ourselves this case: a few well meaning men conceive that they and their fellow subjects labour under some grievance; they assemble peaceably to deliberate on the means of obtaining redress; the numbers increase; the discussion grows animated, eager, and violent; a rash measure is proposed, adopted, and acted upon; who can say where this shall stop, and that these men, who originally assembled peaceably, shall not finally, and suddenly too, involve themselves in the crime of high treason? It is apparent how easily an impetuous man may precipitate such assemblies into crimes of unforeseen magnitude, and danger to the state; but, let it be considered, that bad men may also find their way into such assemblies, and use the innocent purposes of their association as the stalking horse to their purposes of a very different complexion. How easy for such men to practise upon the credulity and the enthusiasm of honest men, lovers of their country, loyal to their prince, but eagerly bent upon some speculative improvements in the frame, and internal mechanism of the government? If we suppose bad men to have once gained an ascendancy in an assembly of this description, popular in its constitution, and having popular objects; how easy is it for such men to plunge such an assembly into the most criminal excesses? Thus far I am speaking in general, merely to illustrate the proposition, that men who assemble in order to procure a reform of parliament may involve themselves in the guilt of high treason.

115: FELIX VAUGHAN (or William Godwin). *Cursory Strictures on the Charge delivered by Lord Chief Justice Eyre to the Grand Jury*

2 October 1794

Felix Vaughan was assistant Counsel for the defence in the trial of Thomas Hardy. The report in *State Trials* describes him as " a young man of great abilities and promise in his profession ", who died soon after, and attributes this pamphlet to him. Other sources give it to Godwin. (*State Trials*, XXIV, p. 219.)

CHIEF JUSTICE EYRE'S charge consists of three parts. The first five pages contain principally a sound and constitutional exposition of the law of treason, as exhibited in the books. In the two following pages we are presented with this portentous speculation, this new treason of " conspiring to subvert the monarchy; " though the chief justice, as has already appeared, has qualified his speculation, with expressions, proving, by accumulated evidence, and in the most precise terms, that this new imaginary treason is no treason by the laws of England.

Here, as the chief justice observes, the charge might have concluded. Here, if a proper regard had been paid to the essential principles of criminal justice, it would have concluded; if not in reality a little sooner. The remainder of the charge is made up of hypothesis, presumption, prejudication, and conjecture. There is scarcely a single line that is not deformed with such phrases as " public notoriety," " things likely," " purposes imputed," " measures supposed," and " imaginary cases."

The plain reason of all this is, that the chief justice suspected, that the treason described in the statute 25 Edward 3rd, and those founded upon precedent, or deducible from adjudged cases, even with the addition of the chief justice's new constructive treason, founded, as he confesses, upon no law, precedent, or case, and which therefore is in reality no treason, did not afford sufficient ground of crimination against the prisoners. He is therefore obliged to leave the plain road, and travel out of the record. No law, no deduction, or construction of law, that could be forced or drawn out of a mere view of the statute, would answer the purposes of the special commission. He is therefore obliged to indulge himself in conjecture, as to what the prisoners may have done, and what are " the facts likely to be laid before the jury."

116: SIR JOHN SCOTT (Attorney-General). Speech for the Prosecution at the Trial of Thomas Hardy

28 October–5 November 1794

Sir John Scott, later Lord Eldon (1751–1838), was the son of a Newcastle-on-Tyne coal factor, who eloped with Betty Surtees, the daughter of a wealthy banker, and took to the law. Given a seat in Parliament by Thurlow as a King's Friend, he became in turn Solicitor-General, Attorney-General, Lord Chief Justice and Chancellor (1807–27). Handsome, fascinating, he had a genius for managing men, consuming port, and getting and retaining office. He was responsible for the Treason and Sedition Acts, but conducted the prosecutions under them fairly. He became the symbol of unreasoning opposition to all change and gave its name to " Eldonian Toryism ". (*State Trials*, XXIV, pp. 264–5.)

GENTLEMEN, I think the evidence, that I shall lay before you, will most abundantly satisfy you that the convention, which the persons charged conspired to form, was a convention to alter the whole form of the sovereign power of this country, that it was to form, or to devise the means of forming, *a representative government*—to vest in a body, founded upon universal suffrage, and the alleged unalienable, and, as they are called, imprescriptible rights of man, *all the legislative and executive government of the country*; that a conspiracy to this end would be an overt act of high treason, I presume cannot be disputed; it deposes the king in the destruction of the regal office in the constitution of the state.

Gentlemen, I go farther: if it had been intended to have retained the name and office of the king in the country, and to have retained it in the person of the present king, creating, however, by the authority of the intended convention, a new legislature, to act with him, provided they would allow him to act with such new legislature, and thus calling upon him to act against the express obligations of his coronation oath, if he could forget it, it still would have been a conspiracy to depose him from his royal authority, as now established; if he refused to act, he must necessarily be deposed from that authority; if he did accept, he was not the king of England, as he is established by law the king of England. But he could not accept; he could not so govern; he is sworn not so to govern; he must refuse, must resist, and, in consequence of resisting, his life must be in danger.

117: ROBERT BURNS. Letter to Mrs. Dunlop

1794

Burns' republican sympathies and support for the French Revolution nearly lost him his post as a Government exciseman at Dumfries. (*Letters of Robert Burns*, edited by J. de L. Ferguson, 1931, II, 281–2.)

ENTRE nous, you know my Politics; & I cannot approve of the honest Doctor's whining over the deserved fate of a certain pair of Personages.—What is there in the delivering over a perjured Blockhead & an unprincipled Prostitute to the hands of the hangman, that it should arrest for a moment, attention, in an eventful hour, when, as my friend Roscoe in Liverpool gloriously expresses it—

" When the welfare of Millions is hung in the scale
" And the balance yet trembles with fate! "

But our friend is already indebted to People in power, & still looks forward for his Family, so I can apologise for him; for at bottom I am sure he is a staunch friend to liberty.—Thank God, these London trials have given us a little more breath, & I imagine that the time is not far distant when a man may freely blame Billy Pitt, without being called an enemy to his Country.

118: RICHARD BRINSLEY SHERIDAN. Speech on his Motion for the Repeal of the Habeas Corpus Suspension Act, House of Commons

5 January 1795

Richard Brinsley Sheridan (1751–1816), besides being one of the greatest of English dramatists, was a Whig politician with an outstanding reputation as an orator even in the eighteenth century House of Commons. His speech in 1787 on the Begums of Oudh lasted five hours and forty minutes. Fox, fifteen years later, said it was the best speech he had ever heard in the House. Sheridan supported Fox's stand for freedom throughout the War, but drank himself into debt and deterioration. " It was Sheridan's irreparable misfortune to have been honoured with the friendship of the Prince of Wales." Pitt asked for and secured the suspension of Habeas Corpus in the summer of 1794, at the time of the arrest of Thomas Hardy, Horne Tooke and the others tried later that year. See also Nos. 122–126. (*Parliamentary History*, XXXI, p. 1,065.)

WITH regard to the manner in which the proceedings had been conducted, at least no labour had been spared. The first speech on the trials had taken up nine hours. Had he been a juryman, the very circumstance of an attorney-general taking nine hours to tell him of an overt act of treason, would have been a reason why he could not have believed it true. The whole procedure on the prosecution, was a piece of delicate clock-work, a sort of filigree or net-work too slight to hold a robust traitor, and yet so contrived as to let all the lesser cases of libel and sedition escape. The very intricacy and labour of the proceeding was, to his mind, the most satisfactory testimony that the case could not be supported on the grounds of substantial evidence and constitutional principles. If he were asked, did there not appear, from these trials, instances of sedition? He had no hesitation to say, that they exhibited instances of many gross and scandalous libels. He was ready to admit that there were in the societies mischievous men intent on mischievous purposes. There were others actuated by enthusiasm, whom he could not consider in the same light because it was that sort of enthusiasm which had actuated men of the purest minds. As to the phrases Convention, Citizen, &c. in which they had affected an imitation of the proceedings of the French, the worst that could be said of them was, that they were contemptibly foolish. He had attended the trials he said, from a principle of duty. He was of opinion that every man who loved the constitution, and who thought that it was endangered by false alarms, would feel it incumbent to attend trials which he considered as originating from ministerial artifice; and to watch the conduct of the crown lawyers, and of the judges in order to avert those calamities from the country, in which, at former times, it had been involved, and to prevent that most dreadful of all wars—a war of plots and conspiracies; wars in which the purest blood had been shed by the most destructive of all weapons, the perjured tongues of spies and informers.

119: THOMAS HOLCROFT. *A Letter to the Rt. Hon. William Windham, on the Intemperance and Dangerous Tendency on his Public Conduct*

1795

(Pp. 23–4, 26–7.)

AND here, Sir, aware of the personal odium against myself which I am almost certain to create, in these times of political superstition, conscious that I shall again have the cry of Jacobin, Leveller, and perhaps Traitor, echoed in my ear, I still cannot forbear to suggest how necessary it is for men to inquire accurately what they mean, when they speak, in terms rather of bigotry than of sound understanding, of what they call the constitution. Philosophers themselves have erected many an imaginary being, each as their idol. They have figured Time, Space, Motion, Nature, and various other terms of mere classification, to themselves as real existences; and on such assumed data have systematized. Statesmen have followed their example, and Monarchy, Aristocracy, Republic, Constitution, the Rights of nations, and other abstract words and phrases, equally denoting arrangement and relative ideas, have been personified so often that, at last, they have been understood, not to signify a number of customs classed under these different heads, and which though preserving a degree of resemblance were continually varying, but each an identical and permanent existence: a thing perfectly well defined, and which every schoolboy could explain; so that to ask, What do you mean by Monarchy, or Republic? would have been an insult to common sense. I can only say, give to superstition, religious, philosophic, or political, that which you imagine to be superstition's due. Let it endure no persecution. Do you, Sir, as a statesman, worship Baal in your own way. Proclaim the constitution on the high places, in language as incomprehensible and absolute as its perfections. Only suffer those, who are not thus amused by words, to inquire into facts.

This constitution either does or does not relate to all the actions of civil society; it does or it does not regulate them; it does or it does not execute justice in all possible cases. Exert your faculties, Sir; think but a little and you will find that, when we thus amuse ourselves with words, we act like children. The sole inquiry worthy of man is, What are the best means of increasing his happiness? To discover these we must see things as they are, speak of them as they are, and suffer each other to shew how we individually suppose they may become better. However you may deceive yourself, the laws that you and your partisans have made or abrogated, the wars you have excited, the trials you have instituted, and the acrimony you have sowed, have all been directed against this very thing, inquiry, by which alone that public felicity which you imagine you pant to promote can be promoted.

120: WILLIAM GODWIN. *Considerations on Lord Grenville's and Mr. Pitt's Bills concerning Treasonable and Seditious Practices, by a Lover of Order*

1795

(Pp. 80–3.)

NO infatuation can be more extraordinary than that which at present prevails among the alarmed adversaries of reform. Reform must come. It is a resistless tide; and, if we endeavour to keep it out too long, it will overwhelm us. You are friends to the peace and tranquillity of human society. So is every reasonable and conscientious man that lives. But, take heed lest your mistaken friendship should produce the effects of hatred. In order to maintain the peace and tranquillity of society, it is necessary to temporize. We must both accommodate ourselves to the empire of old prejudices, and to the strong and decisive influx of new opinions. We must look far before us. To promote greatly our own interest, we must think a little of the interest of posterity. We must not spend the whole capital of our estate, in the first year that we came into possession. If we would preserve in the community any reverence for authority, we must exercise it over them with frugality. We must not stretch the strings of our instrument so far, as to put them in instant danger to snap.

The London Corresponding Society has been thoughtlessly pursuing a conduct, which was calculated sooner or later to bring on scenes of confusion. They have been to blame. But it is scarcely possible for a serious enquirer to pronounce, that the king's ministers, and the opulent and titled alarmists, are not much more to blame. These were men who, by their situation and influence in the country, were peculiarly bound to hold the balance even, and to consult for the interests of the whole. But, they have been the first to violate the general compact. They have thrown down the gauntlet. They have had recourse to every kind of irritation. They have laid aside the robes and insignia of authority; and leaped, like a common wrestler, upon the stage. They have been loudest in increasing the broil; they have urged on the animosity of the combatants; and they have called for blood. Neither the present times nor posterity will forget the trials for high treason last year at the Old Bailey; a measure which, for precipitation, folly, and an unscrupulous and sanguinary spirit, has never been exceeded. This was one of the early measures, by which government conspicuously forced the moderate and the neutral, to take their station in the ranks of the enemy.

But the present bills will have still more strongly, and, if they pass into a law, much more permanently, the same effect. . . . We must part with the Bill of Rights, with the liberty of the press, and the liberty of speech. . . . We must admit a national militia of spies and informers. . . . The present bills force men into the extremest state of hostility; they leave no opening for treaty; they offer no compromise; they inculcate an obstinate and impracticable temper upon both parties. At a time when conciliation is most necessary, they most deeply inspire into us sentiments of animosity.

121: CHARLES JAMES FOX. Speech on his Motion for the Repeal of the Treason and Sedition Acts, House of Commons

19 May 1797

(*Parliamentary History*, XXXIII, pp. 621–2.)

IN proportion as opinions are open, they are innocent and harmless. Opinions become dangerous to a state only when persecution makes it necessary for the people to communicate their ideas under the bond of secrecy. Do you believe it possible that the calamity which now rages in Ireland would have come to its present height, if the people had been allowed to meet and divulge their grievances? Publicity makes it impossible for artifice to succeed, and designs of a hostile nature lose their danger by the certainty of exposure. But it is said that these bills will expire in a few years; that they will expire when we shall have peace and tranquillity restored to us. What a sentiment to inculcate! You tell the people, that when every thing goes well, when they are happy and comfortable, then they may meet freely, to recognize their happiness, and pass eulogiums on their government; but that in a moment of war and calamity, of distrust and misconduct, it is not permitted them to meet together, because then, instead of eulogizing, they might think proper to condemn ministers. What a mockery is this! What an insult to say that this is preserving to the people the right of petition! To tell them that they shall have a right to applaud, a right to rejoice, a right to meet when they are happy, but not a right to condemn, not a right to deplore their misfortunes, not a right to suggest a remedy! I hate these insidious modes of undermining and libelling the constitution of the country. If you mean to say, that the mixed and balanced government of England is good only for holidays and sunshine, but that it is inapplicable to a day of distress and difficulty, say so. If you mean that freedom is not as conducive to order and strength as it is to happiness, say so; and I will enter the lists with you, and contend, that among all the other advantages arising from liberty, are the advantages of order and strength in a supereminent degree, and that too, in the moment when they are most wanted. Liberty is order. Liberty is strength. Good God, Sir, am I, on this day, to be called upon to illustrate the glorious and soothing doctrine? Look round the world and admire, as you must, the instructive spectacle! You will see that liberty not only is power and order, but that it is power and order predominant and invincible; that it derides all other sources of strength; that the heart of man has no impulse, and can have none that dares to stand in competition with it; and if, as Englishmen, we know how to respect its value, surely the present is the moment of all others, when we ought to secure its invigorating alliance.

THE SUSPENSION OF HABEAS CORPUS

122: AN ACT TO EMPOWER HIS MAJESTY TO SECURE AND DETAIN SUCH PERSONS AS HIS MAJESTY SHALL SUSPECT ARE CONSPIRING AGAINST HIS PERSON AND GOVERNMENT

23 May 1794

(*Statutes at Large*, 34 Geo. 3. c. 54.)

WHEREAS a traitorous and detestable Conspiracy has been formed for subverting the existing Laws and Constitution, and for introducing the System of Anarchy and Confusion which has so fatally prevailed in *France*:

Therefore, for the better Preservation of his Majesty's sacred Person, and for securing the Peace and the Laws and Liberties of this Kingdom; be it enacted by the King's most Excellent Majesty, by and with the advice and consent of the Lords Spiritual and Temporal, and Commons, in this present Parliament assembled, and by the Authority of the same, that every Person or Persons that are or shall be in Prison within the Kingdom of *Great Britain* at or upon the Day on which this Act shall receive his Majesty's Royal Assent, or after, by Warrant of his said Majesty's most Honourable Privy Council, signed by six of the said Privy Council, for High Treason, Suspicion of High Treason, or treasonable Practices, or by Warrant, signed by any of his Majesty's Secretaries of State, for such Causes as aforesaid, may be detained in safe Custody, without Bail or Mainprize, until the first Day of *February* one thousand seven hundred and ninety-five; and that no Judge or Justice of the Peace shall bail or try any such Person or Persons so committed, without Order from his said Majesty's Privy Council, . . . any Law or Statute to the contrary notwithstanding.

123: DEBATE IN THE HOUSE OF COMMONS ON THE HABEAS CORPUS SUSPENSION BILL

16–17 May 1794

(*Parliamentary History*, XXXI, pp. 497, 533, 536, 546–7.)

Pitt

Gentlemen would perceive that that report, so expeditiously laid before the House, contained a general view of the transactions referred to the committee, without waiting for a more minute investigation, and was shortly this:—that it appeared to them that a plan had been digested and acted upon, and at that moment was in forwardness towards its execution, the object of which was nothing less than to assemble a pretended convention of the people, for the purposes of assuming to itself the character of a general representation of the nation; superseding, in the first place, the representative capacity of that House, and arrogating, in the next place, the legislative power of the country at large. It would be for the House to consider whether the circumstances contained in the report, impressed their minds with the same conviction with which they had impressed the minds of the committee. If they did, he could not have a doubt but that they would lead to the same practical conclusion, namely, that, if such designs existed, if such designs had been acted upon and were in forwardness, there was not one moment to be lost in arming the executive power with those additional means, which might be sufficient effectually to stop the farther progress of such a plan, and to prevent its being carried into final execution.

GREY

What was the object of these people? "Their ostensible object," said the minister, "is parliamentary reform; but their real object is the destruction of the government of the country." How was that explained? "By the resolutions," said the minister, "of these persons themselves; for they do not talk of applying to parliament, but of applying to the people for the purpose of obtaining a parliamentary reform." If this language be criminal, said Mr. Grey, I am one of the greatest criminals. I say, that from the House of Commons I have no hope of a parliamentary reform; that I have no hope of a reform, but from the people themselves; that this House will never reform itself, or destroy the corruption by which it is supported, by any other means than those of the resolutions of the people, acting on the prudence of this House, and on which the people ought to resolve. This they can only do by meeting in bodies. This was the language of the minister in 1782; but I do not know what his sentiments are now; for who can know the sentiments of an apostate, who has no rule for his guidance but his own conscience? These were the sentiments of the duke of Richmond at that time; but he accompanied these sentiments with a plan, precisely what these societies now recommend, universal suffrage, and annual parliaments. What, then, have these persons done, more than the chancellor of the exchequer and the duke of Richmond? And what has been discovered by examining the fine velvet bag which the minister brought into the House in so solemn a manner? Nothing, but what every body knew twelve years ago, and what these societies thought fit to reprint and publish in 1794. It is for this that the Habeas Corpus act is to be suspended, and the personal liberty of every individual in the kingdom is to be in the hands of the king's minister.

CANNING

He then adverted to the conduct of Mr. Pitt respecting parliamentary reform. What he himself thought on that subject signified but little to the question in debate. He, however, entertained the same opinions with his right hon. friend; and agreed with him, that though such a reform might be not improper for discussion in time of peace, yet it was a proposition that ought not to be agitated in times of tumult and storm. This was not a period when gentlemen should take a partial view of the subject: they should not look to a part, but the whole. The observations which had been made on the supposed political apostacy of his right hon. friend, had no relation to the question in debate, and were in themselves so weak and futile as to be hardly worth notice.

WINDHAM

For his part, he was surprised how men of sense could so far attempt to impose upon themselves and others, as to allege that the words parliamentary reform, were used by the seditious societies for any other purpose than as a mark for their real intention of a total annihilation of all property, constitution, and religion. It was perfectly puerile to impute to them innocent intentions; for taking the whole chain and tenor of their proceedings and resolutions, it was plain as the sun that what they meant by reform was the wildest anarchy.

124: CHARLES JAMES FOX. Debate in the House of Commons on the Habeas Corpus Suspension Bill

17 May 1794

(*Parliamentary History*, XXXI, pp. 559–60.)

TO deny to the people the right of discussion because upon some occasions, that right had been exercised by indiscreet or bad men, was what he could not subscribe to. The right of popular discussion was a salutary and an essential privilege of the subject. He would not answer long for the conduct of parliament, if it were not subject to the jealousy of the people. They all entertained becoming respect for the executive government, that was, for the chief magistrate of the kingdom, but their respect for the king did not supersede the vigilance of parliament. In his opinion, the best security for the due maintenance of the constitution, was in the strict and incessant vigilance of the people over parliament itself. Meetings of the people, therefore, for the discussion of public objects, were not merely legal, but laudable; and, unless it was to be contended that there was some magic in the word convention, which brought with it disorder, anarchy, and ruin, he could perceive no just ground for demolishing the constitution of England, merely because it was intended to hold a meeting for the purpose of obtaining a parliamentary reform. With respect to their plan, that of universal suffrage, he never had but one opinion on the subject. He had constantly and uniformly considered universal suffrage as a wild and ridiculous idea. When his noble relation, the duke of Richmond, had one day taken pains to explain his ideas on this subject, a learned and ingenious friend of his said to him, with as much truth as wit, "My lord, I think the best part of your grace's plan is its utter impracticability." He had always thought that it was impracticable; and though he could not agree with the opinion, that rather than continue the present state of representation, he would incur all the hazards of universal suffrage, yet he was ready to say, that the measures of last year, the horrid and detestable prosecutions, the scandalous sentences that had been passed, and the scandalous way in which they had been executed, did not tend to make him wish less than heretofore for some reform, that should protect the country against these violations of good sense, propriety, and justice.

125: RICHARD BRINSLEY SHERIDAN. Speech on his Motion for the Repeal of the Habeas Corpus Suspension Act, House of Commons

5 January 1795

(*Parliamentary History*, XXXI, pp. 1,065–9.)

If, then, a suspension of the Habeas Corpus can be compared to nothing but a measure which suspends the whole of the constitution, it ought only to take place in cases of the most absolute necessity. Was the present a case of such extreme emergency? If any man believed that the people of this country were infected with treasonable principles, and disposed to overturn the government, he might be justified in holding such an opinion; but if he believed that the characteristic feature of the English nation was a sober, settled, and steady attachment to the constitution, it was incumbent on him to call for an immediate repeal of the act suspending the Habeas Corpus. Such was the opinion, which had been confirmed by repeated verdicts of a jury; verdicts which went completely to do away the idea of any conspiracy having ever existed in the country.

I can suppose the case of a haughty and stiff-necked minister, who had never mixed in a popular assembly, who had therefore no common feeling with the mass of the people, no knowledge of the mode in which their intercourse is conducted, who was not a month in the ranks in this House before he was raised to the first situation, and though on a footing of equality with any other member, elevated with the idea of fancied superiority: such a minister can have no communication with the people of England except through the medium of spies and informers; he is unacquainted with the mode in which their sentiments are expressed, and cannot make allowance for the language of toasts and resolutions adopted in an unguarded and convivial hour. Such a minister, if he lose their confidence, will bribe their hate; if he disgust them by arbitrary measures, he will not leave them till they are completely bound and shackled; above all, he will gratify the vindictive resentment of apostacy, by prosecuting all those who dare to espouse the cause which he has betrayed, and he will not desist from the gratification of his malignant propensities, and the prosecution of his arbitrary schemes, till he has buried in one grave, the peace, the happiness, the glory, and the independence of England.

126: WILLIAM LAMBTON. Speech on the Bill for Continuing the Habeas Corpus Suspension Act, House of Commons

23 January 1795

William Lambton, who died in 1797, was M.P. for Durham City and a supporter of Fox. He was the father of John Lambton, Earl of Durham, famous as the author of the Durham Report. (*Parliamentary History*, XXXI, pp. 1, 150–1.)

LET men of honour and conscience declare, then, whether it was a fit thing that the people of England should, without any reason, be deprived of their rights. He could not help thinking the system pursued by ministers most alarming. What was this system ? The adoption of intriguing measures, calculated to separate the higher and lower classes of society,—a system which he was in hopes would have been left to the despotism of Russia and Germany; where the proud nobles, as if formed of different flesh and blood, were but too apt to consider their inferiors as mere beasts of burthen. This was the baneful exotic transplanted by ministers into this land of freedom; and fatal must be its fruits, unless nipped and blasted in the bud. Fear was their successful engine, and we all knew that fear begat jealousy, jealousy partial oppression; that partial oppression led to general tyranny and tyranny to a resistance big with consequences, equal, perhaps, to those which had produced those scenes of horror, which had laid low the monarchy of France, and had shaken to their very centers every government in Europe. This, he repeated, was the trick, the legerdemain of their Machiavellian policy, and they had succeeded. Was this the good old sterling policy of Englishmen? Certainly not. The minister had filled the men of wealth with fear for the possession of their darling property, for the purpose of making them look with distrust on the poor, and thereby to gain his object in taking away the liberty of all. This might pass for a time: for a time the opinion of the rich would appear to be the entire opinion of the country; and give a certain tone to its politics; but this was a fugitive and transitory cloud; and the whole people of England, seeing with their own eyes, would before long speak with their own tongues; and when they should speak, they would speak with a voice that would rouse the most lethargic, and intimidate the most corrupt and profligate of their enemies. He had no pleasure in saying these things; he could wish there was no foundation for them; but these were not times to mince matters; they were times in which every honest man should speak the real dictates of his heart.—Such were the grounds on which this bill was to be opposed by him.

PART V

CHANGING VIEWS ON THE REVOLUTION

127: EDMUND BURKE. *Reflections on the Revolution in France*

1790

(*Works*, II, pp. 282–3)

I FLATTER myself that I love a manly, moral, regulated liberty as well as any gentleman of that society, be he who he will; and perhaps I have given as good proofs of my attachment to that cause, in the whole course of my public conduct. I think I envy liberty as little as they do, to any other nation. But I cannot stand forward, and give praise or blame to anything which relates to human actions, and human concerns, on a simple view of the object, as it stands stripped of every relation, in all the nakedness and solitude of metaphysical abstraction. Circumstances (which with some gentlemen pass for nothing) give in reality to every political principle its distinguishing colour and discriminating effect. The circumstances are what render every civil and political scheme beneficial or noxious to mankind. Abstractedly speaking, government, as well as liberty, is good; yet could I, in common sense, ten years ago, have felicitated France on her enjoyment of a government (for she then had a government) without enquiry what the nature of that government was, or how it was administered? Can I now congratulate the same nation upon its freedom? Is it because liberty in the abstract may be classed amongst the blessings of mankind, that I am seriously to felicitate a mad-man, who has escaped from the protecting restraint and wholesome darkness of his cell, on his restoration to the enjoyment of light and liberty? Am I to congratulate a highwayman and murderer, who has broke prison, upon the recovery of his natural rights? This would be to act over again the scene of the criminals condemned to the galleys, and their heroic deliverer, the metaphysic knight of the sorrowful countenance.

When I see the spirit of liberty in action, I see a strong principle at work; and this, for a while, is all I can possibly know of it. The wild *gas*, the fixed air, is plainly broke loose; but we ought to suspend our judgment until the first effervescence is a little subsided, till the liquor is cleared, and until we see something deeper than the agitation of a troubled and frothy surface. I must be tolerably sure, before I venture publicly to congratulate men upon a blessing, that they have really received one. Flattery corrupts both the receiver and the giver; and adulation is not of more service to the people than to kings. I should therefore suspend my congratulations on the new liberty of France, until I was informed how it had been combined with government; with public force; with the discipline and obedience of armies; with the collection of an effective and well-distributed revenue; with morality and religion; with the solidity of property; with peace and order; with civil and social manners. All these (in their way) are good things too; and, without them, liberty is not a benefit whilst it lasts, and is not likely to continue long. The effect of liberty to individuals is, that they may do what they please: we ought to see what it will please them to do, before we risk congratulations, which may be soon turned into complaints. Prudence would dictate this in the case of separate, insulated, private men; but liberty, when men act in bodies, is *power*. Considerate people, before they declare themselves, will observe the use which is made of *power*; and particularly of so trying a thing as *new* power in *new* persons, of whose principles, tempers, and dispositions they have little or no experience, and in situations, where those who appear the most stirring in the scene may possibly not be the real movers.

128: EDMUND BURKE. *Reflections on the Revolution in France*

1790

(*Works*, II, pp. 396–7.)

I DO not know under what description to class the present ruling authority in France. It affects to be a pure democracy, though I think it in a direct train of becoming shortly a mischievous and ignoble oligarchy. But for the present I admit it to be a contrivance of the nature and effect of what it pretends to. I reprobate no form of government merely upon abstract principles. There may be situations in which the purely democratic form will become necessary. There may be some (very few, and very particularly circumstanced) where it would be clearly desirable. This I do not take to be the case of France, or of any other great country. Until now, we have seen no examples of considerable democracies. The ancients were better acquainted with them. Not being wholly unread in the authors, who had seen the most of those constitutions, and who best understood them, I cannot help concurring with their opinion, that an absolute democracy, no more than absolute monarchy, is to be reckoned among the legitimate forms of government. They think it rather the corruption and degeneracy, than the sound constitution of a republic. If I recollect rightly, Aristotle observes, that a democracy has many striking points of resemblance with a tyranny. Of this I am certain, that in a democracy, the majority of the citizens is capable of exercising the most cruel oppression upon the minority, whenever strong divisions prevail in that kind of polity, as they often must; and that oppression of the minority will extend to far greater numbers, and will be carried on with much greater fury, than can almost ever be apprehended from the dominion of a single sceptre. In such a popular persecution, individual sufferers are in a much more deplorable condition than in any other. Under a cruel prince they have the balmy compassion of mankind to assuage the smart of their wounds; they have the plaudits of the people to animate their generous constancy under their sufferings: but those who are subjected to wrong under multitudes, are deprived of all external consolation. They seem deserted by mankind, overpowered by a conspiracy of their whole species.

129: EDMUND BURKE. *Reflections on the Revolution in France*

1790

(*Works*, II, p. 456.)

So far from this able disposition of some of the old republican legislators, which follows with a solicitous accuracy the moral conditions and propensities of men, they have levelled and crushed together all the orders which they found, even under the coarse unartificial arrangement of the monarchy, in which mode of government the classing of the citizens is not of so much importance as in a republic. It is true, however, that every such classification, if properly ordered, is good in all forms of government; and composes a strong barrier against the excesses of despotism, as well as it is the necessary means of giving effect and permanence to a republic. For want of something of this kind, if the present project of a republic should fail, all securities to a moderated freedom fail along with it; all the indirect restraints which mitigate despotism are removed; insomuch that if monarchy should ever again obtain an entire ascendency in France, under this or under any other dynasty, it will probably be, if not voluntarily tempered, at setting out, by the wise and virtuous counsels of the prince, the most completely arbitrary power that has ever appeared on earth. This is to play a most desperate game.

130: JAMES MACKINTOSH: *Vindiciæ Gallicæ*

1791

(Pp. 174–6.)

THE massacres of war, and the murders committed by the sword of justice, are disguised by the solemnities which invest them. But the wild justice of the people has a naked and undisguised horror. Its slightest exertion awakens all our indignation, while murder and rapine, if arrayed in the gorgeous disguise of acts of State, may with impunity stalk abroad. Our sentiments are reconciled to them in this form, and we forget that the evils of anarchy must be short lived, while those of despotic government are fatally permanent.

Let us correct that illusion of *moral optics* which makes near objects so disproportionately large. Let us place the scene of the French Revolution in a remote age, or in a distant nation, and then let us calmly ask our own minds, whether the most reasonable subject of wonder be not its unexampled mildness, and the small number of individuals crushed in the fall of so vast a pile.

131: SAMUEL ROMILLY. Letter to Madame G———

15 May 1792

(Romilly, *Memoirs*, II, pp. 1–2.)

MY opinion, however, is not in the least altered with respect to your Revolution. Even the conduct of the present Assembly has not been able to shake my conviction that it is the most glorious event, and the happiest for mankind, that has ever taken place since human affairs have been recorded; and though I lament sincerely the miseries which have happened, and which still are to happen, I console myself with thinking that the evils of the revolution are transitory, and all the good of it is permanent.

132: ARTHUR YOUNG. *Travels in France*

1792

(Pp. 358–9, 552.)

IT is impossible to justify the excesses of the people on their taking up arms; they were certainly guilty of cruelties; it is idle to deny the facts, for they have been proved too clearly to admit of a doubt. But is it really the people to whom we are to impute the whole?—Or to their oppressors, who had kept them so long in a state of bondage? He who chooses to be served by slaves, and by ill-treated slaves, must know that he holds both his property and life by a tenure far different from those who prefer the service of well treated freemen; and he who dines to the music of groaning sufferers, must not, in the moment of insurrection, complain that his daughters are ravished, and then destroyed; and that his sons' throats are cut. When such evils happen, they surely are more imputable to the tyranny of the master, than to the cruelty of the servant. The analogy holds with the French peasants —the murder of a seigneur, or a chateau in flames is recorded in every newspaper; the rank of the person who suffers, attracts notice; but where do we find the register of that seigneur's oppressions of his peasantry, and his exactions of feudal services, from those whose children were dying around them for want of bread? Where do we find the minutes that assigned these starving wretches to some vile petty-fogger, to be fleeced by impositions, and a mockery of justice, in the seigneural courts? Who gives us the awards of the intendant and his *sub-delegués*, which took off the taxes of a man of fashion, and laid them with accumulated weight, on the poor, who were so unfortunate as to be his neighbours? Who has dwelt sufficiently upon explaining all the ramifications of despotism, regal, aristocratical, and ecclesiastical, pervading the whole mass of the people; reaching, like a circulating fluid, the most distant capillary tubes of poverty and wretchedness? In these cases, the sufferers are too ignoble to be known; and the mass too indiscriminate to be pitied. But should a philosopher feel and reason thus? should he mistake the cause for the effect? and giving all his pity to the few, feel no compassion for the many, because they suffer in his eyes not individually, but by millions? The excesses of the people cannot, I repeat, be justified; it would undoubtedly have done them credit, both as men and christians, if they had possessed their new acquired power with moderation. But let it be remembered, that the populace in no country ever use power with moderation; excess is inherent in their aggregate constitution; and as every government in the world knows, that violence infallibly attends power in such hands, it is doubly bound in common sense, and for common safety, so to conduct itself, that the people may not find an interest in public confusions. They will always suffer much and long, before they are effectually roused; nothing, therefore, can kindle the flame, but such oppressions of some classes or order in the society, as give able men the opportunity of seconding the general mass; discontent will soon diffuse itself around; and if the government take not warning in time, it is alone answerable for all the burnings, and plunderings, and devastation, and blood that follow. The true judgment to be formed of the French revolution, must surely be gained, from an attentive consideration of the evils of the old government: when these are well understood—and when the extent and universality of the oppression under which the people groaned—oppression which bore upon them from every quarter, it will scarcely be attempted to be urged, that a revolution was not absolutely necessary to the welfare of the kingdom.

The candid reader will, I trust, see, that in whatever I have ventured to advance on so critical a subject as this great and unexampled revolution, I have assigned the merit I think due to it, *which is the destruction of the old government*, and not the establishment of the new. All that I saw, and much that I heard, in France, gave me the clearest conviction, that *a change* was necessary for the happiness of the people; a change, that should limit the royal authority; that should restrain the feudal tyranny of the nobility; that should reduce the church to the level of good citizens; that should correct the abuses of finance; that should give purity to the administration of justice; and that should place the people in a state of ease, and give them weight enough to secure this blessing. Thus far I must suppose every friend of mankind agreed. But whether, in order to effect thus much, all France were to be overthrown, ranks annihilated, property attacked, the monarchy abolished, and the king and royal family trampled upon; and, above all the rest, the whole effect of the revolution, good or bad, put on the issue of a conduct which, to speak in the mildest language, made a civil war probable:—this is a question absolutely distinct. In my private opinion, these extremities were not necessary; France might have been free without violence; a necessitous court, a weak ministry, and a timid prince, could have refused nothing to the demands of the states, essential to public happiness. The power of the purse would have done all that ought to have been done. The weight of the commons would have been predominant; but it would have had checks and a controul, without which *power* is not CONSTITUTION, but *tyranny*.—While, however, I thus venture to think that the revolution might have been accomplished upon better principles, because probably more durable ones, I do not therefore assign the first National Assembly in the gross to that total condemnation, they have received from some very intemperate pens, and for this plain reason, because it is certain that they have not done much which was not called for by the people.

133: SAMUEL ROMILLY. Letter to M. Dumont

10 September 1792

(Romilly, *Memoirs*, II, p. 4.)

I OBSERVE that, in your letter, you say nothing about France, and I wish I could do so too, and forget the affairs of that wretched country altogether; but that is so impossible, that I can scarcely think of anything else. How could we ever be so deceived in the character of the French nation as to think them capable of liberty! wretches, who, after all their professions and boasts about liberty, and patriotism, and courage, and dying, and after taking oath after oath, at the very moment when their country is invaded and the enemy is marching through it unresisted, employ whole days in murdering women, and priests, and prisoners!

134: JOHN CARTWRIGHT. Letter of January 1793

(*Life and Correspondence of Major Cartwright*, p. 195.)

I AM amongst those who entertain doubts as to the competency of human authority, in any case whatever, deliberately to punish with death. In this particular case[1] I can the less excuse it, as, so far from having been necessary or prudent, it seems to have been in the highest degree impolitic. And when I reflect on the disservice it is likely to do to the cause of freedom, which I must ever hold to be the cause of virtue and of man, most sincerely do I lament it. The true cause of this event I can no where discover, but in the mean, revengeful, murderous spirit of a small faction, the demagogues of an ignorant rabble, contaminated by all the vices which, in a succession of ages, grow out of DESPOTISM, in a vicious and overgrown capital; a faction who are a disgrace to human kind, and the enemies to justice, to humanity and virtue.

[1] The execution of Louis XVI.

135: ROBERT BURNS. Letter to Robert Graham

5 January 1793

(*Letters*, edited by J. de L. Ferguson, 1931, II, pp. 143–4.)

IT has been said, it seems, that I not only belong to, but head a disaffected party in this place.—I know of no party in this place, Republican or Reform, except an old party of Borough Reform; with which I never had any thing to do.

I never uttered any invectives against the king.—His private worth, it is altogether impossible that such a man as I, can appreciate; and in his Public capacity, I always revered, & ever will, with the soundest loyalty, revere, the Monarch of Great Britain, as, to speak in Masonic, the sacred KEYSTONE OF OUR ROYAL ARCH CONSTITUTION.—

As to REFORM PRINCIPLES, I look upon the British Constitution, as settled at the Revolution, to be the most glorious Constitution on earth, or that perhaps the wit of man can frame; at the same time, I think, & you know what High and distinguished Characters have for some time thought so, that we have a good deal deviated from the original principles of that Constitution; particularly, that an alarming System of Corruption has pervaded the connection between the

Executive Power and the House of Commons.—This is the Truth, the Whole truth, of my Reform opinions; opinions which, before I was aware of the complection of these innovating times, I too unguardedly (now I see it) sported with: but henceforth, I seal up my lips.

As to France, I was her enthusiastic votary in the beginning of the business.—When she came to shew her old avidity for conquest, in annexing Savoy, &c. to her dominions, & invading the rights of Holland, I altered my sentiments.

136: BISHOP OF LLANDAFF. *An Appendix to the Bishop of Llandaff's Sermon, preached in Charlotte street Chapel, April* 1785

25 January 1793

Richard Watson, Bishop of Llandaff (1737–1816), was elected Professor of Chemistry at Cambridge in 1764, having, according to himself, " never read a syllable on the subject nor seen a single experiment ". In 1771 he transferred to the Regius Chair of Divinity, for which he had, to begin with, almost as little qualification. He wrote " A Letter by a Christian Whig ", and an " Apology for Christianity ", and was attached to the Grafton interest. Appointed Bishop of Llandaff by Shelburne in 1782, he visited his diocese at least once every three years. During the Revolution he wrote an " Apology for the Bible " and supported Pitt's war policy.

I HAVE no hesitation in declaring, that the object which the French seemed to have in view at the commencement of their revolution, had my hearty approbation. The object was to free themselves and their posterity from arbitrary power. . . . I did not approve of the means by which the first revolution was effected in France. . . . I considered them certainly as evils of importance; but at the same time as evils inseparable from a state of civil commotion, and which I conceived would be more than compensated by the establishment of a limited monarchy.

The French have abandoned the constitution they had at first established, and have changed it for another. No one can reprobate with more truth than I do both the means, and the end of this change.—The end has been the establishment of a republic.—Now, a republic is a form of which, of all others, I most dislike —and I dislike it for this reason: because of all forms of government, scarcely excepting the most despotic, I think a republic the most oppressive to the bulk of the people: they are deceived in it with the shew of liberty; but they live in it, under the most odious of all tyrannies, the tyranny of their equals.—With respect to the means by which this new republic has been erected in France, they have been sanguinary, savage, more than brutal. They not merely fill the heart of every individual with commiseration for the unfortunate sufferers; but they exhibit to the eye of contemplation, an humiliating picture of human nature, when its passions are not regulated by religion, or controlled by law.

137: ARTHUR YOUNG. *The Example of France a Warning to Britain*

1793

(Pp. 3–4.)

IN attempting to give expressions inadequate to the indignation every one must feel at the horrible events now passing in France, I am sensible that I may be reproached with changing my politics, my "principles", as it has been expressed.

The Revolution before the 10th of August, was as different from the Revolution after that day as light from darkness; as clearly distinct in principle and practice as liberty and slavery; for the same man to approve therefore of both, he must either be uncandid or changeable; uncandid in his approbation before that period—changeable in his approbation after it.

138: LORD GRENVILLE. Letter to Lord Auckland

11 November 1793

William Wyndham Grenville, Lord Grenville (1759–1834), was Home Secretary, June 1789–June 1791, and Pitt's Secretary of State for Foreign Affairs, 1791—1801. (Historical Manuscripts Commission: *The Manuscripts of J. B. Fortescue, Esq., preserved at Dropmore*, 1892–1927, II, p. 464.)

DO I flatter myself with the hope of what I so strongly wish, or does it strike you as it does me that every fresh account from France brings decisive proofs that the system is drawing to its close, and cannot longer support itself. Consider only the violent and continued effort which the interior requires, and it is surely not being too sanguine to pronounce that this is incompatible with the maintenance of their external defence.

139: LORD ROBERT STEPHEN FITZGERALD.
Letter to Lord Grenville

13 January 1795

Lord Robert Stephen Fitzgerald was Secretary of the Paris Embassy from 1789 to 1791, and Minister to Switzerland from 1792 to 1795. (*Dropmore Papers*, III, p. 7.)

I MAY add, *par parenthèse*, that if this Revolution has been attended with misery and wretchedness to nations and millions of individuals, that it has also been productive of some good in opening the eyes of men on the real character of Frenchmen, and of exhibiting to the world in its true colours that horrid mass of infamy, perfidy, and wickedness of every description, which had been so long concealed under the veil of politeness and urbanity, to the great misfortune, at all ages, of those who mistook the appearance for the reality. Sorry am I to say that I think there are but very few exceptions to be made amongst them, but how can it be otherwise with men who are become the agents of the Devil, and who, openly disavowing God and the truth, harden their hearts against every thing that has hitherto been held sacred amongst men. They are become like a second race on earth, and it may truly be said that the world is inhabited by two sets of human beings, by men and Frenchmen. And unfortunately these monsters are not confined to their own limits, for those who are expelled are as exceptionable as those who remain in France.

140: HELEN MARIA WILLIAMS. *Letters containing a Sketch of the Politics of France*

1795

Helen Maria Williams (1762–1827), was a poetess and woman of letters, who, from 1788, resided in France. Her writings on the Revolution are enthusiastic and unreliable, but they attracted much contemporary notice. She remained attached to revolutionary principles even after imprisonment for her Girondin associations during the Terror. (p. 211.)

IN the first days of the Revolution, when Liberty and Property went hand-in-hand together, what a moral revolution was instantly effected throughout Europe, by the sublime and immortal principles which this great change seemed about to introduce into government! But what eternal regrets must the lovers of liberty feel, that her cause should have fallen into the hands of monsters, ignorant of her charms, by whom she has been transformed into a fury, who, brandishing her snaky whips and torches, has enlarged the limits of wickedness and driven us back into regions of guilt hitherto unknown! . . .

Yet it is some consolation, amidst this mighty mass of evil, that France is at length beginning to learn wisdom from the things she has suffered. . . . We may now approach the altar of liberty with confidence and hope; the hideous spectres that haunted it have fled for ever; and its incense in future will rise grateful to heaven, and spread fragrance over a regenerated land.

141 : WILLIAM COBBETT. *The Bloody Buoy, Thrown out as a Warning to the Political Pilots of America,* by Peter Porcupine

1796

William Cobbett (1763–1835). Gardener, lawyer's clerk, regimental sergeant-major and author, Cobbett was at the time of the Revolution a British propagandist in America. Among his pamphlets were *A Bone to Gnaw for Democrats*, *A Kick for a Bite*, *The Cannibal's Progress* and *A Letter to the Infamous Tom Paine*. Returning to England in 1805, he found that the picture drawn from childhood days at " The Jolly Farmer ", Farnham, did not correspond to the reality, and though an old Tory by nature, in reaction against the new Toryism, he turned Radical.

IT has been asserted, again and again, by the partizans of the French revolution, that all the crimes which have disgraced it are to be ascribed to the hostile operations of their enemies. They have told us, that, had not the Austrians and Prussians been on their march to Paris, the prisoners would not have been massacred on the 2d and 3d of September, 1792. But, can we possibly conceive how the murder of 8000 poor prisoners, locked up and bound, could be necessary to the defence of a capital, containing a million of inhabitants? Can we believe that the sabres of the assassins would not have been more effectively employed against the invaders, than against defenceless priests and women? . . . Where could be the necessity of massacring them? Where could be the necessity of hacking them to pieces, tearing out their bowels, and biting their hearts? . . .

Their butcheries at Lyons, and in its neighbourhood, did not begin till they were completely triumphant. It was then, at the moment when they had no retaliation to fear, that they commenced their bloody work. Carrier, lolling at his ease, sent the victims to death by hundreds. The blood never flowed from the guillotine in such torrents as at the very time when their armies were driving their enemies before them in every direction.

142: ROBERT BURNS. "*Does Haughty Gaul Invasion Threat?*"

1795

(*Works*, edited by A. Cunningham, 1842, pp. 436–7.)

I

Does haughty Gaul invasion threat?
Then let the louns beware, Sir;
There's WOODEN WALLS upon our seas,
And VOLUNTEERS on shore, Sir;
The *Nith* shall run to *Corsincon*,
And *Criffel* sink in *Solway*,
Ere we permit a Foreign Foe
On British ground to rally!

IV

The wretch that would a *tyrant* own
And the wretch, his true-born brother,
Who would set the *Mob* above the *Throne*,
May they be damn'd together!
Who will not sing "God save the King",
Shall hang as high's the steeple;
But while we sing "God save the King",
We'll ne'er forget THE PEOPLE!

143: JOHN THELWALL. *Speech at the General Meeting of the Friends of Parliamentary Reform*

26 October 1795

(Pp. 12–3.)

I VENERATE, I esteem, I adore the principles upon which the French Revolution has been established. But those principles, though talked of by a few, have unhappily never been considered by the many; and the people of *France*, though they were sensible of their wrongs, and easily found out the way to rid themselves of one tyranny, have not yet found out the effectual means of preventing the usurpations of another. . . . What has been the consequence? Faction after faction has triumphed in the blood of its predecessors . . . and during the space of six successive years they have been cutting each others throats, upon personal disputes, and questions of ambitious ascendancy, till the public mind appears to have grown sick and weary of the contest, and the real object of their first and wise pursuit has vanished almost out of sight. . . . Look at their newly accepted Constitution, and tell me—what have they done at last? Have they not abandoned the glorious principle of equality? Have they not quietly resigned the principle of universal suffrage?

144: SAMUEL TAYLOR COLERIDGE. Letter to Charles Lloyd Sen.

15 October 1796

Samuel Taylor Coleridge (1772–1824), poet and philosopher, was an enthusiast for an idealized Revolution. His political theories at this time were Utopian (or Pantisocratic), and hostile to the Government. Jacobinism and French conquests however completely alienated him from the Revolution. (*Biographia Epistolaris*, edited by A. Turnbull, 1911, I, p. 107.)

I HAVE accordingly snapped my squeaking baby-trumpet of sedition, and have hung up its fragments in the Chamber of Penitences.

145: WILLIAM WORDSWORTH. *The Prelude*, Book XI

(Book XI, lines 206–12.)

But now, become oppressors in their turn,
Frenchmen had changed a war of self-defence
For one of conquest, losing sight of all
Which they had struggled for: up mounted now,
Openly in the eye of earth and heaven,
The scale of liberty. I read her doom,
With anger vexed, with disappointment sore.

146: EDMUND BURKE. *Letters on a Regicide Peace*

1796

(*Works*, V, p. 255.)

FRANCE differs essentially from all those governments, which are formed without system, which exist by habit, and which are confused with the multitude, and with the complexity of their pursuits. What now stands as government in France is struck out at a heat. The design is wicked, immoral, impious, oppressive; but it is spirited and daring; it is systematic; it is simple in its principle; it has unity and consistency in perfection. In that country entirely to cut off a branch of commerce, to extinguish a manufacture, to destroy the circulation of money, to violate credit, to suspend the course of agriculture, even to burn a city, or to lay waste a province of their own, does not cost them a moment's anxiety. To them the will, the wish, the want, the liberty, the toil, the blood of individuals, is as nothing. Individuality is left out of their scheme of government. The state is all in all. Everything is referred to the production of force; afterwards, everything is trusted to the use of it. It is military in its principle, in its maxims, in its spirit, and in all its movements. The state has dominion and conquest for its sole objects; dominion over minds by proselytism, over bodies by arms.

147: ROBERT SOUTHEY. Letter to John May

26 June 1797

Robert Southey (1774–1843), was at first an ardent revolutionary. He wrote *Wat Tyler* in 1794, but soon sought safety as a Quarterly Reviewer and historian. " Mr. Southey," said Hazlitt, rather unfairly, " missed his way in Utopia; he has found it at Old Sarum." (*Life and Correspondence of Robert Southey*, edited by C. C. Southey, 1849–50, I, p. 317.)

THERE was a time when I believed in the persuadability of man, and had the mania of man-mending. Experience has taught me better. . . . The ablest physician can do little in the great lazar house of society; it is a pest-house that infects all within its atmosphere.

148: WILLIAM COBBETT. *Democratic Principles Illustrated, Part II, containing an instructive essay, Tracing all the Horrors of the French Revolution to their real Causes, the licentious Politics and infidel Philosophy of the Present Age* by Peter Porcupine

1798

(P. 48.)

THE whole history of the French Revolution presents us with nothing but a regular progress in robbery and murder. The first Assembly, for instance, wheedling their King out of his title and his power; they then set him at defiance, proscribe or put to death his friends, and then shut him up in his palace, as a wild beast in his cage. The second Assembly send a gang of ruffians to insult and revile him, and then they hurl him from his throne. The third Assembly cut his throat. What is there in all this but a regular and natural progression from bad to worse, and so with the rest of their abominable actions.

149: SAMUEL TAYLOR COLERIDGE. "*France*," *An Ode*

February 1798

(*Poetical Works*, edited by E. A. Coleridge, 1912, I, pp. 245–7.)

When France in wrath her giant-limbs upreared,
  And with that oath, which smote air, earth, and sea,
  Stamped her strong foot and said she would be free,
Bear witness for me, how I hoped and feared!
With what a joy my lofty gratulation
  Unawed I sang, amid a slavish band:
And when to whelm the disenchanted nation,
  Like fiends embattled by a wizard's wand,
    The Monarchs marched in evil day,
    And Britain joined the dire array;
  Though dear her shores and circling ocean,
Though many friendships, many youthful loves
  Had swoln the patriot emotion
And flung a magic light o'er all her hills and groves;
Yet still my voice, unaltered, sang defeat
  To all that braved the tyrant-quelling lance,
And shame too long delayed and vain retreat!
For ne'er, O Liberty! with partial aim
I dimmed thy light or damped thy holy flame;
  But blessed the pæans of delivered France,
And hung my head and wept at Britain's name.

. . .

Forgive me, Freedom! O forgive those dreams!
  I hear thy voice, I hear thy loud lament,
  From bleak Helvetia's icy caverns sent—
I hear thy groans upon her blood-stained streams!
  Heroes, that for your peaceful country perished,
And ye that, fleeing, spot your mountain-snows

With bleeding wounds; forgive me, that I cherished
One thought that ever blessed your cruel foes!

. . .

The Sensual and the Dark rebel in vain,
Slaves by their own compulsion! In mad game
They burst their manacles and wear the name
Of Freedom, graven on a heavier chain!
O Liberty! with profitless endeavour
Have I pursued thee, many a weary hour;
But thou nor swell'st the victor's strain, nor ever
Didst breathe thy soul in forms of human power,
Alike from all, howe'er they praise thee,
(Nor prayer, nor boastful name delays thee)
Alike from Priestcraft's harpy minions,
And factious Blasphemy's obscener slaves,
Thou speedest on thy subtle pinions,
The guide of homeless winds, and playmate of the waves!
And there I felt thee!—on that sea-cliff's verge,
Whose pines, scarce travelled by the breeze above,
Had made one murmur with the distant surge!
Yes, while I stood and gazed, my temples bare,
And shot my being through earth, sea, and air,
Possessing all things with intensest love,
O Liberty! my spirit felt thee there.

150: GEORGE CANNING. Speech in the Debate on Mr. Tierney's Motion respecting Peace with the French Republic, House of Commons

11 December 1798

(*Parliamentary History*, XXXIV, p. 49.)

I WOULD ask the hon. gentleman, I would ask every man in the House, whether he does not know—personally and intimately know—many individuals in this country, the whole course and current of whose ideas, with respect to France, have of late been entirely changed? Does he not believe that the invasion of Switzerland, for instance, that the profligate, swindling transaction with America, that the event of the negotiation at Lisle, worked a great change in the public mind in this country?

PART VI

THE DEFENCE OF THE ESTABLISHED ORDER

Equality and Property

151: MARY WOLLSTONECRAFT. *A Vindication of the Rights of Woman*

1792

(Pp. 91–2.)

BIRTH, riches, and every intrinsic advantage that exalt a man above his fellows, without any mental exertion, sink him in reality below them. In proportion to his weakness, he is played upon by designing men, till the bloated monster has lost all traces of humanity. And that tribes of men, like flocks of sheep, should quietly follow such a leader, is a solecism that only a desire of present enjoyment and narrowness of understanding can solve. Educated in slavish dependence, and enervated by luxury and sloth, where shall we find men who will stand forth to assert the rights of man;—or claim the privilege of moral beings, who should have but one road to excellence? Slavery to monarchs and ministers, which the world will be long in freeing itself from, and whose deadly grasp stops the progress of the human mind, is not yet abolished.

Let not men then in the pride of power, use the same arguments that tyrannic kings and venal ministers have used, and fallaciously assert that woman ought to be subjected because she has always been so.—But, when man, governed by reasonable laws, enjoys his natural freedom, let him despise woman, if she do not share it with him; and, till that glorious period arrives, in descanting on the folly of the sex, let him not overlook his own.

152: MARY WOLLSTONECRAFT. *A Vindication of the Rights of Woman*

1792

(Pp. 335–6.)

I MAY excite laughter, by dropping an hint, which I mean to pursue, some future time, for I really think that women ought to have representatives, instead of being arbitrarily governed without having any direct share allowed them in the deliberations of government.

But, as the whole system of representation is now, in this country, only a convenient handle for despotism, they need not complain, for they are as well represented as a numerous class of hard working mechanics, who pay for the support of royalty when they can scarcely stop their children's mouths with bread. How are they represented whose very sweat supports the splendid stud of an heir apparent, or varnishes the chariot of some female favourite who looks down on shame? Taxes on the very necessaries of life, enable an endless tribe of idle princes and princesses to pass with stupid pomp before a gaping crowd, who almost worship the very parade which costs them so dear. This is mere gothic grandeur, something like the barbarous useless parade of having sentinels on horseback at Whitehall, which I could never view without a mixture of contempt and indignation.

153: WILLIAM GODWIN. *Political Justice*

1793

(Book V, Chapter XIII; Book VIII, Chapters I, II, IV.)

NO man can be an useful member of society except so far as his talents are employed in a manner conducive to the general advantage. In every society the produce, the means of contributing to the necessities and conveniences of its members, is of a certain amount. In every society the bulk at least of its members contribute by their personal exertions to the creation of this produce. What can be more reasonable and just than that the produce itself should with some degree of equality be shared among them? What more injurious than the accumulating upon a few every means of superfluity and luxury to the total destruction of the ease and plain, but plentiful, subsistence of the many? It may be calculated that the king even of a limited monarchy receives as the salary of his office an income equivalent to the labour of fifty thousand men.[1] Let us set out in our estimate from this point and figure to ourselves the shares of his counsellors, his nobles, the wealthy commoners by whom the nobility will be emulated, their kindred and dependents. Is it any wonder that in such countries the lower orders of the community are exhausted by all the hardships of penury and immoderate fatigue?

[1] Taking the average price of labour at one shilling per diem.

When we see the wealth of a province spread upon the great man's table, can we be surprised that his neighbours have not bread to satiate the cravings of hunger ?

What is the criterion that must determine whether this or that substance capable of contributing to the benefit of a human being ought to be considered as your property or mine ? To this question there can be but one answer—Justice. Let us then recur to the principles of justice.

I have an hundred loaves in my possession, and in the next street there is a poor man expiring with hunger to whom one of these loaves would be the means of preserving his life. If I withhold this loaf from him, am I not unjust ? If I impart it, am I not complying with what justice demands ? To whom does the loaf justly belong ?

I suppose myself in other respects to be in easy circumstances, and that I do not want this bread as an object of barter or sale, to procure me any of the other necessaries of a human being. Our animal wants have long since been defined, and are stated to consist of food, clothing and shelter. If justice have any meaning, nothing can be more iniquitous than for one man to possess superfluities, while there is a human being in existence that is not adequately supplied with these.

It has been alleged that we find among different men very different degrees of labour and industry, and that it is not just they should receive an equal reward.

It cannot indeed be denied that the attainments of men in virtue and usefulness ought by no means to be confounded. How far the present system of property contributes to their being equitably treated it is very easy to determine. The present system of property confers on one man immense wealth in consideration of the accident of his birth. He that from beggary ascends to opulence is usually known not to have effected this transition by methods very creditable to his honesty or his usefulness. The most industrious and active member of society is frequently with great difficulty able to keep his family from starving.

But, to pass over these iniquitous effects of the unequal distribution of property, let us consider the nature of the reward which is thus proposed to industry. If you be industrious, you shall have an hundred times more food than you can eat and an hundred times more clothes than you can wear. Where is the justice of this? If I be the greatest benefactor the human species ever knew, is that a reason for bestowing on me what I do not want, especially when there are thousands to whom my superfluity would be of the greatest advantage? With this superfluity I can purchase nothing but gaudy ostentation and envy, nothing but the pitiful pleasure of returning to the poor under the name of generosity that to which reason gives them an irresistible claim, nothing but prejudice, error and vice.

If superfluity were banished, the necessity for the greater part of the manual industry of mankind would be superseded; and the rest, being amicably shared among all the active and vigorous members of the community, would be burthensome to none. Every man would have a frugal yet wholesome diet; every man would go forth to that moderate exercise of his corporal functions that would give hilarity to the spirits; none would be made torpid with fatigue, but all would have leisure to cultivate the kindly and philanthropical affections of the soul and to let loose his faculties in the search of intellectual improvement. What a contrast does this scene present us with the present state of human society, where the peasant and the labourer work till their understandings are benumbed with toil, their sinews contracted and made callous by being forever on the stretch, and their bodies invaded with infirmities and surrendered to an untimely grave? What is the fruit of this disproportioned and unceasing toil? At evening they return to a family famished with hunger, exposed half-naked to the inclemencies of the sky, hardly sheltered, and denied the slenderest instruction, unless in a few instances where it is dispensed by the hands of ostentatious charity and the first lesson communicated is unprincipled servility.

In reply, it may be observed in the first place that the equality for which we are pleading is an equality that would succeed to a state of great intellectual improvement. So bold a revolution cannot take place in human affairs till the general mind has been highly cultivated. The present age of mankind is greatly enlightened, but it is to be feared is not yet enlightened enough. Hasty and undigested tumults may take place under the idea of an equalisation of property; but it is only a calm and clear conviction of justice, of justice mutually to be rendered and received, of happiness to be produced by the desertion of our most rooted habits, that can introduce an invariable system of this sort. Attempts without this preparation will be productive only of confusion. Their effect will be momentary, and a new and more barbarous inequality will succeed. Each man with unaltered appetite will watch his opportunity to gratify his love of power or his love of distinction by usurping on his inattentive neighbours.

154: *THE LONDON GAZETTE.* Offer of a Reward by the Home Secretary

22 October 1793

(*The London Gazette*, 1793, p. 926.)

WHEREAS it has been humbly represented to the King, that a seditious Hand-Bill has been posted up on the Walls of Norwich, and circulated among the Inhabitants of that Town and it's Vicinity, of which the following is a Copy, viz.:

"To all real Lovers of liberty My Friends and Fellow Citizens.—It is with the greatest Joy I congratulate You on the Defeat of the combined Tyrants—Be assured that Liberty and Freedom will at last prevail. Tremble O thou Oppressor of the People, that reigneth upon the Throne, and ye Ministers of State, weep for ye shall fall, Weep oh ye Conductors of this vile and wicked War, ye who grind the Face of the Poor, oppress the People, and starve the Industrious Mechanic—My Friends, you are oppressed, you know it,—Revenge it, Lord Buckingham who died the other Day, had Thirty Thousand Pounds, yeerly For setting his Arse in the House of Lords, and doing nothing—Think of this, ye who work hard, and have hardly a Crust to put in your Mouths, think how many Wretches it would have made happy, in short my Friends Liberty calls aloud, ye who will hear her

Voice may you be free, and happy, He who does not let him starve and be *damned.*

Sunday, Sept. 14th.

N.B. Be resolute, and you shall be happy, he who wishes well to the Cause of Liberty, let him repair to
Chaple Field at
Five oClock
This Afternoon
to begin a Glorious Revolution."

His Majesty, for the better apprehending and bringing to Justice the Persons concerned in writing and publishing the Hand-Bill abovementioned, is hereby pleased to promise . . . a Reward of TWO HUNDRED POUNDS to any Person who shall make such Discovery as aforesaid, . . . upon the Conviction of One or more of the Offenders.

HENRY DUNDAS.

Whitehall, October 22, 1793.

155: THOMAS SPENCE. *The Restorer of Society to its Natural State, in the Important Trial of Thomas Spence, on May 27th, 1801*

Thomas Spence (1750–1814), bookseller, devoted his life to the advocacy of land nationalization and phonetic spelling. He was the founder of the Society of Spencean Philanthropists. (2nd ed., pp. 16, 48.)

BUT I contend that many Things are too sacred, and of too great Importance to the Happiness and Dignity of the human Race to be trafficked in, and in order to put a Stop to all illicit Trade, I begin with prohibiting all Commerce in Land, for that is the root of all the other Branches of injurious Trade. . . . It is natural enough of you to wonder why none of the modern Champions for the Rights of Man, should take Notice of my Scheme in their Books and Harangues, though I have been diligently publishing it these Five and Twenty Years, in great variety of shapes, and have sold many thousands of Copies. . . . Your surprise will cease when you reflect on the purity of the Plan, and the selfishness and avarice of the human Heart.

156: DEPOSITION ON THE SALE OF SPENCE'S PUBLICATIONS

17 May 1797

An anonymous letter to the Duke of Portland complains of the sale of ballads in Marylebone for ½d., entitled "The Rights of Man in verse", by children of 5 or 6 years. Evidence taken by the Constable is appended (Record Office, H. O. 119/1).

Substance of the Boy's Deposition

CHARLES CONNALLY aged about eleven years says he lodges with his Mother at the House of Mr. Spence No. 9 Oxford St.—that he this Dept. is employed by Spence to sell the Hand Bills called "the Rights of Man" for which Spence allows Deponent four pence out of every shilling being one third, that upon an average he makes four shillings per diem or thereabouts.

That there is another Boy employed daily to sell Publications called "The Rights of Man" who has the same allowance as Deponent, that they have been employed for this purpose about two months.

157: WILLIAM WINDHAM: Letter to W. J. Gurney

2 May 1792

(*Windham Papers*, I, pp. 104–5.)

WHAT are all the laws of property but the mere creatures of arbitrary appointment? And who shall be able to derive any one of them by a regular deduction from natural rights, so at least, as not to admit endless disputes about the authenticity of the pedigree? Suppose some one should take it into their head to write a work addressed to the labouring people, exposing to them the iniquity of that system which condemns half the world to labour for the other, and pleading for such a partition of goods, as may give to every one a competence and leave to none a superfluity. I am certainly not meaning to say that such arguments would be good ones: I am not meaning to say, that they might not be easily answered, but I should be sorry to undertake to answer them, in an auditory such as composes the majority of every parish in England. For some time the habitual respect which the laws have taught for property, would perhaps prevail: but when you have once well taught men to consider the power from which such laws proceed, as an usurpation, how much longer will the respect remain for regulations, unfavourable to their interests, which that power has ordained? How long will men acquiesce in laws, which condemn them to poverty, when they are to be maintained on no other ground than such agreement, as they can discern in them, with natural rights? Why publications of this sort should not be put forth, I don't see. You cannot punish them on any principles which permit the publication of many works now circulating; and you cannot dispute the competency of the common people to judge of the question of property, when you allow them to be judges of what are certainly not less difficult, the first principles of Government.

158: SHORT HINTS UPON LEVELLING, EXTRACTED FROM DR. VINCENT'S DISCOURSE ON MAY 13, 1792

See note to No. 95. (*Publications of the Society for preserving Liberty and Property.* At the Crown and Anchor in the Strand, 1793.)

ALL History and all experience prove, that wherever Society exists, there must exist a class of poor. . . . However it is the object and the interest of every good Government to alleviate poverty, all attempts to eradicate it, tend finally to the dissolution of society, and not to the removal of the evil. . . . I wish to speak a language which the meanest individual may understand; I wish to teach the poor that every plan of this sort is delusive, that even their own interest is concerned in the well-being of their superiors, and that whatever tends to dissolve the tie, instead of relieving their wants, would add tenfold to their misery. . . . I say then, that extensive commerce implies extensive capitals; that capitals are employed in the commerce of our own country equal to the property of Princes; that if the merchant was compelled to divide his substance by any law whatever, exclusive of the check it would be on his own industry, it would destroy the possibility of conducting any extensive commerce; and that if the merchant is driven from his profession, the manufacturer must fail, the loom must stand still, and the ploughshare rest in the furrow. . . . And the Poor themselves may learn, that if the ties which bind all orders together in this country were once dissolved, whatever calamities the wealthy might be involved in, would fall with double weight upon themselves, when there would be no recourse to look to—no friend, no protector, no benefactor.

159: ARCHDEACON PALEY. *Reasons for Contentment*

1792

William Paley, Archdeacon of Carlisle and philosopher (1743–1805), was the author of *Principles of Moral and Political Philosophy*, which includes the famous pigeon analogy, *Evidences of Christianity*, *Reasons for Contentment*, etc. He was regarded by Coleridge, not with approval, as the great exponent of "other-worldly" utilitarian morality. (Pp. 5–7, 13, 20.)

THE Laws which accidentally cast enormous estates into one great man's possession, are, after all, the self same laws which protect and guard the poor man. . . . Of the two, it is rather more the concern of the poor to stand up for the laws than of the rich; for it is the Law which defends the weak against the strong, the humble against the powerful, the little against the great. . . . Service in England is, as it ought to be, voluntary and by contract; a fair exchange of work for wage; an equal bargain, in which each party has his rights and his redress; wherein every servant chuses his master. Can this be mended? . . . Religion smoothes all inequalities, because it unfolds a prospect which makes all earthly distinctions nothing.

160: THE EARL OF RADNOR. Charge to the Grand Jury of the County of Berks.

15 January 1793

Jacob Pleydell-Bouverie, Earl of Radnor (1750–1829), was Lord Lieutenant of Berkshire, 1791–1819. He is described by a contemporary as a "grand Borer after forms and precedents in the House of Lords and Dictator at Quarter Sessions and Turnpike meetings, by way of relaxation in the Country." (*Liberty and Property preserved against Republicans and Levellers, a collection of Tracts*, No. IX, 1793. See note to No. 95.)

THERE are people senseless or wicked enough to propagate notions of Equality, and by disturbing the public with "false alarms of imaginary evils, and foolish conceits of imaginary good," endeavour to destroy all subordination. *But a disparity of conditions I hold to be universally necessary*, for it universally exists.

It is an obvious objection to us who are seated on this Bench, that we are interested in maintaining the distinctions of Rank and Fortune. It is an objection of an invidious kind, but it is one to which we ought and are able and willing to give a direct and sufficient answer. True, we are personally interested in maintaining them, but with respect to that of Fortune, all the members of every great community whatever are likewise interested, for it is evident that no community can have either happiness or respectability (if indeed it can exist) unless some members of it have that distinction; and, with respect to Difference of Rank, all the inhabitants of this kingdom are interested in the maintenance of it, for it is essential and fundamental to our form of Government, and *it remains to be proved that any Government in the world is, or ever was, comparable to ours.*

161: THE ENGLISHMAN'S POLITICAL CATECHISM

1793

(*Liberty and Property preserved against Republicans and Levellers, a collection of Tracts*, No. X, 1793. See note to No. 95.)

Q. What is meant by the word *Reform*?

A. It is a *suspicious* word.

Q. Why?

A. Because I hear it made use of by the same people who want to deceive me with the terms *Liberty*, *Equality*, and the *Rights of Man*.

Q. What is their intention?

A. They have shewn it by their seditious speeches and writings. Their endeavours are to make us dissatisfied with our condition, and weary of being happy; to raise a spirit of discontent in the nation.

Q. But do you not think the manner of Representation of the People in Parliament ought to be altered?

A. No.

Q. Why?

A. Because, if the mode of election be altered, and the scale of it extended, *men of property*, interested *by that property* in the real welfare and stability of the nation, would not be chosen; but *cunning, low-minded men, who had nothing to lose.* Actuated by the lust of *power* and *gain*, under the mask of *Equality*, they would give the watch-word to their Friends without doors—declare the King and Lords useless (as the case was in the days of Cromwell), and fabricate what *they would call a Republic*, but, in other words, a *violent usurpation of all the lands and property of the kingdom*, which would be at the disposal of them and their adherents.

162: ARTHUR YOUNG. *The Example of France a Warning to Britain*

1793

(Pp. 32–3.)

LET the farmers of this kingdom represent to themselves a picture of what their situation would be, if their labourers, their servants, and the paupers whom they support by poor's rates, were all armed, and, in some measure, regimented, and in possession of the vestry, voting not only the money to be raised by rates, but the division of it among themselves; decreeing what the price of all the farmer's products should be; what wages should be paid to servants, and what pay to labourers. Under such a system of government, I beg to ask, what security would remain for a single shilling in the pockets of those who are at present in a state of ease and affluence?

163: ARTHUR YOUNG. *The Example of France a Warning to Britain*

1793

(P. 48.)

IN any representative government, if persons only are represented,—that is to say, if a man without a shilling deputes equally with another, who has property, and if men in the former situation are ten times more numerous than those in the latter; and if the representatives, so chosen, sit for so short a time as to vote truely the wills of their constituents, it follows, by direct consequence, that all the property of the society is at the mercy of those who possess nothing; and could theory have blundered so stupidly, as to suppose for a moment, that attack and plunder would not follow power in such hands; let it recur to France for *fact*, to prove what reason ought to have foreseen.

164: JOSEPH TOWERS. *A Dialogue between an Associator and a well-informed Englishman*

1793

Joseph Towers (1737–99), was a bookseller, a dissenting minister, and the editor of *British Biography*, as well as author of many political and other pamphlets. An Associator was a member of the *Association for preserving Liberty and Property against Republicans and Levellers*. For this, see note to No. 95. (Towers, *Tracts on Political and Other Subjects*, 1796, III, pp. 201–2.)

Mr. Grantley. One idea which has prevailed, and which has contributed to enflame the minds of some persons, is, that pains had been taken to propagate among the common people the doctrine of *equality*; or, that all persons should be rendered equal in point of fortune, or property; a doctrine which would certainly lead to great confusion, and to very serious evils.

Mr. Mordaunt. The doctrine of an equality of property has not been propagated by any of the societies of the friends of liberty in Great Britain. . . . If the doctrine has been at all disseminated among the people, it has been by those truly libellous publications, which have been issued by the pretended associators against republicans and levellers. In order to calumniate the real friends of freedom, they have undertaken to refute a doctrine which no man advanced.

165: WILLIAM THOMSON. *A Letter to Dr. Parr*

(Date uncertain)

William Thomson (1746–1817), a former Scottish minister, took up a literary career in London. He was connected with the *Annual Register* and *The English Review.*

THAT all men are equal by nature, is a fiction that may be innocent enough, so long as it is not made a lever for subverting constitutions that have actually grown up and flourished in inequality. . . . Sound policy often can recognize no other right than that of long and uninterrupted occupancy. But if a nicer and more general foundation of property exists, on what is it founded? If it be said, Providence, equally concerned for all his children, bestows equal rights and privileges on all, it is most obvious to answer, that neither are equal rights and privileges, in fact, extended to all men; nor human happiness greatly, if at all, affected by the circumstance of disparity of rank in life. . . . There is no human state in which a certain degree of enjoyment is not found; none in which there is not room for the exercise of virtue; none that is entirely excluded from hope, the greatest balm of life, either in the lowest or the most exalted stations.

166: EDMUND BURKE. *Thoughts and Details on Scarcity*

1795

(*Works*, V, pp. 83–109.)

OF all things, an indiscreet tampering with the trade of provisions is the most dangerous, and it is always worst in the time when men are most disposed to it; that is, in the time of scarcity. Because there is nothing on which the passions of men are so violent, and their judgment so weak, and on which there exists such a multitude of ill-founded popular prejudices.

To provide for us in our necessities is not in the power of government. It would be a vain presumption in statesmen to think they can do it. The people maintain them, and not they the people. It is in the power of government to prevent much evil; it can do very little positive good in this, or perhaps in anything else. It is not only so of the state and statesman, but of all the classes and descriptions of the rich—they are the pensioners of the poor, and are maintained by their superfluity. They are under an absolute, hereditary, and indefeasible dependence on those who labour, and are miscalled the poor.

The labouring people are only poor, because they are numerous. Numbers in their nature imply poverty. In a fair distribution among a vast multitude none can have much. That class of dependent pensioners called the rich is so extremely small, that if all their throats were cut, and a distribution made of all they consume in a year, it would not give a bit of bread and cheese for one night's supper to those who labour, and who in reality feed both the pensioners and themselves.

But the throats of the rich ought not to be cut, nor their magazines plundered; because in their persons they are trustees for those who labour, and their hoards are the banking houses of these latter. Whether they mean it or not, they do, in effect, execute their trust—some with more, some with less, fidelity and judgment. But, on the whole, the duty is performed, and everything returns, deducting some very trifling commission and discount, to the place from whence it arose. When the poor rise to destroy the rich, they act as wisely for their own purposes, as when they burn mills, and throw corn into the river, to make bread cheap.

It is therefore the first and fundamental interest of the labourer, that the farmer should have a full incoming profit on the product of his labour. The proposition is self-evident, and nothing but the malignity, perverseness, and ill-governed passions of mankind, and particularly the envy they bear to each other's prosperity, could prevent their seeing and acknowledging it, with thankfulness to the benign and wise Disposer of all things, who obliges men, whether they will or not, in pursuing their own selfish interests, to connect the general good with their own individual success.

And, first, I premise that labour is, as I have already intimated, a commodity, and, as such, an article of trade. If I am right in this notion, then labour must be subject to all the laws and principles of trade, and not to regulations foreign to them, and that may be totally inconsistent with those principles and those laws. When any commodity is carried to market, it is not the necessity of the vender, but the necessity of the purchaser, that raises the price. The extreme want of the seller has rather (by the nature of things with which we shall in vain contend) the direct contrary operation. If the goods at market are beyond the demand, they fall in their value; if below it, they rise. The impossibility of the subsistence of a man, who carries his labour to a market, is totally beside the question in this way of viewing it. The only question is, what is it worth to the buyer?

I beseech the government (which I take in the largest sense of the word, comprehending the two Houses of parliament) seriously to consider that years of scarcity or plenty do not come alternately, or at short intervals, but in pretty long cycles and irregularly, and consequently that we cannot assure ourselves, if we take a wrong measure, from the temporary necessities of one season; but that the next, and probably more, will drive us to the continuance of it; so that, in my opinion, there is no way of preventing this evil, which goes to the destruction of all our agriculture, and of that part of our internal commerce which touches our agriculture the most nearly, as well as the safety and very being of government, but manfully to resist the very first idea, speculative or practical, that it is within the competence of government, taken as government, or even of the rich, as rich, to supply to the poor those necessaries which it has pleased the Divine Providence for a while to withhold from them. We, the people, ought to be made sensible, that it is not in breaking the laws of commerce, which are the laws of nature, and consequently the laws of God, that we are to place our hope of softening the Divine displeasure to remove any calamity under which we suffer, or which hangs over us.

Tyranny and cruelty may make men justly wish the downfall of abused powers, but I believe that no government ever yet perished from any other direct cause than its own weakness. My opinion is against an over-doing of any sort of administration, and more especially against this most momentous of all meddling on the part of authority; the meddling with the subsistence of the people.

167: CHARLES JAMES FOX. Speech in the Debate on the High Price of Corn, House of Commons

3 November 1795

(*Parliamentary History*, XXXII, pp. 240–2.)

AN hon. gentleman has thrown out some ideas with respect to the state of agriculture. Much of what he said I highly approve. But though I admit the facts which he has stated, as well as the exigency of the crisis, I cannot agree with him as to the propriety of resorting to any system of coercion by way of remedy. I doubt whether such a remedy would be effectual; I fear it might increase the evil. Scope must always be left to the exertions of industry: attempt to fetter and you always destroy them. The proprietor must be allowed to let his land, the farmer to conduct his business and bring his grain to market, in the way which they find most convenient for their own interest. In the course of investigating the subject, I have found some of my friends to whose authority I pay great deference, who thought that the state of the country required coercive measures. I, however, have not been able to coincide with them in this opinion. The state of a country which calls for such measures, must be one nearly approaching to famine. Even then, their effect could only be temporary, and extorted by the exigency of the moment: they might last perhaps for a week or a fortnight, or a month, but then they must necessarily cease. I object to them, not merely because they are inefficient, but because they are, in themselves inconsistent with that just and liberal protection which ought to be afforded to industry, and with that wise and sound policy which best secures the interests of the public, by keeping up a spirit of competition in the market.

There are some who think that the price of labour has not kept pace with the increased price of provisions. I am afraid that this disproportion too much takes place in almost all the counties of England, and that while provisions have been rapidly rising to an unexampled height, labour has by no means advanced in proportion. It is, indeed, a melancholy and alarming fact, that the great majority of the people of England—an enormous and dreadful majority—are no longer in a situation in which they can boast that they live by the produce of their labour; and that it does regularly happen, during the pressure of every inclement season, that the industrious poor are obliged to depend for subsistence on the supplies afforded by the charity of the rich. I agree in opinion with those who think that the price of labour ought to be advanced, and the great majority of the people of England, freed from a precarious and degrading dependence. But I much question whether any compulsory measures ought to be adopted for this purpose. Disapproving, as I do, in every instance of coercion, excepting where it is called for by the last necessity, and justified by the occasion which gives it birth, I wish this salutary measure, of advancing the wages, to proceed, rather from the justice and humanity of the gentlemen in the different counties, than from the obligation of a legislative act.

168: THOMAS PAINE. *Agrarian Justice*

1796

NOTHING could be more unjust than Agrarian Law[1] in a country improved by cultivation; for though every man, as an inhabitant of the earth, is a joint proprietor of it in its natural state, it does not follow that he is a joint proprietor of cultivated earth. The additional value made by cultivation, after the system was admitted, became the property of those who did it, or who inherited it from them, or who purchased it. It had originally an owner. Whilst, therefore, I advocate the right, and interest myself in the hard case of all those who have been thrown out of their natural inheritance by the introduction of the system of landed property, I equally defend the right of the possessor to the part which is his.

[1] The *loi agraire* was the eighteenth-century French term for communism of property. It was derived from the Agrarian Laws of the Gracchi

169: EDMUND BURKE. *Letters on a Regicide Peace*

1796

(*Works*, V, p. 207.)

JACOBINISM is the revolt of the enterprising talents of a country against its property. When private men form themselves into associations for the purpose of destroying the pre-existing laws and institutions of their country; when they secure to themselves an army, by dividing amongst the people of no property the estates of the ancient and lawful proprietors; when a state recognises those acts; when it does not make confiscations for crimes, but makes crimes for confiscations; when it has its principal strength, and all its resources, in such a violation of property; when it stands chiefly upon such a violation; massacring by judgments, or otherwise, those who make any struggle for their old legal government, and their legal, hereditary, or acquired possessions—I call this *Jacobinism by establishment.*

170: HANNAH MORE. Charge to the Women of the Shipham Club

1801

(*Mendip Annuals, the Journal of Martha More*, edited by A. Roberts, 1859, pp. 243–4.)

YET, let me remind you that probably that very scarcity has been permitted by an all-wise and gracious Providence to *unite* all ranks of people *together*, to shew the *poor* how immediately they are dependent on the *rich*, and to shew both *rich* and *poor* that they are all dependent on *Himself*. It has also enabled you to see more clearly the advantages you derive from the government and constitution of this country—to observe the benefits flowing from the distinction of rank and fortune, which has enabled the high so liberally to assist the low; for I leave you to judge what would have been the state of the poor of this country in this long, distressing scarcity had it not been for your superiors. . . . *You* are not the *only* sufferers . . . it has fallen in some degree on all ranks. . . . We trust the poor in general, especially those that are well instructed, have received what has been done for them as a matter of *favour*, not of *right*.

Church and State

171: *THE GENTLEMAN'S MAGAZINE.* A Review of the Case of the Protestant Dissenters with Reference to the Corporation and Test Acts

1790

(*Gentleman's Magazine*, 1790, Part I, pp. 248–51.)

THAT a dissenter, whatever may be his integrity and piety, whatever may be the grounds of his dissent, is an unfit person to be entrusted with command, authority, and influence, in any state in which the civil magistrate takes a particular church under his protection, is an axiom in politics of which, it is hoped, a regular proof is not at this time wanting. Ill-will to the establishment must, in all governments, belong to the character of a Dissenter, if he be an honest man.

172: MRS. BARBAULD. *An Address to the Opposers of the Repeal of the Corporation and Test Acts*

1790

(Pp. 11–13, 15–16.)

We could wish to be considered as children of the State, though we are not so of the Church. She must excuse us if we look upon the alliance between her and the State as an ill-sorted union, and herself as a mother-in-law who, with the too frequent arts of that relation, is ever endeavouring to prejudice the State, the common father of us all, against a part of his offspring, for the sake of appropriating a larger portion to her own children. We claim no share in the dowry of her who is not our mother, but we may be pardoned for thinking it hard to be deprived of the inheritance of our father.

But it is objected to us that we have sinned in the manner of making our request, we have brought it forward as a claim instead of asking it as a favour. We should have sued, and crept, and humbled ourselves. Our preachers and our writers should not have dared to express the warm glow of honest sentiment, or, even in a foreign country glance at the downfall of a haughty aristocracy. As we were suppliants, we should have behaved like suppliants, and then perhaps—No, Gentlemen, we wish to have it understood, that we *do* claim it as a right. It loses otherwise half its value.

We claim it as men, we claim it as citizens, we claim it as good subjects. We are not conscious of having brought the disqualification upon ourselves by a failure in any of these characters.

But this it is again imputed to us is no contest for religious liberty, but a contest for power, and place, and influence. We want civil offices—And why should citizens *not* aspire to civil offices ? Why should not the fair field of generous competition be freely opened to every one ?—A contention for power—It is not a contention for power between Churchmen and Dissenters, nor is it as Dissenters we wish to enter the lists; we wish to bury every name of distinction in the common appellation of Citizen. We wish not the name of Dissenter to be pronounced, except in our theological researches and religious assemblies. It is you, who by considering us as Aliens, make us so. It is you who force us to make our dissent a prominent feature in our character. It is you who give relief, and cause to come out upon the canvas what we modestly wished to have shaded over, and thrown into the background. If we are a party, remember it is you who force us to be so.

173: EDMUND BURKE. Speech on Mr. Fox's Motion for the Repeal of the Test and Corporation Acts, House of Commons

2 March 1790

(*Parliamentary History*, XXVIII, p. 437.)

MR. Burke dwelt on the destruction of the establishment of the French church as a circumstance peculiarly shameful and scandalous. Those who had compared the church of Rome to the whore of Babylon, the kirk of Scotland to a kept mistress, and the church of England to something between a prostitute and a modest woman, would probably be preaching up the same doctrines to their congregations, while the rising race of dissenters were, perhaps, imbibing those principles so pernicious in themselves, and so dangerous to the safety of the established church of this country; and how could he tell but that it would end in the acting the same shameful scene, respecting the plunder of the wealth and revenues, and the accompanying demolition of our church, as it had done in the case of the church of France?

174: HANNAH MORE. *Remarks on the Speech of M. Dupont*

1793

(*Works*, VI, pp. 315–6.)

IT is much to be suspected, that certain opinions in politics have a tendency to lead to certain opinions in religion. Where so much is at stake, they will do well to keep their consciences tender, in order to which they should try to keep their discernment acute. They will do well to observe, that the same restless spirit of innovation is busily operating under various, though seemingly unconnected forms; to observe, that the same impatience of restraint, the same contempt of order, peace, and subordination, which makes men bad citizens, makes them bad Christians; and that to this secret, but almost infallible connexion between religious and political sentiment, does France owe her present unparalleled anarchy and impiety.

175: JOSEPH PRIESTLEY. *An Appeal to the Public, on the Subject of the Riots in Birmingham*

1791

Joseph Priestley (1733–1804), Unitarian minister, theologian, scientist and political pamphleteer, was the chief victim of the Birmingham " Church and King " Riots of July 1791. During these disturbances, the two Unitarian meeting houses and Priestley's own house were sacked and burned. In 1794 he withdrew to America. (Pp. 59–60.)

THAT the true source of the late riots in Birmingham was *religious bigotry*, and the animosity of the high church party against the Dissenters, and especially against the Presbyterians and Unitarians, and not the commemoration of the French Revolution, is evident from all that has passed *before*, *at*, and *after*, the day.

In the public houses where the people were inflaming themselves with liquor, all that day, and some time before, there were heard execrations of the most horrid kind against *the Presbyterians*. One person was heard not only to wish *damnation* to them, but that " God Almighty would make a week's holiday for the purpose of damning them." The mob did not arrive at the Hotel till more than two hours after the company had left it, and there they demanded only *myself*, who had not been there. No part of their vengeance fell upon any churchman, whether at the dinner or not. After demolishing the two meeting-houses, and every thing belonging to *me*, their next objects were the houses of Mr. Taylor and Mr. John Ryland, who were well known to have been much averse to the scheme of the Dinner; and during the whole course of the outrages, the constant cry was CHURCH AND KING, and DOWN WITH THE PRESBYTERIANS.

176: DR. HORSLEY. *A Sermon preached before the Lords Spiritual and Temporal on January* 23, 1793; *being the Anniversary of the Martyrdom of King Charles the First*

1793

IT was a signal instance of God's mercy, not imputing to the people of this land the atrocious deed of a desperate faction; it was a signal instance of God's mercy, that the goodly fabric was not crushed, in the middle of the last century, ere it had attained its finished perfection, by the phrensy of that fanatical banditti, which took the life of the First Charles. In the madness and confusion, which followed the shedding of that blood, our History holds forth an edifying example of the effects, that are ever to be expected—in that example, it gives warning of the effects, that ever are INTENDED, by the dissemination of those infernal maxims, that Kings are the servants of the people, punishable by their Masters. The same lesson is confirmed by the horrid example, which the present Law exhibits, in the unparalleled misery of a neighbouring Nation; once great in Learning, Arts and Arms! Now torn by contending factions! Her Government demolished! Her Altars overthrown! Her First-born despoiled of their Birth right! Her Nobles degraded! Her best Citizens exiled! Her riches, sacred and profane, given up to the pillage of sacrilege and rapine!

Athiests directing her Councils! Desperados conducting her Armies! Wars of unjust and chimerical ambition consuming her Youth! Her Granaries exhausted! Her Fields uncultivated! Famine threatening her multitudes! Her Streets swarming with Assassins, filled with violence, deluged with blood! . . . A monarch deliberately murdered!

Let us remember that a conscientious submission to the Sovereign Powers is, no less than brotherly love, a distinctive badge of Christ's disciples. Blessed be God, in the Church of England both those marks of genuine Christianity have ever been conspicuous. Perhaps in the exercise of brotherly love, it is the amiable infirmity of Englishmen, to be too easy to admit the claim of a spiritual kindred. The times compel me to remark, that brotherly love embraces only brethren. . . . If any enjoying the blessings of the British Government, living under the protection of its free Constitution, and its equal Laws, have DARED to avow the WICKED sentiment, that this day of national contrition, this rueful day of guilt and shame, " is a PROUD day for England, to be remembered as such by the latest posterity of freemen," with such persons it is meet that we abjure all brotherhood.

177: JOSEPH PRIESTLEY. Preface to Fast Sermon of 1794

(*Memoirs of Joseph Priestley*, 1806, p. 145.)

AFTER what has taken place with respect to Birmingham, all idea of much hazard for insulting and abusing the Dissenters is entirely vanished; whereas the disposition to injure the Catholics was effectually checked by the proceedings of the year 1781. From that time *they* have been safe, and I rejoice in it. But from the year 1791, the Dissenters have been more exposed to insult and outrage than ever.

If, then, my real crime has not been *sedition*, or *treason*, what has it been ? . . . In my opinion, it cannot have been any thing but my open hostility to the doctrines of the established church, and more especially to all civil establishments of religion whatever. This has brought upon me the implacable resentment of the great body of the clergy.

178: DR. PARR

(*Memoirs of the Rev. Samuel Parr*, by the Rev. W. Field, 1828, I, 309.)

IT happened, at this period, that, dining in a public company, Dr. Parr was called upon to drink " Church and King "—the watch-word of a party, and the reigning toast of the times. At first, he resolutely declined. But the obligation of compliance being urgently pressed upon him—rising, at length, with firmness and dignity—with a manner of impressive solemnity, and with a voice of powerful energy, he spoke thus—" I am compelled to drink the toast given from the chair; but I shall do so, with my own comment. Well, then, gentlemen—Church and King.—Once it was the toast of Jacobites; now it is the toast of incendiaries. It means a church without the gospel—and a king above the law! "

179: EDMUND BURKE. *Reflections on the Revolution in France*

1790

(*Works*, II, pp. 363–6.)

WE know, and it is our pride to know, that man is by his constitution a religious animal; that atheism is against, not only our reason, but our instincts; and that it cannot prevail long. But if, in the moment of riot, and in a drunken delirium from the hot spirit drawn out of the alembic of hell, which in France is now so furiously boiling, we should uncover our nakedness, by throwing off that Christian religion which has hitherto been our boast and comfort, and one great source of civilization amongst us, and amongst many other nations, we are apprehensive (being well aware that the mind will not endure a void) that some uncouth, pernicious, and degrading superstition might take place of it.

First, I beg leave to speak of our church establishment, which is the first of our prejudices, not a prejudice destitute of reason, but involving in it profound and extensive wisdom. I speak of it first. It is first, and last, and midst in our minds. For, taking ground on that religious system, of which we are now in possession, we continue to act on the early received and uniformly continued sense of mankind. That sense not only, like a wise architect, hath built up the august fabric of states, but like a provident proprietor, to preserve the structure from profanation and ruin, as a sacred temple purged from all the impurities of fraud, and violence, and injustice, and tyranny, hath solemnly and forever consecrated the commonwealth, and all that officiate in it. This consecration is made, that all who administer in the government of men, in which they stand in the person of God himself, should have high and worthy notions of their function and destination; that their hope should be full of immortality; that they should not look to the paltry pelf of the moment, nor to the temporary and transient praise of the vulgar, but to a solid, permanent existence, in the permanent part of their nature, and to a permanent fame and glory, in the example they leave as a rich inheritance to the world.

Such sublime principles ought to be infused into persons of exalted situations; and religious establishments provided, that may continually revive and enforce them. Every sort of moral, every sort of civil, every sort of politic institution, aiding the rational and natural ties that connect the human understanding and affections to the divine, are not more than necessary, in order to build up that wonderful structure Man; whose prerogative it is, to be in a great degree a creature of his own making; and who, when made as he ought to be made, is destined to hold no trivial place in the creation. But whenever man is put over men, as the better nature ought ever to preside, in that case more particularly, he should as nearly as possible be approximated to his perfection.

The consecration of the state, by a state religious

establishment, is necessary also to operate with a wholesome awe upon free citizens; because, in order to secure their freedom, they must enjoy some determinate portion of power. To them therefore a religion connected with the state, and with their duty towards it, becomes even more necessary than in such societies, where the people, by the terms of their subjection, are confined to private sentiments, and the management of their own family concerns. All persons possessing any portion of power ought to be strongly and awfully impressed with an idea that they act in trust: and that they are to account for their conduct in that trust to the one great Master, Author, and Founder of society.

This principle ought even to be more strongly impressed upon the minds of those who compose the collective sovereignty, than upon those of single princes. Without instruments, these princes can do nothing. Whoever uses instruments, in finding helps, finds also impediments. Their power is therefore by no means complete; nor are they safe in extreme abuse. Such persons, however elevated by flattery, arrogance, and self-opinion, must be sensible, that, whether covered or not by positive law, in some way or other they are accountable even here for the abuse of their trust. If they are not cut off by a rebellion of their people, they may be strangled by the very janissaries kept for their security against all other rebellion. Thus we have seen the king of France sold by his soldiers for an increase of pay. But where popular authority is absolute and unrestrained, the people have an infinitely greater, because a far better founded, confidence in their own power. They are themselves, in a great measure, their own instruments. They are nearer to their objects. Besides, they are less under responsibility to one of the greatest controlling powers on earth, the sense of fame and estimation. The share of infamy, that is likely to fall to the lot of each individual in public acts, is small indeed; the operation of opinion being in the inverse ratio to the number of those who abuse power. Their own approbation of their own acts has to them the appearance of a public judgment in their favour. A perfect democracy is therefore the most shameless thing in the world. As it is the most shameless, it is also the most fearless. No man apprehends in his person that he can be made subject to punishment. Certainly the people at large never ought: for as all punishments are for example towards the conservation of the people at large, the people at large can never become the subject of punishment by any human hand.[1] It is therefore of infinite importance that they should not be suffered to imagine that their will, any more than that of kings, is the standard of right and wrong. They ought to be persuaded that they are full as little entitled, and far less qualified, with safety to themselves, to use any arbitrary power whatsoever; that therefore they are not, under a false show of liberty, but in truth, to exercise an unnatural, inverted domination, tyrannically to exact, from those who officiate in the state, not an entire devotion to their interest, which is their right, but an abject submission to their occasional will; extinguishing thereby, in all those who serve them, all moral principle, all sense of dignity, all use of judgment, and all consistency of character; whilst by the very same process they give themselves up a proper, a suitable, but a most contemptible prey to the servile ambition of popular sycophants, or courtly flatterers.

[1] Quicquid multis peccatur inultem.

When the people have emptied themselves of all the lust of selfish will, which without religion it is utterly impossible they ever should, when they are conscious that they exercise, and exercise perhaps in a higher link of the order of delegation, the power, which to be legitimate must be according to that eternal, immutable law, in which will and reason are the same, they will be more careful how they place power in base and incapable hands. In their nomination to office, they will not appoint to the exercise of authority, as to a pitiful job, but as to a holy function; not according to their sordid, selfish interest, nor to their wanton caprice, nor to their arbitrary will; but they will confer that power, (which any man may well tremble to give or to receive) on those only, in whom they may discern that predominant proportion of active virtue and wisdom, taken together and fitted to the charge, such, as in the great and inevitable mixed mass of human imperfections and infirmities, is to be found.

180: WILLIAM BELSHAM. *Observations on the Test Laws*

(Date Uncertain)

(Belsham, *Essays Philosophical and Moral*, 1799, II, pp. 129–30.)

THE spirit of the church, in a political view, differs indeed most essentially from the spirit of the constitution, or rather it is diametrically opposite to it. For the existence of its legislative powers it is dependent entirely upon the crown, which by virtue of its supremacy has wisely suspended, or rather annihilated the exercise of them. Its executive powers are subject to no regular superintendency or control, and its judicial powers are universally execrated as dark, oppressive, and despotic. The church presumptuously claims indeed to be *an ally* of the state, as if it were a co-ordinate or independent power: and talks of the two-fold nature of the constitution, as if the Act of Toleration was not as much a part of the constitution as the Act of Uniformity. But the church is, in a civil view, the mere creation of the state, which supports what it originally formed, not as ALLY, which is only a softer term for a rival to itself, but as a mere human institution, established for the purpose of instructing the people in the principles of morality and religion.

181: JOSEPH PRIESTLEY. *Letters to the Rt. Hon. Edmund Burke*

1791

(Pp. 52–3.)

THAT our readers may see at one view what it is that you maintain with respect to civil establishments of religion, I shall, before I enter upon the discussion of them, give our readers a summary view of all your positions. Confounding, as you evidently do, the idea of *religion* itself, with that of the *civil establishment* of it, you say, " It is the basis of civil society, and essential to every state," insomuch that you even question whether it be *lawful* to be without one. So far, you think, is the church from having any dependence upon the state, that the state has not even " the property, or dominion," of any thing belonging to the church, being only the " guardian " of the revenues of the church, and holding them in trust for its use. You, therefore, hold that the property of the church is unalienable, and not to be touched in any emergency of state whatever. Religion, you maintain, derives its estimation and effect, from the riches and magnificence of its establishment; that such establishment is calculated for the multitude, that it is peculiarly useful both to the poor and the rich, and, though necessary to all states, is more proper for a democratical, than any other form of government.

Now, Sir, strange as it may appear to you, my ideas, in all these respects, are the very reverse of yours. Religion I consider as a thing that requires no civil establishment whatever, and that its beneficial operation is injured by such establishment, and the more in proportion to its riches. I am satisfied that such an establishment, instead of being any advantage, is a great incumbrance to a state, and in general highly unfavourable to its liberties. Civil establishments of christianity were altogether unknown in the early ages, and gained ground by very slow degrees, as other corruptions and abuses in the system did. I am clearly of opinion, that the state has a right to dispose of *all* property within itself; that of the church, as well as of every thing else of a public nature, and that religion has naturally nothing at all to do with any particular form of civil government; being useful indeed to all persons, the rich as well as the poor, but only as individuals.

182: JOSEPH PRIESTLEY. *Letters to the Rt. Hon. Edmund Burke*

1791

(Pp. 58–60.)

YOU, Sir, appear to defend church establishments on the latter of these principles. " The christian statesman ", you say, " must first provide for the multitude, because it is the multitude, and is therefore, as such, the first object in the ecclesiastical institution, and in all institutions." But how does this apply to the case of your country of Ireland. For the very same reason that episcopacy ought to be established in England, and presbyterianism in Scotland, the Roman catholic ought to be the established religion of Ireland, because, as I apprehend, it is unquestionably the religion of a very great majority of the inhabitants. As to the great mass of the oppressed Irish, if they be asked whether it be *their* religion, that which they really approve, that they are obliged to maintain, they will say it is a *foreign* one, one that they disbelieve and detest, and yet are compelled to support, whilst from genuine zeal, they think it their duty to maintain their own. It is not supposed that more than one in ten of the inhabitants of Ireland are of the church of England, and yet the iron hand of power compels them to maintain it. Is this, think you, the way to recommend your religion ? Judge by the effect. What converts have been made to it in the last two centuries ?

The zealous members of your church, in the reign of the two Charles's of blessed memory, imposed episcopacy also upon Scotland, when not more than one in a hundred of the Scots would attend the service; but the generous spirit of that nation at length threw off the oppressive yoke. The Irish also have the will, but, alas, not the power.

If you will have an establishment, and act upon the principles that you profess, viz. to provide for the *multitude*, or the great mass of the people, do you, of your own accord, change the established religion of Ireland, to one more consonant to the genius and wishes of the nation; and let it not be said that the church of England would have the impudence, if it had the power, to collect its tithes from every country in christendom, though every parish should be a *sinecure*, and all their bishops be denominated *in partibus*. Let there be an appearance at least which now there is not, of some regard to *religion* in the case, and not to mere *revenue*. Often as I have urged this subject, and many as have been those who have animadverted upon my writings, hardly any have touched upon *this*. They feel it to be tender ground. They can, however, keep an obstinate silence, they can shut their ears, and turn their eyes to other objects, when it is not to their purpose to attend to this.

Admitting that religion must be *established*, or supported by civil power, in order to its efficiency, will *any* species of religion answer the purpose, the heathen, or the Mahometan, as well as the christian, and one species of christianity as well as another? Must we have no *discussion* concerning the nature, and influence, of the different kinds of religion, in order that, if we happen to have got a worse, we may relieve ourselves by substituting a better in its place? Must every thing once established be, for that reason only, ever maintained? This is said, indeed, to be your maxim, openly avowed in the House of Commons, and, it is perfectly agreeable to every thing advanced in this publication. For you condemn the French National Assembly, for innovating in *their* religion, which is Catholic, as much as you could do the English Parliament, for innovating in *ours*, which is Protestant. You condemn them for lowering the state of archbishops, bishops and abbots, though they have improved that of the lower orders of the clergy; and therefore you would, no doubt, be equally offended at any diminution of the power of cardinals, or of the pope. We may therefore presume, that had you lived in Turkey, you would have been a mahometan, and in Tartary, a devout worshipper of the grand lama.

PART VII

THE REVOLUTIONARY WAR

183: LORD GRENVILLE. Letter to the Marquis of Buckingham

14 September 1789

(The Duke of Buckingham, *Courts and Cabinets of George III*, 1853, II, p. 165.)

WE have no sort of news. The French Assembly is going on with endless disputes about their Constitution; but one ought to be much more interested than I feel myself in the event of these disputes, not to be heartily tired of hearing of them. The main point appears quite secure, that they will not for many years be in a situation to molest the invaluable peace which we now enjoy.

184: HENRY DUNDAS. Letter to Richard Burke

20 September 1791

Henry Dundas, Viscount Melville (1742–1811), was for nearly thirty years the political manager and chief dispenser of patronage for Scotland. Lord Advocate in 1775, he held many offices until his impeachment for corruption in 1805. As Home Secretary from 1791 to 1794 he was responsible for the sedition trials. His influence on military operations as Secretary of State for War, 1794 to 1801, is bitterly criticized by Fortescue. (*Memorials and Correspondence of Charles James Fox*, III, 9–10.)

YOU will naturally feel that my situation prevents me entering into any of the discussions you are so good as to lay before me. The line of the British Government, to adhere to an honest and fair neutrality, being taken, and everywhere announced, it is impossible for any member of Government to give way to any indulgence of any speculations on the subject of French affairs.

185: REV. RICHARD WORTHINGTON. *Thoughts on the Manifesto of the French to all States and Nations*

1792

Rev. Richard Worthington, of Worcester, a dissenting minister, was the author of *Letters to the Jews*, *Thoughts on the Manifesto of the French*, *Treatise on the Dorsal Spasm*, *Invitation to the Inhabitants of Great Britain to manufacture Wines from the Fruits of their own Country*, etc. (Pp. 27–8.)

HOW far the constitutional principles of France, so moral in their original conception, so pledged by the solemnity of engagement, may be counted on as the beginning of good and lasting fellowship among nations, it is not in human foresight to determine. But it would be an insult to the justice and benevolence, conspicuous in her present address to the world, should we hesitate to acknowledge, that it is hardly possible to imagine any political avowal more admirably adapted—in the inspired and soothing phrase of the Prophet—to convert " Swords into Ploughshares, and Spears into Pruning hooks ".

186: JOEL BARLOW. *Advice to the Privileged Orders*

1792

Joel Barlow (1754–1812), an American writer, came to England in 1791. He was associated with the Constitutional Society and published political writings of a democratic and republican nature. To escape prosecution he crossed to France, where by avoiding politics and engaging in commerce and speculation he made a fortune. He subsequently acted as a diplomatic agent for the United States in France, and was on a mission to Napoleon when he was involved in the retreat from Moscow and died of privations. (Barlow, *Political Writings*, 1796, pp. 64–6)

THOUGH infinite praise is due to the constituent assembly of France for the temperate revolution and manly firmness which mark their operations in general; yet it must be confessed that some of their reforms bear the marks of too timorous a hand. Preserving an hereditary King with a tremendous accumulation of powers, and providing an unnecessary number of priests to be paid from the national purse, and furnished with the means of rebuilding the half-destroyed ruins of the hierarchy, are circumstances to be pardoned for reasons which I have already hinted. But the enormous military force, which they have decreed shall remain as a permanent establishment, appears to me not only unnecessary, and even dangerous to liberty, but totally and directly subversive of the end they had in view. . . .

I hope I shall not be understood to mean, that the

nature of man is totally changed by living in a free republic. I allow that it is still *interested* men and *passionate* men, that direct the affairs of the world. But in national assemblies, passion is lost in deliberation, and interest balances interest; till the good of the whole community combines the general will. Here then is a great moral entity, acting still from interested motives; but whose interest it can never be, in any possible combination of circumstances, to commence an offensive war.

187: EDMUND BURKE. Letter to Lord Grenville

18 August 1792

(*Correspondence, III*, pp. 508–9.)

I DO not see what a nation loses in reputation or in safety, by keeping its conduct in its own power. I think such a state of freedom in the use of a moral and political reserve in such unheard-of circumstances, can be well justified to any sovereign abroad, or to any person or party at home. I perceive that much pains are taken by the Jacobins of England to propagate a notion, that one state has not a right to interfere according to its discretion in the interior affairs of another. This strange notion can only be supported by a confusion of ideas, and by not distinguishing the case of rebellion and sedition in a neighbouring country, and taking a part in the divisions of a country when they do prevail, and are actually formed. In the first case there is undoubtedly more difficulty than in the second, in which there is clearly no difficulty at all. To interfere in such dissentions requires great prudence and circumspection, and a serious attention to justice, and to the policy of one's own country, as well as to that of Europe. But an abstract principle of public law, forbidding such interference, is not supported by the reason of that law, nor by the authorities on the subject, nor by the practice of this kingdom, nor by that of any civilized nation in the world. This nation owes its laws and liberties, His Majesty owes the throne on which he sits, to the contrary principle. The several treaties of guarantee to the Protestant succession more than once reclaimed, affirm the principle of interference, which in a manner forms the basis of the public law in Europe. A more mischievous idea cannot exist, than that any degree of wickedness, violence, and oppression, may prevail in a country, that the most abominable murderous, and exterminating rebellions may rage in it, or the most atrocious and bloody tyranny may domineer, and that no neighbouring power can take cognizance of either, or afford succour to the miserable sufferers.

188: LORD GRENVILLE. Letter to Lord Auckland

6 November 1792

William Eden, first Lord Auckland (1744–1814), was the British envoy at the Hague at this time. In his almost daily official correspondence with Grenville, British reactions to French aggressions against the Netherlands can be traced, from the initial determination to refuse to be provoked into war to a final acceptance of its inevitability. (*Journal and Correspondence of William, Lord Auckland*, 1860–2, II, pp. 464–5.)

WITH respect to any steps to be taken by this country, I continue fixed in my opinion, or rather I am every day more and more confirmed in it, that both in order to preserve our own domestic quiet, and to secure some other parts at least of Europe free from the miseries of anarchy, this country and Holland ought to remain quiet as long as it is possible to do so, even with some degree of forbearance and tolerance beyond what would in other circumstances have been judged right....

I cannot but remain in the persuasion that the re-establishment of order in France, under any form, can be effected only by a long course of intestine struggles; and that foreign intervention, while it retards the free course of the principles now prevalent in France, and their natural operation on the people there, serves the course of anarchy by giving both an excuse for its disorders and the means of collecting military force to support them. In this situation I see nothing for us to fear but the introduction of the same principles amongst ourselves.

189: LORD GRENVILLE. Letter to the Marquis of Buckingham

7 November 1792

(Duke of Buckingham, *Courts and Cabinets of George III*, II, pp. 222–4.)

I BLESS God, that we had the wit to keep ourselves out of the glorious enterprize of the combined armies, and that we were not tempted by the hope of sharing the spoils in the division of France, nor by the prospect of crushing all democratical principles all over the world at one blow. . . .

All my ambition is that I may at some time hereafter, when I am freed from all active concern in such a scene as this is, have the inexpressible satisfaction of being able to look back upon it, and to tell myself that I have contributed to keep my own country at least a little longer from sharing in all the evils of every sort that surround us. I am more and more convinced that this can only be done by keeping wholly and entirely aloof, and by watching much at home, but doing very little indeed; endeavouring to nurse up in the country a real determination to stand by the Constitution when it is attacked, as it most infallibly will be if these things go on; and, above all, trying to make the situation of the lower orders among us as good as it can be made.

190: ROBERT BANKS JENKINSON. Speech on Mr. Fox's Motion for sending a Minister to Paris, House of Commons

15 December 1792

Robert Banks Jenkinson, later Lord Liverpool (1770–1828), was the son of the first Earl of Liverpool, a country gentleman who had risen in politics by making himself useful to Lord North and George III. The younger Jenkinson began his parliamentary career as a strong advocate of war with France and opponent of reform. Except for a short interval in 1806 he was in office from 1793 to 1827, and Prime Minister from 1812. (*Parliamentary History*, XXX, pp. 87–8.)

HE had on a former occasion remarked, that we might always consider France as our natural enemy and rival, whether its government were despotic or free; with this difference, that, under a despotism, we should be more liable to wars from intrigue; but under a good and free government, very different indeed from the present, though we should be less subject to wars, whenever they did happen, they would be more formidable. In the same way he held it to be true with respect to ambition. The ambition of a monarch was no farther formidable than as it was supported by the power of the people; but when a whole people, and those powerful, were ambitious, as was now the case in France, the alarm became serious, and the consequences might be dreadful. In every point of view in which the subject could be regarded, it concerned the independence and existence of this country to exert itself strenuously in opposing the progress of the French arms.

191: WILLIAM PITT. Speech on the King's Message for an Augmentation of the Forces, House of Commons

1 February 1793

(*Parliamentary History*, XXX, pp. 278–83.)

THEIR decree of the 15th of December contains a fair illustration and confirmation of their principles and designs. They have by that decree expressly stated the plan on which they mean to act. Whenever they obtain a temporary success, whatever be the situation of the country into which they come, whatever may have been its antecedent conduct, whatever may be its political connexions, they have determined not to abandon the possession of it, till they have effected the utter and absolute subversion of its form of government, of every ancient, every established usage, however long they may have existed, and however much they may have been revered. They will not accept, under the name of liberty, any model of government, but that which is conformable to their own opinions and ideas; and all men must learn from the mouth of their cannon the propagation of their system in every part of the world. They have regularly and boldly avowed these instructions, which they sent to the commissioners who were to carry these orders into execution. They have stated to them what this house could not believe, they have stated to them a revolutionary principle and order, for the purpose of being applied in every country in which the French arms are crowned with success. They have stated, that they would organize every country by a disorganizing principle; and afterwards, they tell you all this is done by the will of the people. Wherever our arms come, revolutions must take place, dictated by the will of the people. And then comes this plain question, what is this will of the people? It is the power of the French. They have explained what that liberty is which they wish to give to every nation; and if they will not accept of it voluntarily, they compel them. They take every opportunity to destroy every institution that is most sacred and most valuable in every nation where their armies have made their appearance; and under the name of liberty, they have resolved to make every country in substance, if not in form, a province dependent on themselves, through the despotism of jacobin societies. This has given a more fatal blow to the liberties of mankind, than any they have suffered, even from the boldest attempts of the most aspiring monarch. We see, therefore, that France has trampled under foot all laws, human and divine. She has at last avowed the most insatiable ambition, and greatest contempt for the law of nations, which all independent states have hitherto professed most religiously to observe; and unless she is stopped in her career, all Europe must soon learn their ideas of justice—law of nations—models of government—and principles of liberty from the mouth of the French cannon.

I would next proceed to their confirmed pledge, not

to interfere in the government of other neutral countries. What they have done here is in countries which, under some pretence or other, they have made their enemies. I need not remind the house of the decree of the 19th of November, which is a direct attack on every government in Europe, by encouraging the seditious of all nations to rise up against their lawful rulers, and by promising them their support and assistance. By this decree, they hold out an encouragement to insurrection and rebellion in every country in the world. They shew you they mean no exception, by ordering this decree to be printed in all languages.—And therefore I might ask any man of common sense, whether any nation upon earth could be out of their contemplation at the time they passed it? And whether it was not meant to extend to England, whatever might be their pretences to the contrary? It is most manifest they mean to carry their principles into every nation, without exception, subvert and destroy every government, and to plant on their ruins their sacred tree of liberty.

To all this I shall only observe, that in the whole context of their language, on every occasion, they shew the clearest intention to propagate their principles all over the world. Their explanations contain only an avowal and repetition of the offence. They have proscribed royalty as a crime, and will not be satisfied but with its total destruction. The dreadful sentence which they have executed on their own unfortunate monarch, applies to every sovereign now existing.

France can have no right to annul the stipulations relative to the Scheldt, unless she has also the right to set aside, equally, all the other treaties between all the powers of Europe, and all the other rights of England, or of her allies. England will never consent that France shall arrogate the power of annulling at her pleasure, and under the pretence of a natural right of which she makes herself the only judge, the political system of Europe, established by solemn treaties, and guaranteed by the consent of all the powers. Such a violation of rights as France has been guilty of, it would be difficult to find in the history of the world. The conduct of that nation is in the highest degree arbitrary, capricious, and founded upon no one principle of reason and justice.

192: WILLIAM WINDHAM. Speech on Mr. Fox's Resolutions against the War with France, House of Commons

18 February 1793

(*Parliamentary History*, XXX, 451.)

IT had been a great question of morality among writers, how far any country was justified in interfering in the internal affairs of another; and the only danger to result from establishing the doctrine seemed to be, that it might be of dangerous consequence, as proceedings which in one instance were dictated by pure benevolence, might serve as a cover to other interferences of a very different nature. When we talked of the internal government of France, we talked of it as it concerned ourselves; we talked of the proceedings and principles in that country as affecting our own. When opinions were propagated by force of arms, it became necessary that they should be opposed. When armies and navies were employed to disseminate principles, armies and navies became the proper means of resisting them.

193: EDMUND BURKE. Letter to the Comte de Mercy

August 1793

(*Correspondence*, IV, pp. 138–40.)

THE present evil of our time, though in a great measure an evil of ambition, is not one of common political ambition, but in many respects entirely different. It is not the cause of nation as against nation; but, as you will observe, the cause of mankind against those who have projected the subversion of that order of things, under which our part of the world has so long flourished, and indeed, been in a progressive state of improvement; the limits of which, if it had not been thus rudely stopped, it would not have been easy for the imagination to fix. If I conceive rightly of the spirit of the present combination, it is not at war with France, but with Jacobinism. They cannot think it right, that a second kingdom should be struck out of the system of Europe, either by destroying its independence, or by suffering it to have such a *form* in its independence, as to keep it, as a perpetual fund of revolutions, in the very centre of Europe, in that region which alone touches almost every other, and must influence, even where she does not come in contact. As long as Jacobinism subsists there, in any form, or under any modification, it is not, in my opinion, the gaining a fortified place or two, more or less, or the annexing to the dominion of the allied powers this or that territorial district, that can save Europe, or any of its members. We are at war with a *principle*, and with an example, which there is no shutting out by fortresses, or excluding by territorial limits. No lines of demarcation can bound the Jacobin empire. It must be extirpated in the place of its origin, or it will not be confined to that place. In the whole circle of military arrangements and of political expedients, I fear that there cannot be found any sort of *merely defensive plan* of the least force, against the effect of the *example* which has been given in France. That *example* has shown, for the first time in the history of the world, that it is very possible to subvert the whole frame and order of the best constructed states, by corrupting the common people with the spoil of the superior classes. It is by that instrument that the French orators have accomplished their purpose, to the ruin of France; and it is by that instrument that, if they can establish themselves in France, (however broken or curtailed by themselves or others,) sooner or later, they will subvert every government in Europe. The effect of *erroneous doctrines* may be soon done away; but the example of *successful pillage* is of a nature more permanent, more applicable to use, and a thing which speaks more forcibly to the interests and passions of the corrupt and unthinking part of mankind, than a thousand theories.

194: ROYAL DECLARATION PUBLISHED IN *THE LONDON GAZETTE*

29 October 1793

(*The London Gazette*, 1793, pp. 947–50.)

THE following DECLARATION has been sent, by His Majesty's Command, to the Commanders of His Majesty's Fleets and Armies employed against France, and to His Majesty's Ministers residing at Foreign Courts.

The Circumstances, in consequence of which His Majesty has found Himself engaged in a Defensive War against France, are known already to all Europe. . . . It has become daily more and more evident how much the Internal Situation of France obstructs the conclusion of a solid and permanent Treaty. . . .

The Designs which had been professed of reforming the Abuses of the Government of France, of establishing personal liberty and the Rights of Property on a solid Foundation, of securing to an extensive and populous country the Benefit of a wise Legislation, and an equitable and mild Administration of it's Laws; all these salutory Views have unfortunately vanished. In their place has succeeded a System destructive of all Public Order, maintained by Proscriptions, Exiles, and Confiscations without Number, by arbitrary Imprisonments, by Massacres, which cannot even be remembered without Horror, and at length, by the execrable Murder of a just and beneficent Sovereign, and of the Illustrious Princess, who, with an unshaken Firmness, has shared all the misfortunes of her Royal Consort. . . Neighbouring Nations, instead of deriving a new Security for the Maintenance of general Tranquillity from the Establishment of a wise and moderate Government, have been exposed to the repeated Attacks of a ferocious Anarchy, the natural and necessary Enemy of all Public Order. . . .

This State of Things cannot exist in France without involving all the surrounding Powers in one common Danger, without giving them the Right, without imposing it upon them as a Duty, to stop the progress of an Evil which exists only by the successive Violation of all Law and all Property, and which attacks the fundamental Principles by which Mankind is united in the Bonds of Civil Society. His Majesty by no means disputes the Right of France to reform it's Laws. It never would have been his wish to employ the Influence of external Force with respect to the particular Forms of Government to be established in an independent Country. Neither has He now that Wish, except in so far as such Interference is become essential to the Security and Repose of other Powers. Under these Circumstances, He demands from France, and He demands with Justice, the Termination of a System of Anarchy, which has no Force but for the Purposes of Mischief. . . . The King demands that some legitimate and stable Government should be established, founded on the acknowledged Principles of universal Justice, and capable of maintaining with other Powers the accustomed Relations of Union and Peace. . . .

It is then in order to deliver themselves from this

unheard of Oppression, to put an end to a System of unparalleled crimes, and to restore at length Tranquillity to France, and Security to all Europe, that His Majesty invites the Co-operation of the People of France. It is for these Objects that He calls upon them to join the Standard of an hereditary Monarchy, not for the purpose of deciding, in this Moment of Disorder, Calamity, and Public Danger, on all the Modifications of which this Form of Government may hereafter be susceptible, but in order to unite themselves once more under the Empire of Law, of Morality, and of Religion. . . .

Whitehall, 29 October 1793.

195: EARL OF MORNINGTON. Speech on the Address of Thanks, House of Commons

21 January 1794

William Wellesley-Pole, Earl of Mornington (1763–1845), was the brother of Lord Wellesley and the Duke of Wellington. He was Member of Parliament for East Looe, 1790–94. (*Parliamentary History*, XXX, pp. 1,112–3.)

THE views which we attributed to France previous to the war, were views of aggrandizement and ambition, connected with the propagation of principles incompatible with the existence of any regular government. The particular acts, by which those views had been manifested, were, 1st, the decree of the 19th of November, in which France made (according to her own language) a grant of universal fraternity and assistance, and ordered her generals every where to aid and abet those citizens who had suffered, or might suffer hereafter, in the cause of what she called liberty. Her sense of liberty, as applied to England, was shown by the reception of seditious and treasonable addresses, and by the speeches of the president of the National Convention, expressing his wish for the auspicious Institution of a British Convention, founded, as such an institution must have been, upon the destruction of every branch of our happy constitution. 2nd, The conduct of France, in incorporating the territories of other powers with her own, under colour of voluntary acts of union, pretended to have been freely voted by the people; particularly in the cases of Savoy and of the Netherlands, of both which countries France had assumed the sovereignty. 3d. The opening of the Scheldt, in direct violation of the most solemn treaties guaranteed by France herself; and lastly; her general designs of hostility against Holland.

196: EARL OF MANSFIELD. Speech on the Address of Thanks, House of Lords

21 January 1794

David Murray, Earl of Mansfield (1727–1796), held various diplomatic posts. He energetically supported Pitt and the war against France. (*Parliamentary History*, XXX, pp. 1,077–8.)

OUR great aim is to resist and defeat the wild attempts of those who have declared it to be their deliberate purpose to " disorganize " Europe, as they call it: that is, to subvert this and every other regular government; to trample upon all property; to break all the ties of civil society; to deprive men of every present comfort, of every future hope, and reduce them to the same wretched level with themselves. We wage war with those who are not our enemies alone, but who have declared themselves *hostes humani generis* by their avowed conspiracy against the general interests of mankind. I recollect at the moment, that in a vapouring letter, addressed by a M. Fouche to the committee of safety, he says, " let the republic act as one great volcano pouring forth its destructive lava upon this infamous island." Strong as the expression may seem, it gives an imperfect idea of the mischief they would certainly bring upon us, if God, in his vengeance, should give them the power. Torrents of lava, as we all know, work but partial destruction but if they could effect their purpose by the dissemination of their principles, the contagion of their example, and the introduction of anarchy like theirs, the certain consequences must be immediate universal ruin.

197: WILLIAM WORDSWORTH. *The Prelude*

(Book X, lines 263–8, 276–310.)

What, then, were my emotions, when in arms
Britain put forth her freeborn strength in league,
Oh, pity and shame! with those confederate Powers!
Not in my single self alone I found,
But in the minds of all ingenuous youth,
Change and subversion from that hour.

. . . As a light
And pliant harebell, swinging in the breeze
On some grey rock—its birthplace—so had I
Wantoned, fast rooted on the ancient tower
Of my belovèd country, wishing not
A happier fortune than to wither there:
Now was I from that pleasant station torn
And tossed about in whirlwind. I rejoiced,
Yea, afterwards—truth most painful to record!—
Exulted, in the triumph of my soul,
When Englishmen by thousands were o'erthrown,
Left without glory on the field, or driven,
Brave hearts! to shameful flight. It was a grief,—
Grief call it not, 'twas anything but that,—
A conflict of sensations without name,
Of which *he* only, who may love the sight
Of a village steeple, as I do, can judge,
When, in the congregation bending all
To their great Father, prayers were offered up,
Or praises for our country's victories;
And, 'mid the simple worshippers, perchance
I only, like an uninvited guest
Whom no one owned, sate silent, shall I add,

Fed on the day of vengeance yet to come.
Oh! much have they to account for, who could tear,
By violence, at one decisive rent,
From the best youth in England their dear pride,
Their joy, in England; this, too, at a time
In which worst losses easily might wear
The best of names, when patriotic love
Did of itself in modesty give way,
Like the Precursor when the Deity
Is come Whose harbinger he was; a time
In which apostasy from ancient faith
Seemed but conversion to a higher creed.

198: MARQUIS OF LANSDOWNE. Speech on his Motion for Peace with France, House of Lords

17 February 1794

(*Parliamentary History*, XXX, p. 1,395.)

YOU ought to look at the consequences which are likely to follow from your keeping up in France that enthusiasm of spirit and energy of execution which they at present display. You will run the hazard of establishing in the centre of Europe a military republic; you will cherish and confirm a spirit, that it will be impossible for Europe afterwards to extinguish. You will give a new turn to their thoughts, a new pursuit, a new genius, a new character to the people.

Thus, if we persevere to goad, to attack, and to hunt the French, we should only confirm a military republic in the very heart of Europe. And do not let us proudly conceive, that our combination will make us formidable, because it is opposed to a single people; when we sharpen talents by irascibility, when we inflame the natural energies of the soul, when we call forth and rouse every faculty of nature, while every individual man becomes a god, the consequences are not to be calculated by the arithmetic of common events. And such has ever been the experience of ages. Great moments have always produced great men, and great actions.

199: DUKE OF BEDFORD. Speech on his Motion for ending the War with France, House of Lords

30 May 1794

Francis Russell, fifth Duke of Bedford (1765–1802), was the head of the great Whig family and a devoted friend and follower of Fox. He was one of the small pro-French group in the House of Lords, and has been immortalized in Burke's *Letter to a Noble Lord*. (*Parliamentary History*, XXXI, pp. 661–2.)

THE present was called a war of humanity, and incessant appeals were made to their lordships' feelings in favour of a war that had for its object the preservation of order, of religion, and humanity; but it would be well for their lordships to recollect, whether, in our very conduct to the king of Prussia, we did not act upon the contrary principle, and pay him a subsidy only to enable him to wage the most cruel and inhuman war that ever was undertaken against any people. When we had the cry of humanity for ever in our mouths, it would be well that we felt its true and genuine emotions. While we stood by to see the people of Poland, loyal, faithful to their neighbours, respectful to the rights of nations, and honourable in every part of their conduct, made the savage prey of our allies; nay, when we granted subsidies to enable our allies to prosecute their injustice with effect, to trample upon the necks of this brave and gallant people, without remorse and without pity, what pretension had we to the true feeling of humanity, or how could we claim to ourselves praise for honest and conscientious regards to the well-being of society? If we made it a plea that the principles of the French tended to attack the independence of nations, and that no neighbouring power was safe from their restless ambition, and their arrogant tyranny, could we shut our eyes to the same practices in the conduct of those powers with whom we were leagued? Did we not assist those powers in assailing the independence of their neighbours, in trampling down order, in confounding establishments, and in spreading ruin and desolation over whole countries? It was idle and hypocritical to assume the pretext of humanity in the one instance, while we laughed it to scorn in the other. There was no integrity in our proceeding. One part of the war of Europe was at variance in its principle with the other. The pretended defender of social order and of national independence in one place, was the assailant and violator of independence in another; and while the people of this country were taught to believe that it was for virtue, and religion, and humanity, that we were at war, they were called upon for a subsidy to one of our allies, enormous beyond all precedent in British history, to enable him to carry on an unprovoked and unjust war against the brave and virtuous people of Poland.

200: WILLIAM WILBERFORCE. Speech on the Address of Thanks, House of Commons

30 December 1794

(*Parliamentary History*, XXXI, pp. 1,016–7.)

IT was his firm belief, on a most deliberate review of all the circumstances of our present situation, that peace was now desirable, if it could be effected on terms consistent with our honour and our interests. But though such was his clear opinion, he should most likely have thought it best not to interrupt the unanimity of that day's proceedings, if the Address had been couched in terms at all moderate or pacific; but its language was of a quite contrary character, and he thought no one could adopt it who was not prepared to say, that Great Britain ought never to treat with France till a counter-revolution should be effected.

201: EARL STANHOPE. Protest against interfering in the Internal Affairs of France, House of Lords

6 January 1795

(*Parliamentary History*, XXXI, pp. 1,141–3.)

THE following Protest was entered on the Journals:

" Dissentient,

1. " Because the motion made for the House to adjourn, was professedly intended to get rid of the following Resolution, viz. ' Resolved that this country ought not, and will not, interfere in the internal affairs of France: and that it is expedient explicitly to declare the same.'

2. " Because I hold that it is contrary both to equity and policy for any foreign country to interfere in the internal affairs or constitution of the French republic or of any other independent nation.

3. " Because the government of Great Britain (not having been elected by the citizens of France), can have no more right to give to France a monarchical, aristocratical, or other form of government whatever, than the crowned despots of Prussia and of Russia had to overturn the free constitution of now unhappy Poland.

4. " Because I heartily disapprove and reprobate the doctrine advanced by ministers in the debate, namely, ' That to restore the ancient and hereditary monarchy of France no expense should be spared.'

"Having upon this most important and momentous subject, frequently stood alone; and having also been, upon this last occasion, totally unsupported in the division, if I should therefore cease, at present to attend this House (where I have been placed by the mere accident of birth) such of my fellow-citizens as are friends to freedom, and who may chance to read this my solemn Protest, will find that I have not altered my sentiments or opinions; and that I have not changed any of my principles; for my principles never can be changed."

202: JOHN BOWLES. *The Dangers of Premature Peace, with cursory strictures on the declaration of the King of Prussia*

1795

Bowles, a lawyer, was a prolific political writer. (Pp. 8–9.)

A VERY little attention to the nature of the different forms of government known to mankind, and to the effects, both internal and external, which those forms have a tendency to produce, will demonstrate that France cannot be a Republic consistently with this balance of power. It is suggested by reason, as well as by history and experience, that nations where the Republican system prevails, are abundantly the most prone to war. They are peculiarly subject to agitation and disquiet, and exposed in a remarkable degree to those influences, which tend incessantly to produce domestic broils and foreign disputes. They contain no principle which can restrain the workings of ambition, or the machinations of intrigue: no superintending controul to limit, as in a Monarchy, the aspiring views of individuals, or the daring projects of party; and to declare to each restless spirit "thus far mayest thou go, but no farther." They present on the contrary a boundless horizon to the ambitious, and give a free scope to the most violent struggles for ascendancy. Such a state is therefore, unavoidably, in constant fermentation, and the passions of the people, which, in a republic, are the only engines of power, are perpetually excited by the machinations of faction, the operations of cabal, and the artifices of popularity. The effects produced on the disposition and manners of a people by Republican principles and habits, are also unfavourable to tranquillity, foreign and domestic. The character of Republicanism, from the Roman Brutus, down to the British Cromwell, and from him to the more modern Robespierre of France, has ever been conspicuously distinguished as stern — morose — haughty—ambitious—turbulent—impatient of contradiction and controul—insidious—malicious—hypocritical—irritable—ferocious—intolerant—greedy of power—tyrannical under the mask and pretext of liberty—implacable—vindictive and sanguinary.

203: WILLIAM WINDHAM. Letter to Edmund Burke

17 January 1796

(*The Windham Papers*, II, p. 2.)

THE moment of Peace is yet, I hope, so far distant, that chance may still do much to save us from so dreadful a catastrophe: I mean, of course, Peace with a Jacobin Republick; yet everything has a dreadful tendency that way: and the great impediment is wanting; a conviction of the extent of the danger which from that moment will begin to operate against the Country. It really does not appear to me that, from the moment that such a Peace is made, the shame and degradation of this country will be any longer supportable.

204: EDMUND BURKE. *Letters on a Regicide Peace*

1796

(*Works*, V, pp. 214–9, 223.)

AS to war, if it be the means of wrong and violence, it is the sole means of justice amongst nations. Nothing can banish it from the world. They who say otherwise, intending to impose upon us, do not impose upon themselves. But it is one of the greatest objects of human wisdom to mitigate those evils which we are unable to remove. The conformity and analogy of which I speak, incapable, like everything else, of preserving perfect trust and tranquillity among men, has a strong tendency to facilitate accommodation, and to produce a generous oblivion of the rancour of their quarrels. With this similitude, peace is more of peace, and war is less of war. I will go further. There have been periods of time in which communities, apparently in peace with each other, have been more perfectly separated than, in latter times, many nations in Europe have been in the course of long and bloody wars. The cause must be sought in the similitude throughout Europe of religion, laws, and manners. At bottom, these are all the same. The writers on public law have often called this *aggregate* of nations a commonwealth. They had reason. It is virtually one great state having the same basis of general law, with some diversity of provincial customs and local establishments. The nations of Europe have had the very same Christian religion, agreeing in the fundamental parts, varying a little in the ceremonies and in the subordinate doctrines. The whole of the polity and economy of every country in Europe has been derived from the same sources. It was drawn from the old Germanic or Gothic custumary, from the feudal institutions which must be considered as an emanation from that custumary; and the whole has been improved and digested into system and discipline by the Roman law.

This violent breach of the community of Europe we must conclude to have been made (even if they had not expressly declared it over and over again) either to force mankind into an adoption of their system, or to live in perpetual enmity with a community the most potent we have ever known. Can any person imagine, that, in offering to mankind this desperate alternative, there is no indication of a hostile mind, because men in possession of the ruling authority are supposed to have a right to act without coercion in their own territories? As to the right of men to act anywhere according to their pleasure, without any moral tie, no such right exists. Men are never in a state of *total* independence of each other. It is not the condition of our nature: nor is it conceivable how any man can pursue a considerable course of action without its having some effect upon others; or, of course without producing some degree of responsibility for his conduct. The *situations* in which men relatively stand produce the rules and principles of that responsibility, and afford directions to prudence in exacting it.

Distance of place does not extinguish the duties or the rights of men: but it often renders their exercise impracticable. The same circumstance of distance renders the noxious effects of an evil system in any community less pernicious. But there are situations where this difficulty does not occur; and in which, therefore, these duties are obligatory, and these rights are to be asserted. It has ever been the method of public jurists to draw a great part of the analogies, on which they form the law of nations, from the principles of law which prevail in civil community. Civil laws are not all of them merely positive. Those, which are rather conclusions of legal reason than matters of statutable provision, belong to universal equity, and are universally applicable. Almost the whole prætorian law is such. There is a *Law of Neighbourhood* which does not leave a man perfectly master on his own ground. When a neighbour sees a *new erection*, in the nature of a nuisance, set up at his door, he has a right to represent it to the judge; who, on his part, has a right to order the work to be stayed; or, if established, to be removed. On this head the parent law is express and clear, and has made many wise provisions, which, without destroying, regulate and restrain the right of *ownership*, by the right of *vicinage*.

Such is the law of civil vicinity. Now, where there is no constituted judge, as between independent states there is not, the vicinage itself is the natural judge. It is, preventively, the assessor of its own rights, or remedially, their avenger. Neighbours are presumed to take cognizance of each other's acts. "*Vicini vicinorum facta presumuntur scire.*" This principle, which, like the rest, is as true of nations as of individual men, has bestowed on the grand vicinage of Europe a duty to know, and a right to prevent, any capital innovation which may amount to the erection of a dangerous nuisance.

I have therefore been decidedly of opinion, with our declaration at Whitehall, in the beginning of this war, that the vicinage of Europe had not only a right, but an indispensable duty, and an exigent interest, to denunciate this new work before it had produced the danger we have so sorely felt, and which we shall long feel. The example of what is done by France is too important not to have a vast and extensive influence; and that example, backed with its power, must bear with great force on those who are near it; especially on those who shall recognise the pretended republic on the principle upon which it now stands. It is not an old structure which you have found as it is, and are not to dispute of the original end and design with which it had been so fashioned. It is a recent wrong, and can plead no prescription. It violates the rights upon which not only the community of France, but those on which all communities are founded. The principles on which they proceed are *general* principles, and are as true in England as in any other country. They, who (though with the purest intentions) recognise the authority of these regicides and robbers upon principle, justify their acts and establish them as precedents. It is a question not between France and England. It is a question between property and force.

And is then example nothing? It is everything. Example is the school of mankind, and they will learn at no other. This war is a war against that example. It is not a war for Louis the Eighteenth, or even for the property, virtue, fidelity of France. It is a war for George the Third, for Francis the Second, and for the dignity, property, honour, virtue, and religion of England, of Germany, and of all nations.

205: WILLIAM WINDHAM. Letter to Mrs. Crewe

30 September 1796

(*The Windham Papers*, II, pp. 19–20.)

THERE can be no doubt about the matter. Peace made, and the Republick established, there is an end of the power, independence, government, morals, of this country, as well as of every other throughout Europe. It is another Roman Republick that is coming into existence, equally fatal to the independence of other nations and infinitely more so to their virtue and happiness. Yet this is the consummation,—a consummation from which nothing but new wars can save us,—that the booby politicians in this country are all wishing for, and holding out as the only means by which our ruin is to be averted.

206: WILLIAM PITT. Speech on the King's Message respecting a Subsidy to Russia, House of Commons

7 June 1799

(*Parliamentary History*, XXXIV, pp. 1,047, 1,050–2.)

THE hon. gentleman has told us, that his deliverance of Europe is the driving of France within her ancient limits; but it is assumed by the hon. gentleman, that we are not content with wishing to drive France within her ancient limits, that we seek to overthrow the government of France; and he would make us say, that we never will treat with it as a republic. Now I neither meant any thing like this, nor expressed myself so as to lead to such inferences. Whatever I may in the abstract think of the kind of government called a republic, whatever may be its fitness to the nation where it prevails, there may be times when it would not be dangerous to exist in its vicinity. But while the spirit of France remains what at present it is, its government despotic, vindictive, unjust, with a temper untamed, a character unchanged, if its power to do wrong at all remains, there does not exist any security for this country or Europe. In my view of security, every object of ambition and aggrandisement is abandoned. Our simple object is security, just security, with a little mixture of indemnification. These are the legitimate objects of war at all times; and when we have attained that end, we are in a condition to derive from peace its beneficent advantages; but until then, our duty and our interest require that we should persevere unappalled in the struggle to which we were provoked. We shall not be satisfied with a false security.

I cannot agree to the interpretation the hon. gentleman has thought proper to give to parts of my speech. He has supposed that I said, we persevere in the war in order to restore monarchy to France. I never once uttered any such intention. What I said was, that the France which now exists, affords no promise of security against aggression and injustice in peace, and is destitute of all justice and integrity in war.

The hon. gentleman persists in saying, that we have an intention to wage war against opinion. It is not so. We are not in arms against the opinions of the closet, nor the speculations of the school. We are at war with armed opinions; we are at war with those opinions which the sword of audacious, unprincipled, and impious innovation seeks to propagate amidst the ruins of empires, the demolition of altars, the destruction of every venerable and good and liberal institution, under whatever form of polity they have been raised.

Whilst republican France continues what it is, I make war against republican France; but if I should see any chance of the return of a government that did not threaten to endanger the existence of other governments, far be it from me to breathe hostility to it. I must first see this change of fortune to France and to Europe make its progress with certain steps, before I relax in the assertion of those rights, which are the common property, the links of union of the regular governments of Europe.

207: WILLIAM PITT. Speech on the King's Message respecting Overtures of Peace from the Consular Government of France, House of Commons

3 February 1800

(*Parliamentary History*, XXXIV, pp. 1,308–9.)

WHAT would have been the effect of admitting this explanation?—to suffer a nation, and an armed nation, to preach to the inhabitants of all the countries in the world, that themselves were slaves, and their rulers tyrants: to encourage and invite them to revolution, by a previous promise of French support, to whatever might call itself a majority, or to whatever France might declare to be so. This was their explanation; and this they told you, was their ultimatum. But was this all? Even at that very moment, when they were endeavouring to induce you to admit these explanations, to be contented with the avowal, that France offered herself as a general guarantee for every successful revolution, and would interfere only to sanction and confirm whatever the free and uninfluenced choice of the people might have decided, what were their orders to their generals on the same subject? In the midst of these amicable explanations with you, came forth a decree, which I really believe must be effaced from the minds of gentlemen opposite to me, if they can prevail upon themselves for a moment to hint even a doubt upon the origin of this quarrel, not only as to this country, but as to all the nations of Europe with whom France has been subsequently engaged in hostility. I speak of the decree of the 15th of December. This decree, more even than all the previous transactions, amounted to an universal declaration of war against all thrones, and against all civilized governments. It said, wherever the armies of France shall come (whether within countries then at war or at peace is not distinguished), in all those countries it shall be the first care of their generals to introduce the principles and the practice of the French revolution; to demolish all privileged orders, and every thing which obstructs the establishment of their new system.

208: WILLIAM PITT. Speech on the King's Message respecting Overtures of Peace from the Consular Government of France, House of Commons

3 February 1800

(*Parliamentary History*, XXXIV, pp. 1,326–7.)

ITS first fundamental principle was, to bribe the poor against the rich, by proposing to transfer into new hands, on the delusive notion of equality, and in breach of every principle of justice, the whole property of the country; the practical application of this principle was, to devote the whole of that property to indiscriminate plunder, and to make it the foundation of a revolutionary system of finance, productive in proportion to the misery and desolation which it created. It has been accompanied by an unwearied spirit of proselytism, diffusing itself over all the nations of the earth; a spirit which can apply itself to all circumstances and all situations, which can furnish a list of grievances, and hold out a promise of redress equally to all nations, which inspired the teachers of French liberty with the hope of alike recommending themselves to those who live under the feudal code of the German empire; to the various states of Italy, under all their different institutions; to the old republicans of Holland, and to the new republicans of America; to the catholic of Ireland, whom it was to deliver from protestant usurpation; to the protestant of Switzerland, whom it was to deliver from popish superstition; and to the mussulman of Egypt, whom it was to deliver from Christian persecution; to the remote Indian, blindly bigotted to his ancient institutions; and to the natives of Great Britain, enjoying the perfection of practical freedom, and justly attached to their constitution, from the joint result of habit, of reason, and of experience. The last and distinguishing feature is a perfidy, which nothing can bind, which no tie of treaty, no sense of the principles generally received among nations, no obligation, human or divine, can restrain. Thus qualified, thus armed for destruction, the genius of the French revolution marched forth, the terror and dismay of the world. Every nation has in its turn been the witness, many have been the victims of its principles, and it is left for us to decide, whether we will compromise with such a danger, while we have yet resources to supply the sinews of war, while the heart and spirit of the country is yet unbroken, and while we have the means of calling forth and supporting a powerful co-operation in Europe.

209: WILLIAM PITT. Speech on the King's Message respecting Advances to the Emperor of Germany

17 February 1800

(*Parliamentary History*, XXXIV, pp. 1,442, 1,444–5.)

THE hon. gentleman defies me to state, in one sentence, what is the object of the war. In one word, I tell him that it is security.

As to the first proposition, he has assumed the foundation of the argument, and has left no ground for controverting it, or for explanation, because he says that any attempt at explanation upon this subject is the mere ambiguous language of *ifs* and *buts*, and of special pleading. Now, Sir, I never had much liking to special pleading; and if ever I had any, it is by this time almost entirely gone. He has, besides so abridged me of the use of particles, that though I am not particularly attached to the sound of an *if* or a *but*, I would be much obliged to him if he would give me some others to supply their places. Is this, however, a light matter, that it should be treated in so light a manner? The restoration of the French monarchy, I consider as a most desirable object, because I think that it would afford the best security to this country and to Europe. *But* this object may not be attainable;

and *if* it be not attainable, we must be satisfied with the best security we can find independent of it. Peace is most desirable to this country; *but* negociation may be attended with greater evils than could be counterbalanced by any benefits which would result from it. And *if* this be found to be the case; *if* it afford no prospect of security; *if* it threaten all the evils which we have been struggling to avert; *if* the prosecution of the war afford the prospect of attaining complete security; and *if* it may be prosecuted with increasing commerce, with increasing means, and with increasing prosperity, except what may result from the visitations of the seasons; then, I say, that it is prudent in us not to negociate at the present moment. These are my *buts* and my *ifs*. This is my plea, and on no other do I wish to be tried, by God and my country.

SOME BOOKS FOR FURTHER READING

P. A. Brown: *The French Revolution in English History* (1918).

C. Cestre: *La Révolution française et les poètes anglais (1789–1809)* (1906).

A. Cobban: *Edmund Burke and the Revolt Against the Eighteenth Century* (1929).

E. Halévy: *La formation du radicalisme philosophique* (1901–04). English translation: *The Growth of Philosophical Radicalism* (1928).

W. E. H. Lecky: *A History of England in the Eighteenth Century*, Vols. VI, VII (1877).

A. Lincoln: *Some Political and Social Ideas of English Dissent, 1076–1380* (1938).

H. W. Meikle: *Scotland and the French Revolution* (1912).

J. Holland Rose: *William Pitt and the Great War* (1911).

G. S. Veitch: *The Genesis of Parliamentary Reform* (1913).

INDEX OF NAMES

[Biographical or other notes are given in black figures, extracts in roman, and other references in italics. Merely incidental references are not indexed.]